STRAINING
FORWARD

STRAINING
FORWARD

One woman's journey from oppression to
redemption in the wake of the Vietnam War

Minh Phuong Towner's Story
by Michelle Layer Rahal

XULON PRESS

Xulon Press
2301 Lucien Way #415
Maitland, FL 32751
407.339.4217
www.xulonpress.com

Printed in the United States of America.

ISBN-13: 9781545631638

Praise for
Straining Forward

Michelle Layer Rahal has the voice of a storyteller as she takes us on a journey from war-torn Vietnam, to France, Australia and eventually the United States through the eyes of Minh Phuong Towner as she searches for healing and her place in the world. *Straining Forward* is a beautiful memoir of survival, self-reflection, and faith.

Anna Whiston-Donaldson
Author of the *New York Times* bestseller *Rare Bird*

Minh's Phuong Towner's book, like her life, is a triumph. Her story offers an eye-opening view of the incredible hardships suffered by so many in other parts of the world, but also of the unfathomable redemption and freedom found in Christ. Her account is edifying and encouraging for us all.

Retired Congressman Frank R. Wolf of Virginia
Former co-chair of the Congressional Human Rights Caucus
Author of *Prisoner of Conscience, One Man's Crusade for Global Human and Religious Rights*

In the tradition of Augustine's *Confessions*, Minh Towner makes confession both of her turnings away from God and of her turnings back to God. In the face of evils perpetrated against her and despite her own moments of falling short, Minh testifies to God's unending grace and providence. Here is an account of an ordinary yet extraordinary woman who finds her way home. Her invitation to you to accompany her is deeply moving.

John P. Burgess, Professor of Systematic Theology,
Pittsburgh Theological Seminary
Author of *Holy Rus': The Rebirth of Orthodoxy in the
New Russia*

Straining Forward is an engaging memoir that begins in Vietnam during "The American War" which destroys young Minh's life of privilege. Her family fractured, Minh makes a harrowing escape on a boat and ultimately crosses two continents. She thinks she is searching to better herself, but ultimately realizes she is searching for her salvation, which has been doggedly following her. This lively journey is told with a clear gospel purpose.

Ruth Everhart
Author of *Ruined*

In memory of all those who lost their lives during the
Têt Offensive, and in honor of those who carry
the scars of living through the Vietnam War.

This book is dedicated to my beloved father, Nguyen Xuan Dat,
and brother, Nguyen Xuan Thanh, whose strength and love
gave me the courage to press forward in the darkest of times.

And to my children, Eddie and Emily, for giving my life purpose.
I love you more than words can express.

Emily, Eddie, and Minh

50% of the proceeds from sales of this book
will be donated to individuals and groups
involved in missionary work abroad.

TABLE OF CONTENTS

FORWARD

My most vivid memory of Minh Towner dates back eleven years when I was leading a Sunday evening class at the church where I serve as pastor. I had met her previously after Sunday worship yet only in passing. Things come at me fast at the door after worship, and I was having trouble remembering her uncommon name and placing her distinct accent.

Minh was one of nineteen students in the class I was teaching on Mark's Gospel, and I took notice of her immediately. Her enthusiasm for being there was readily apparent. Her joy cheered me. She was caring and concerned about everyone's welfare, mine included. I was intrigued. *Who exactly is this person, and why does she care so much?*

I asked the class to break into smaller clusters to share their faith journey. "Tell the story of your experience with Christ and his church with others in your small group," I said. Then I circulated among the groups to listen and ensure no one dominated the discussion. I joined Minh's group when she began to share. As she told her improbable story, my jaw dropped. I rocked back in my chair. I could not believe what I was hearing. Hers was the kind of story I had only read about in books—the most riveting story of faith I had ever witnessed.

When Minh finished, there was profound silence in the room. Other groups could sense the moment and turned their heads to listen. Afterward, I leaned forward and said quietly, "Minh, you must share your story with more people."

Well, here we are, reading Minh's story in written form. I promise you, you will not be bored. Her implausible journey will stir something deep in you. At times the pain and horror she endured might prompt you to turn away. Don't stop! Keep going! Her life is a remarkable story of Christ's transformation.

I preach about Christ's transformation each Sunday. Paul writes, "We are being transfigured much like the Messiah, our lives gradually becoming brighter and more beautiful as God enters our lives and we become like him." (2 Corinthians 3:18—*The Message*)

Minh serves for me as a constant reminder that Christ really does change people for the better. May she serve as a constant reminder for you too.

Rev. Dr. Pete James
Vienna Presbyterian Church
Vienna, VA

INTRODUCTION

"I want to write your story." These were the first words I ever spoke to Minh Phuong Towner. I didn't know her. She didn't know me. However, after hearing her testimony at church one Sunday morning that left the congregation stunned and teary, I knew in my soul that God had more to say through her. Minh smiled and giggled like a teenager at my suggestion. She said something I either don't remember or didn't understand due to her broken English and thick Australian accent, but the door had been opened.

This petite, Asian woman had touched a nerve deep inside of me that I did not know existed, and I felt a strange kinship to her. We were close in age, had both attended Catholic schools, and had lost siblings as children; but her story couldn't have been more different than mine. While I was growing up sheltered in a stable family on farmland in upstate New York, Minh was struggling to make sense of her life in the wake of atrocities she endured throughout her childhood in the war-torn country of Vietnam and later as an adult dealing with the aftereffects of post-traumatic stress disorder (PTSD).

According to the U.S. National Archives and Records Administration, the Vietnam War, which the Vietnamese people call the American War, claimed over 58,000 American lives. As high as this number is, it pales in comparison to the number of veterans who returned home carrying the scars of battle—both physically and mentally. A longitudinal study conducted by the U.S. Department of Veterans Affairs found that a large majority of Vietnam veterans struggled with chronic post-traumatic stress disorder symptoms decades after discharge. This equates to around 283,400 veterans.[1] If this is how the Vietnam War afflicted the men and women who had served in the U.S. armed forces, how did it affect the people—especially the children—of Vietnam who were not able to leave their country following the communist takeover?

This was not a question I was ever asked to consider during any of my history classes. I do remember learning a little bit about the Vietnam War in school, but it centered on U.S. military involvement, not the Vietnamese people who were left behind. Minh's testimony forced me to confront my naiveté, or rather my ignorance. Jesus had commanded me to love my neighbor as myself, yet I had looked no further than my backyard. I had no right to write Minh's story, but the call on my heart to do so did not dissipate; it increased. God would not let it rest.

Whenever our paths crossed at church, I would ask Minh, "Are you ready to write your book?" Usually she would laugh. Her bubbly personality perplexed me. Knowing only what she had shared at church that one Sunday morning, I had to wonder: *Why was she always smiling? What made her so resilient? Where did she find the courage and strength to keep going?*

Finally, eight years after we first met and while Minh was studying in seminary school, she gave me an answer: God wanted me to write her story. This was no longer just my desire; it was God's command.

Capturing the memories of Minh's past was no easy feat for her or for me. Many tears were shed and, thus, many prayers were said. It has been a burden and a joy, a torment and a privilege to walk alongside this woman as she relived the pain, the struggles, the grief, and the joys of her life. Both the peaks and valleys have been steep, but every step of this journey has brought us both closer to God and to each other. Though we look nothing alike, I call Minh my sister. (I always wanted an older sister!) It is because I know her so well that I took the liberty of writing Minh's story in first person, as if she were speaking. And indeed, as we painstakingly reviewed each chapter, often through tears, Minh would say, "You said exactly what I was feeling."

I will never truly understand what Minh experienced. There's not even a word for it in the English language. The French word *malheur* comes close. Malheur carries a sense of predestination and doom, a prolonged and frequent attack on the mind and body that affects life at its very core: socially, psychologically, and physically. It identifies someone who has suffered over a great length of time, deeply and without cause.

Simone Weil, a French philosopher and mystic whose essay, *The Love of God and Affliction,* was published after her death states, "In the realm of suffering, affliction (malheur) is something apart, specific, and irreducible."[2] It hardens the heart and discourages the souls of those who are least deserving of it. Like the Biblical character of Job. Like Minh.

Evil was thrust upon them. Love was stripped from them. Pain was their constant companion. They felt no joy in life, but rather felt as if they were being punished for some unknown crime. Weil says that it is in the midst of the darkest of times when the afflicted have the opportunity to truly experience God's love. Though it does not feel as if God is present, He is. He is the light of hope that sustains the soul and protects it from annihilation. Like the seed that has fallen into the soil at the end of the harvest, the soul in anguish remains buried yet protected, in hopeful anticipation of spring.

The joy I often saw — and continue to see — in Minh is a reflection of her growing soul. Buried for far too long, it is now blossoming as it comes into the full light of Christ.

The pages of this book contain just some of the harrowing experiences that Minh encountered in her early life. It was neither important nor God honoring to share them all. What are shared within these pages are those memories that shaped Minh's personality, directed her to Christ, and kept her alive. This book is, after all, a story of redemption, resilience, and forgiveness.

To help the reader place the events in historical context, I've included timeframes at the beginning of each section and chapter. I would caution the reader to use these merely as a point of reference because several could not be verified. Where actual dates were known, they were used within the text itself.

Many of the names and places within these pages have been changed, but not all. Throughout this book I took the liberty of omitting Vietnamese spellings and accent marks for individuals who played a significant role in Minh's story. I did this in order to allow the English reader the ability to easily pronounce the names. However, spellings and accent marks were left intact for specific locations, historical names, and Vietnamese dialogue, which is always followed by an English translation.

My prayer for you as you read Minh's story is that your heart would be moved to contemplate the lives of children all across the world who feel unloved, unworthy, and lost against a backdrop of war, death, and abuse. I pray you do not become complacent and accept injustice as the norm or someone else's problem. Benjamin Mays, a 20th century pastor and American civil rights leader, said, "The tragedy of life is often not in our failure, but rather in our complacency; not in our doing too much, but rather in our doing too little; not in our living above our ability, but rather in living below our capacities." We are all capable of doing something for the betterment of society, and the Gospel calls us to do so.

I pray also that you would allow God to use you to come alongside those in your own communities who are refugees or feel marginalized. And in the process of opening your heart to those who are less fortunate, may you experience the presence of God guiding you. Press on toward the prize for which God is calling you heavenward in Christ Jesus. Forget what is behind and keep *Straining Forward*.

Michelle Layer Rahal, author

PART I
VIETNAM

1964–1975

CHAPTER 1

Children, always obey your parents, for this pleases the Lord.
Fathers, do not aggravate your children,
or they will become discouraged.
Colossians 3:20-21 (NLT)

1964

I woke up in a bed that was not my own. My eyes drifted from
the white ceiling to the white walls and down to the stiff white
sheets covering my body. I had been in a hospital room once before,
but not as a patient. My presence here meant I had not succeeded.

A gentle hum of white noise coming from a machine next to
my bed muffled the voices in the distance. *Were they talking about
me? What did they know?* I slowly turned my head to examine my
surroundings. That's when I saw him, his face buried in a book. All
I could see was the top of his head. Gray hairs. *When had my father
grown old? How long had he been sitting there? Hours? Days?*

He looked up and our eyes met. Putting his book down, he
cautiously approached the side of my bed, staring at me in grateful
wonder. I saw both pain and relief in his dark eyes. I tried to smile,
to tell him I was fine, but I felt terrible. Not physically, but emotionally. What had I done to my beloved Dad?

"*Con khỏe không?*" (Are you alright, child?)

"*Con khỏe bố,*" (I'm fine Dad,) I answered.

He said nothing more. Instead he pulled his chair to the side of my bed and simply watched me. I didn't know what to say or if I should say anything at all. So I just stared back, grateful for his presence.

A few minutes later, an attendant entered the room and asked my father to step outside to speak with the doctor. My father gave me a loving smile that indicated everything would be OK; then he followed the man into the hallway. I heard two voices: my father's and a woman's. Though my French was poor and the voices were faint, I could decipher enough to know that the woman was a doctor and she wanted an explanation.

My father soon returned to his seat next to my hospital bed. He thought for a while before speaking. "*Kể cho bố chuyện gì đã xảy ra,*" (Tell me what happened,) he said.

It wasn't an order. It was a plea. And though I loved my father deeply, I lied. I told him that a terrible headache had driven me to the medicine cabinet. When the headache wouldn't go away, I kept taking more and more pills. I lost track of the number, and I didn't mean to take so many.

I'm sure he wanted to believe my story, but I'm just as sure that he didn't. Nonetheless, he took my explanation back to the doctor waiting in the hallway. Her response was gruff, unaccepting. She didn't buy it. The amount and variety of drugs she had pumped out of my stomach did not support my story. What I had done was no accident, she said. She wanted to send someone to investigate my home life.

I was kept in the hospital for two more days. I don't know if an investigation of my home life was conducted during this time. I never asked, and no one ever said. Nor did anyone ever question me during my hospital stay; but if they had, I would have lied again. To speak the truth would have been shameful. I had no right to be unhappy. I was seven years old and, from all outward appearances, led an ideal life.

I was a privileged Vietnamese child who lived in an upper class section of Saigon in a house that employed a nanny, a cook, a housekeeper, a gardener, and a chauffeur—all of Chinese descent. It was not uncommon for families like mine to hire displaced Chinese nationals as servants of some sort in order to elevate our status in society. We all lived comfortably, though not extravagantly, in a one-story brick house that sat back some distance from the road, surrounded by a high brick wall and accessible through a large, iron gate. I was aware of the neighbors, but other than the occasional wave through the car window, I had little contact with them or anyone else.

My playmates were my siblings—four of them at the time, all younger than me. For fun we were encouraged to read, and so there were always plenty of books to choose from. When not tucked away in our bedrooms, we spent time outside playing hopscotch or a game similar to jacks called chơi chuyền that utilized a small ball and chopsticks.

Our care fell into the hands of the hired staff. The nanny bathed and dressed us and tucked us into bed each night. When we were sick, she would concoct terrible Chinese potions that drove me to feign wellness in order to avoid taking them. The cook served us our meals at the kitchen table and liberally provided us with sweets. The housekeeper cleaned up after us, making sure our rooms and clothing were always clean. This could not have been easy, for the dominant color in my home was white. In her pursuit of perfection, my mother's decorative style focused on the absence of color. The walls were white, the bedding was white, even the tile floor was white. In fact, most of our clothes were white.

The chauffeur did all the driving, which included driving me to school each morning. And the gardener cared for the fruit trees and vegetables that kept us well fed. The staff was kind to us, but I did not like the gardener. He had once touched me inappropriately, and then swore me to secrecy. That secret weighed heavily on my young mind and soul.

I must have been five years old at the time, too young to be in school. It happened one day while I was playing in the garden. I got dirt on my hands and white cotton dress, and the gardener took me into the shed to clean me off. He rinsed my hands and brushed water on my dress. When the stain wouldn't come out, he led me to his room, which was situated in the little extension off the back of the main house. He had me sit on the edge of his bed while he went to get a washcloth. When he returned, he continued to wash my hands, which were already clean. It felt weird. He was too close. I could smell his breath. Then, in one swift motion, he pushed me gently down onto the bed. I tried to sit up, but he wouldn't let me.

"I'm not going to hurt you," he said. So I lay there. Confused.

Once he was sure that I wasn't going to move, he stood up and removed his pants. I had never seen a naked man before, and I couldn't help but stare. He lay down next to me. I didn't like it, yet I stayed completely still and as silent as a lamb. He began rubbing his genitals against me while he ran his hands all over my little body. First, my stomach and chest. Then my legs. His breathing got heavier. I went numb, too afraid to cry out. Then he pulled down my underwear and continued to touch me in places that I had never touched myself. All of a sudden I felt something warm ooze onto my skin.

"Yuck," I whispered, realizing my clean body had now been soiled.

The gardener gently wiped me off with the washcloth he had previously used on my hands. "Be a good girl," he said, "and don't tell anyone what we did." He helped me dress and sent me back into the garden to play.

After that, I avoided the gardener at all costs. I also made it my responsibility to protect my younger siblings from him. Whenever I saw them playing outside, I would usher them into the house to read. Heaven forbid they should get dirt on their hands! I made it my mission to keep them clean, which was a difficult task for a child of my age to enforce. Cleanliness would become an obsession. I believe it was my way of coping with something I did not understand.

To what degree this incident affected my decision to attempt suicide two years later, I do not know. However, I can say with certainty that I felt physically uneasy each time I saw the gardener. I never told the nanny or my father about the incident, and the thought of telling my mother never crossed my mind. Even if I had felt compelled to tell someone, I'm not sure I could have with my five-year-old vocabulary. Besides, the gardener had told me not to tell anyone, and I had been taught to obey my elders without question. I was a compliant child. I had been trained to be seen—perfectly clean and white—but not heard. Such behavioral guidelines may have been introduced at home, but they were enforced tenfold at school.

As the oldest of five children, I was honored with a first-rate education. While I was chauffeured to a private Catholic school six days a week, my younger brothers walked to the local public school. My academic subjects had a western bent and were taught in French, whereas my siblings were instructed in Vietnamese. Unaware of my family's elite social standing, the education I received made me feel ostracized from my siblings and the world around me, not special.

Vietnam was, and remains, an overwhelmingly Buddhist country despite the fact that in 1858 France invaded Vietnam and systematically made it a colony steeped in Catholic dogma and French culture. The French military captured Saigon in 1859 and formed what became known as French Indochina. Once colonial rule was established, citizens who professed allegiance to the Catholic faith were rewarded with government posts, education, and tracts of land that had once belonged to Vietnamese Buddhists. To remain a Buddhist in this Catholic-dominated political setting meant financial ruin. And so, long before I was born, my ancestors aligned with Catholicism, thus paving the way for my privileged lifestyle generations later.

My early education began with the memorization of French nursery rhymes. While the rhythm of the poetry made recitation possible, it didn't guarantee comprehension. Eventually I was able to recite the rhymes, but I didn't always understand what I was saying, nor did my siblings. Though I studied every night for several hours, I was not the strongest student, as evidenced by my rank at school. Vietnamese schools traditionally rank students rather than grade their work. I was always at the bottom of the list and, therefore, shunned by my peers. My academic performance was not only shameful for me, it was embarrassing for my mother. So much of a Vietnamese woman's pride and social standing rests on the success of her children—particularly her oldest child. Suffice it to say, I was not helping my mother move up the social ladder.

Unlike my father, my mother offered me no words of encouragement, only words of disappointment. "Well," she would say looking at my report card, "it looks like good money gone down the drain again!"

In an effort to bring my rank up to a respectable level, my mother hired a French tutor. When the tutor couldn't make headway with me, my mother brought in the big guns: her sister. Auntie Dung did her best to drill French—as well as other subjects—into my young brain. Her main teaching tactic was to pinch my ear whenever I failed a lesson. I often went to sleep with bruised lobes. I am living proof that corporal punishment does not improve aptitude. At the end of my first grade year, I was deemed hopeless. A failure at age six.

Though I truly tried my best, I could not measure up to my mother's expectations. It hurt my heart when she would say with disgust, "I can't believe you're my child." She withheld her love from me; and try as I might, I was unable to earn it. She was so different from my father, who didn't care about my academic performance. He didn't care where I ranked in relation to my peers. He didn't care if I understood French nursery rhymes. He just loved me, and I believe my mother hated him for it.

I was the apple of my father's eye, and I knew it. In the evenings, he would sometimes take me on walks around the yard among the various fruit trees—mango, cherimoya, and banana. He would tell me silly stories, and we would both laugh like children. Other times he would pull me out of school in the middle of the day just to take me for ice cream. If my mother found out about our escapades, a fight would inevitably ensue. I once heard my mother accuse my father of worshipping me in the same manner that a Buddhist worships his idols. She screamed, "The only thing you have not done yet for that girl is build her a shelf to sit on!"

My dad, Nguyen Xuan Dat, was born in 1920 and educated as an architect. He was a self-made man who rose to the high rank of public servant in the office of Central Town Planning and Development in the city of Saigon. He must have made a decent wage to afford the servants and beautiful home in which we lived. I remember my father working long hours, seven days a week. When he was home, he preferred to be alone in his office or in the company of his children.

In contrast, my mother preferred to spend her days socializing, often playing Mahjongg with friends. Her status in society was of utmost importance to her and, to validate her popularity, she surrounded herself with admirers. When my mother had friends over, which was often, we children were relegated to our rooms where we could not be seen or heard. We were not her priority. That is what hired staff was for. With an audience at hand, she demonstrated her power by ordering the staff around and criticizing anyone who didn't see things her way—especially my father.

One thing that seemed to irk my mother intensely was my father's generosity. He spared no expense when it came to his children, and he willingly gave money to anyone in need—particularly, his poorer relatives. My mother, on the other hand, spent lavishly on herself. Later in life, after I had children of my own, my mother told me that my father had been an honest and compassionate man who had a heart to help everyone around him. Then, in the same breath she said, "He was so good that a lot of people took advantage of him. They would borrow money and never pay it back. I lectured him all the time, but he never learned!"

My mother, Nguyen Thi Minh, was my father's second—and much younger—wife. I think his first wife died from tuberculosis, which was a common killer in those days. I had two older step-brothers from his previous marriage who were being raised by my father's cousins in another town. As a child I wondered why they did not live with us; as an adult I learned it was because my mother wanted nothing to do with them. Occasionally they would visit and help me with my schoolwork. I remember doing rather well under their tutelage. I liked them, for they were gentle, like my father. They never pinched my ear or told me I was hopeless.

Dad was 36 and Mom was 22 when they married in 1956, the year before I was born. I'm told my parents had a Catholic wedding ceremony, though I've never seen any pictures to support this claim. Four more children quickly followed over the span of five years: three boys and another girl. My mother had never aspired to bear children. I imagine she was happier before she became a mother. As the second oldest of eleven children and the first girl born to an abusive, alcoholic father, her childhood couldn't have been easy or pleasant. Perhaps her marriage to my father was an escape. I once asked my mother if she had loved my dad, she answered quickly, "No." She explained that she had married him because he was recently widowed and she felt sorry for him, adding, "He was a good catch because he was financially secure."

Despite the lifestyle my father provided and to which my mother had grown accustomed, my mother always seemed unhappy. Jealous, angry arguments were common occurrences in my home. They put me on edge and sent me into hiding. I remember one argument in particular that seemed especially unwarranted, though I wasn't present during the actual incident that instigated the fight. It had taken place in the car. I was able to infer from my parents' heated exchange that my mother had accused my father of having an affair with a woman whom he had waved through an intersection. My father defended himself by telling my mother that he had no idea who the woman was and that he was merely being polite by waving her to cross the street. My mother would not even acknowledge his explanation and continued to berate him for weeks.

I often ached for my dad. Following any one of my mother's tirades, he would go silent and retreat to his office. Our evening walks in the garden would cease, and days might pass before I would see him again. Though I was not the subject of many of their fights, I often blamed myself for their frequency. My mother could be ruthless. Though she had barely completed her high school education, she was quite skilled at slinging insults that hit the mark. Despite her bitter tongue, my father never responded in kind. In fact, I cannot recall hearing my father say an unkind word about anyone—not even my mother.

My mother's heart did not match her looks. Much like the evil queens in fairy tales, she was picture perfect on the outside, as if she had just stepped off the pages of Vogue magazine. Every day she dressed in a traditional Vietnamese *ao dai*—brightly colored satin slacks beneath a form-fitting sheath that extended to her ankles with slits on each side from hem to waist. The high neck-line, long sleeves, and tight bodice accentuated her thin, petite body. Dressed in bright colors, she appeared to shine against the white walls of our home. In well-heeled shoes, she moved with purpose from room to room, barking out orders to the hired help. Her black hair was thick and straight, and she would often pull it back off her face after teasing into a bouffant. She rarely appeared without black eyeliner around her almond-shaped eyes and a shade of ruby lipstick on her perfect, full lips. My mother was impeccable, but unapproachable. I was in awe of her, but she frightened me.

Before bed each night, our nanny would give us a bath in a plastic tub the size of a small pool. After dressing us in clean pajamas, she would line us up to file into my mother's room for inspection. I knew the routine, but it still made me nervous. My mother's dialogue with us was always the same.

"You had your bath, I can see that. Have you brushed your teeth?"

"Yes," we would answer in unison.

Then the two younger children who had not yet begun school would be dismissed. My two older brothers and I remained behind. Beginning with Duc, then Thanh, and finally me, she would ask us one by one, "Have you done your homework?"

We would each answer, "Yes," when it was our turn to speak.

She would squint her eyes, evaluating our responses, which made me feel like an insect under a microscope. Eventually she would say, "OK. It's time for you to go to bed." And off we'd go with our nanny. No goodnight kisses. Not even a smile. Leaving her presence was always a relief.

I was not blessed with a mother you could run to with a cut finger. I don't recall her ever holding me on her lap or kissing away my tears. She never helped me dress for school or greeted me when I came home, and I have no memories of her playing with me, sharing a meal with me, or reading me a book. I don't ever remember seeing my mother in pajamas; perhaps this is because she never once tucked me into bed at night. Though we lived in the same house, we had very little contact with each other, and what contact we did have was not copacetic. She was judge and jury, and I always felt guilty and condemned.

I'd like to believe that I experienced some happy moments with my mother when I was small, but I don't remember any. Two photographs I possess of me with my parents show very different scenarios. In the one with my mother, I appear rigid and off-balance as she pulls my left arm while I cling to my brother's leg for support. Clearly, I am not comfortable; but in the photo of me with my father and siblings, I am laughing. Joyful. This rare photo is one of my prized possessions because moments such as this were few and far between.

It's hard for me to pinpoint the exact motivation for my suicide attempt so long ago. In truth, it may have been for a number of reasons. I did not feel loved by my mother. I was not smart, and she had deemed me hopeless. I felt somewhat responsible for the fights between my mother and my father. Or perhaps it was because the gardener made me extremely uncomfortable. What I do know is that I did not feel wanted or protected. No matter how hard I strove to be obedient, intelligent, and worthy, I felt I always fell short of the mark.

And so I went to the stark white medicine cabinet in the stark white bathroom off the stark white hallway near my stark white bedroom. First I removed every bottle and box of pills on every shelf in the cabinet. Then I sat on the bathroom floor surrounded by a variety of drugs and began to eat each one, slowly and systematically. Surely, I thought, the world would be a better place without me.

My suicide attempt had hurt my father deeply. That had never been my intent. I loved my father, for he was gentle and kind. He made me laugh and said nice things to me. When I was finally released in his care, I made a promise to God and to myself that I would never again attempt suicide and cause my father more pain. We drove home from the hospital in silence. There was nothing to discuss. He knew the truth, and there was nothing he could do to change it.

My beautiful, ice-cold mother was waiting at the door for me with her arms crossed above her waist. "You'd better go to your room and rest," she said. Her compassionate words did not match the look on her face, which told me that I was a disappointment, an embarrassment, a naughty girl.

When my mother was quite advanced in years, I summoned up the courage to ask her how she had felt about motherhood. She struggled to understand the question.

"I took care of you the best I could," she said. "I always made sure you had good clothes and were well fed. I made sure the cook and nanny did their job to care for you."

As I reflect on her statement, I realize that being cared *for* and being cared *about* are two very different things—especially to a young and sensitive child. Striving for my mother's love and acceptance in the hopes that she might some day care about me became a lifelong goal. It was one I would never achieve.

CHAPTER 2

*"Do not store up for yourselves treasures on earth, where moths
and vermin destroy, and where thieves break in and steal.
But store up for yourselves treasures in heaven,
where moths and vermin do not destroy,
and where thieves do not break in and steal.
For where your treasure is, there your heart will be also."*
Matthew 6:19-21 (NIV)

1965–1967

The arguments between my parents intensified following my
suicide attempt. I could always tell when a storm was about
to break. My mother would begin by questioning my father about
something trivial. He would give her a short answer, which was
never good enough. She would then twist and turn his responses,
demanding more information, until she had worked herself into a
frenzy. Eventually she would resort to violence, throwing whatever
was in reach. As the confrontations escalated, my father would
become increasingly passive, which seemed to infuriate my mother
even more. My dad often emerged with bruises on his face. The
very thing I had hoped to avoid—hurting my father—was playing
out in spades.

As time went on, I become more convinced that I was to blame
for their broken relationship and determined that life would be

better for both Dad and me if I were to live elsewhere. I sought my father out in the library, where he often spent many hours alone, to present my plan.

"Dad," I began, "I think it would be good for me to start living at school."

Saint Paul Catholic School had dormitories for girls, yet the boarders were several years older than me. My father listened respectfully as I made my case. I explained that I thought my grades would improve if I lived at the school rather than commute there each day. I also told him that I would like to make friends and that my chances of doing so were greater if I lived in the dormitory. Dad told me he would discuss the matter with my mother and let me know what they decided.

I could tell my father did not fully support the idea. He didn't tell me why, but I assume it was because I was very young and had recently tried to kill myself. Also, he was not a devotee of the Catholic Church, having not been raised in the faith. This did not hinder him, however, from carrying a picture of Jesus and Mother Mary in his wallet. A priest had given him the picture about 20 years earlier when they emigrated together from North Vietnam.

As I suspected, my mother—the proud Catholic—embraced the idea. With me out of the house, she would have one less child to count each night. One less child to disappoint her. And so it was settled. At the beginning of the next school year, I became a boarder at Saint Paul Catholic School. I was already familiar with the educational requirements; what I had to learn were the routines associated with living on campus.

The dorm room of Saint Paul's housed between 20 and 30 girls. Each girl had her own single bed that was separated from the next by a small wooden chair and bedside table. Lights out occurred at 9:00 sharp each evening. To wake us, a nun would walk slowly through our room ringing a bell at 5:00 sharp each morning. How I hated the bell, for it was piercing and abrupt. So unlike the tender shake my nanny used to rouse me. We were required to quickly make our beds, and then kneel beside them in preparation to recite the Morning Prayer of thanks and the Lord's Prayer in unison— in French of course. *Notre Père, qui es aux cieux, que ton nom soit sanctifié… (Our Father who art in Heaven, hallowed be Thy name…)* The theology behind the words was deeply buried in the rote cadence. *Donne-nous aujourd'hui notre pain de ce jour… (Give us this day our daily bread…)* The words meant little more to me than a means of passage to obtain breakfast.

Once God had deemed the prayer acceptable—according to the nuns—we girls were given permission to wash for the day ahead. Forming a line at the sinks, we'd fill our small plastic buckets and cups with water to be used to wash our faces and brush our teeth. The nuns would then inspect each of us individually to make sure we had washed properly. If we met their approval, we were allowed to empty the dirty water, clean our buckets and cups, place them neatly under our bedside table, and get dressed.

We wore the traditional Western uniform for Catholic schools: a white button-down shirt over a navy pleated skirt. White socks were overturned at the ankle, and flat black Mary Janes with a strap and buckle completed the outfit. With our jet-black hair and brown eyes, we were all cookie cutter replicas of each other. The only thing that distinguished us from one another was the book bags and pencil cases we carried with our names on them.

Everything we owned was labeled, from the clothes we wore to the things we carried, from my socks to my soap container. I liked seeing my name engraved on each item. It gave me a sense of belonging and purpose. *Nguyen Thi Minh Phuong.* In Vietnamese, my name means "original, bright path." I was the only child with this particular name, and I was proud of it.

By 6:00 a.m. we were heading to the chapel for confession and mass. Daily confession not only made me aware of my sinfulness, it instilled in me a deep feeling of guilt for the minutest offenses. In my search to find something to confess each morning, I would scrupulously critique my behaviors to the nth degree. This practice had a long-lasting effect on me. To this very day, I feel I am at least partially to blame when situations do not unfold as planned.

Mass was followed by a simple breakfast in the dining hall that consisted of toast or oatmeal and a boiled egg with milk. Adhering to Western practices, we consumed our meals with a fork and knife rather than chopsticks. Eating with these strange utensils was a feat for me to master, but I was determined to excel at it.

We students were allowed to talk as we ate. However, we were not allowed to speak with our mouths full or click our tongues as we chewed. It is a common practice among Asian peoples to make a smacking sound with their tongues as they eat—as common as breathing. Breaking this habit was more difficult than learning how to use a fork and knife. I truly did not know how to eat without making noise. The nuns would have none of it and would walk from table to table during meals enforcing the no-clicking rule. "Minh Phuong," they would say to me, "you are making noise! You need to eat slower."

Ever obedient, I would chew slower, but this did not stop my tongue from clicking. It just became less frequent. As a result, I was never able to finish my meal in a timely manner and often headed to class late and hungry. Roll call was taken at 7:45, and classes promptly started at 8:00. Even after all these years, the morning routine at Saint Paul Catholic School is ingrained in my brain, and I can visualize each step with extreme clarity.

As the youngest boarder at the school, I was an easy target for bullies, one of whom I had the misfortune of eating dinner with each night. Six students were assigned to every dining table, two of which were seniors whose job it was to divvy out the food. One evening I entered the dining hall to discover that cauliflower was on the menu—a vegetable I absolutely detest. I made the mistake of saying aloud, "I hate cauliflower!"

The one senior didn't miss a beat. She looked at the other girls and announced, "I hear Minh Phuong loves cauliflower, so she should have the most." And with that she proceeded to pile my plate sky high with the offending vegetable. When I started to cry, she was encouraged to bully me more. "If you cry," she said, "I will give you more cauliflower to eat, and you will never leave this dining room!"

Choking back the tears, I ate a full plate of the pungent white vegetable and learned a valuable lesson in the process: Never let your enemies know your weakness.

My favorite teacher was Mademoiselle Laurentin. She was not a nun, and in no way resembled a nun. Nor was she Vietnamese. She was French.

Mademoiselle Laurentin wore miniskirts, and her brunette hair was cropped short and fashionable. She spoke in a beautifully clear French voice that flowed like a melody. Every other teacher would conduct lessons while seated in the chair behind her desk—but not Mademoiselle Laurentin. She always stood, leaning over her desk in order to make direct eye contact with each student. The lessons came alive as she spoke French using her hands and her eyes as well as her lips. I adored her and imagined myself as a French teacher when I grew up. Though I never attained this goal, I can say that memories of Mademoiselle Laurentin continue to inspire me to this day. Before she came into my life, I was convinced that all teachers were merely angry wolves, ready to attack. Mademoiselle Laurentin did not fit this mold. She was playful, elegant, and confident, and her laugh was like a beautiful song filling the room with joy.

In addition to the French language, Mademoiselle Laurentin taught us French social skills, such as how to greet people and hold engaging conversations. She would often have us role-play with her so that we might learn how to look people in the eye when speaking with them. This was a true challenge, as Asian children are taught to look down whenever an adult speaks to them. "Let's have a conversation!" she would say to one lucky student. A tête-à-tête would ensue while the rest of us, captivated, watched and listened.

I wasn't Mademoiselle Laurentin's favorite student, but I wasn't her least favorite either. She was fair to everyone, which only increased my admiration for her. One important thing she inadvertently taught me was that it was all right to ask someone how she was feeling. Mademoiselle Laurentin had once put her arm around me and asked, "How do you feel today?"

I must have given her a pat answer like, "Fine," because she informed me that it was OK for people to be themselves and answer honestly. This was contrary to what I had been taught. Conditioned to keep my feelings close to my heart, I knew no other answer than the one I gave.

I also remember Mademoiselle Laurentin teaching the class that it was not appropriate to hug just anyone. You had to read a person's body language in order to determine if a hug would be welcome. She was so clever! In my young mind, I reasoned that I might not have ended up in such a compromising position with the gardener if he had been Mademoiselle Laurentin's student.

Mademoiselle Laurentin never punished me, but other teachers did—mostly the nuns. A common punishment was to put a child in a corner and have her write a thousand times in her notebook: *I will not disobey*. This particular punishment could never be completed in one sitting and could drag on for days.

Another common punishment was to get the palms of your hands slapped with a wooden ruler. A few of the nuns were especially tough and would slap the knuckles instead. That hurt. I had to endure each of these afflictions several times throughout the years. My punishments were usually meted out because of mistakes I had made on my homework. "How many times have I told you how to do this?" was a common plea I heard from my teachers before the ruler came down.

Despite the use of corporal punishment by some of the nuns, I felt that overall they were compassionate to my situation. Most of the girls went home each weekend and over the summer months. Not me. Though my home was less than 30 minutes away by car, I was a permanent fixture at the school for almost three years straight. Many nights I slept alone in the large dormitory room. Without the breathing and movement of other girls, I found it could be a scary place. Every squeak and creak frightened me. I would lay perfectly still in my bed, reciting the Lord's Prayer in my head, hoping the fear would subside so I could fall asleep. When I would look up and see a nun poking her head through the door to check on me, I knew that God had answered my prayer.

During the loneliest of times, the nuns would concoct simple craft projects for me to do. I remember once creating a type of flowerpot out of wooden craft sticks by stacking them one on top of the other. Then I drew some flowers, pasted them to more sticks, and stuck them in the pot. I gave the completed art project to my father who raved over it and displayed it prominently on his desk at home. It was quite ugly, and it wasn't white, so I'm sure my mother hated it, but my father treasured it because he treasured me.

Several times each year, the nuns would call both of my parents in to conference. Listening outside the door, I would hear the principal ask them if things were all right at home. My mother would say that everything was fine, and my father—to avoid confrontation—would simply not dispute her claim. However, Dad would later return to the principal's office alone and share information that I was not privy to.

The nuns served as my protectors. Collectively, they were the surrogate mothers I so desperately needed. Under their constant care and tutelage, my rank at school began to improve, as did my self-esteem. By the end of my second year, I ranked in the top three students for mathematics at my grade level. I remember my father telling me that he was proud of me. My mother, on the other hand, never said a word.

I was also a good athlete—especially in the relay race. Though I was never selected as a team captain, I was often chosen to run first or last. If we needed a strong start, I was appointed to run the baton first. If we needed a strong finish, I was appointed to take the baton last and cross the finish line. Running was the one area in school in which age didn't matter. I loved to run! It made me feel powerful and free.

I don't recall making any true friends at school. This could be attributed to several things. One, I never had any friends when I lived at home and wasn't sure how to make them. Two, there were no other girls my age who were boarders. Three, I was a natural loner who kept to myself. Whatever the reason, I was perfectly content living at Saint Paul Catholic School, away from the tense atmosphere of home where arguments and insults were a daily and nightly occurrence. School was a safe and predictable place. I knew the routine and had learned how to fit in. If I was punished, I knew why and accepted it as just. At times I missed my siblings, but the advantages of boarding at school far outweighed my desire to live with them at home.

My father visited me every week. Occasionally, he would take me away for the weekend. This would usually occur when things had become quite bad at home as evidenced by the bruises on his face. Then I'd pack a small bag, and off we'd go. Sometimes we'd spend a day or two in the country visiting one of Dad's wealthier friends. Other times, we'd visit his sons who were being raised by my father's first cousin. My father's parents were dead, so his cousins were the only family he had. They were materially poor, but emotionally rich—more joyful than anyone I knew.

Dad's cousins and sons always seemed happy to see us and praised me for my accomplishments in school, no matter how trivial they were. They especially loved to hear me sing the French song, *Frère Jacques*, over and over again. I would willingly oblige whenever asked, and they would cheer me on as if I was a famous recording artist. I felt so admired!

My father always gave his cousins money when we left. Their sincere gratefulness made me proud to be my father's daughter. I secretly hoped that one day I would have enough money to help others the way he did.

During one of my father's visits I learned that my mother was pregnant again. Several months later, she gave birth to another boy. I often wondered why my father stayed with my mother and continued to have children with her or why he allowed her to abuse him. At the time, I viewed his behavior as a sign of weakness, but now I see it as a sign of strength.

How hard it must have been for him to live with her and put up with the abuse. How hard it must have been for him to engage in arguments every day when his inherent personality was gentle and upbeat. How hard it must have been for him to watch his children treated as objects rather than beloved offspring. How hard it must have been for him to be separated from me—the daughter he truly loved—and watch me struggle under the care of Catholic nuns who taught a religion he did not embrace. But when we were together, oh, how he loved me!

The first time I had any inclination that something was terribly wrong with the world was the day my father told me that he had let our housekeeper, chauffeur, and gardener go. I was relieved at the gardener's dismissal, though I couldn't imagine how my mother was raising my four siblings with such limited help. I'm sure she had put up a fight.

Boarding school was expensive, and continuing to live at Saint Paul Catholic School seemed selfish. It was time for me to move back home. When I reflect on the clarity with which I arrived at this conclusion, I see God directing me. As I would later realize, He knew what was ahead and what would be best.

Both my father and the principal were visibly elated with my decision to move home, which made it easier for me to pack my small bag and leave. My reentry into family life was uneventful. My mother was not at the house when I arrived; instead, my Chinese nanny joyfully welcomed me in. "Minh Phuong," she said, "it is so good to have you home!" I think she really meant it.

I moved back into the simple white bedroom I shared with my little sister, Chau. We slept together in a typical Vietnamese platform bed with a single, thin mattress atop a hard wooden frame. I found her presence next to me at night to be comforting.

It took a few days for me to realize the subtle changes that had occurred in my absence. My father was no longer in charge of anything. My mother now ran the entire household. With the staff cut in half, she was forced to pick up some of the slack, which included learning how to drive. The extra duties did not slow her down. She would bark orders at the cook and nanny before grabbing the car keys to head out the door on her round of social calls. I knew my mother's status in society had probably diminished along with the hired help, yet this seemed to improve her temperament. My mother's newfound authority and freedom seemed to soften her somewhat, as evidenced by the fact that she fought less with my father.

I fell into the new routine quickly, and life seemed bearable, almost pleasant. I was almost unaware that I was living in the midst of a war.

The Vietnam War, which the Vietnamese people call the American War, began in earnest in 1956 and lasted almost 19 years. From my perspective, the war was nothing more than a power-struggle between the communists and the capitalists of the world being played out on Vietnamese soil. The North Vietnamese communists had the backing of the Soviet Union and China; the South Vietnamese had the support of France and the United States. The dividing line was the 17th parallel, identified by the Geneva Accords of 1954 in the aftermath of World War II. The original plan was for the country to reunite with one ruler based on an election that would be held in 1956 under the supervision of neutral countries. When the election did not take place as planned, the split became permanent and fighting ultimately ensued. As a child I would sometimes hear gunshots in the distance—but they were always in the distance. Both sides periodically proclaimed victory that was either battle specific or sheer propaganda.

One day I overheard the cook saying that several of our neighbors were moving away. This worried me. Vietnamese families never leave their homes empty. Even when they take vacations, which are rare, they have someone housesit to deter intruders.

Later that evening, I asked my dad, "Will we have to move?"

"Don't worry," he answered. "We are very safe here."

I believed him. I lived in a home surrounded by a high wall in an elite section of downtown Saigon, the capital of South Vietnam and the center of my world. I knew the enemy was North Vietnam and the ally was the United States of America. I had grown up with American and Vietnamese military police working alongside each other on every street. I recognized them by the "MP" emblazoned on their helmets and shirtsleeves. Saigon seemed more American than Vietnamese or even French, with restaurants, nightclubs, and hotels sporting American names. The news announcers spoke in English, and the radio played American songs that were more familiar to me than *Frère Jacques*. The Americans were everywhere and would surely protect us if the enemy ever made it as far as the city limits. Even when my mother began stocking up on foodstuffs—canned food and rice—I was not worried.

As a child of 11, I trusted my parents to take care of everything.

When the new school year started, I found myself expectantly looking forward to the most important celebration of the year: New Year, or Têt. It would begin on the first day of the lunar calendar (around late January or early February) and last for three days. During this time, special foods would be eaten, ancestors would be worshipped, and "lucky money" would be given to children in small red envelopes.

A few days before the start of Têt, my father and I took an evening walk in the garden. The faint smell of chrysanthemums filled the air. Dad asked me if I was hopeful about the New Year, and I responded with an emphatic, "Yes!"

"Why?" he asked.

I told him that I was excited thinking about all the lucky money I would receive. He was quiet for a moment. Then he said, "Minh Phuong, you have to think about more than just money."

I looked at him, not quite understanding the lesson he had for me. He took my hand and led me into the garden off the back porch. It was a clear night, and the sky was speckled with thousands of stars. Pointing up he asked, "Do you see that star?"

"Yes," I answered, though I wasn't quite sure which one he meant.

"You have to like that star more than you like money," he said. "Money will buy you a lot of things, but no amount of money can buy you a star. If you have wishes and a star, you won't need money."

What he said didn't make any sense to me at the time, but now I see that my father was teaching me something very important. He was trying to tell me not to rely on things of this world, which can be taken away in the blink of an eye. He was trying to tell me that money could not buy what is priceless: love, or compassion, or hope. The lesson he was trying to teach me was too big for my young mind to fathom. Years later, however, it was the gift that sustained me in dark times. It was the last—and most valuable—gift my father ever gave me.

CHAPTER 3

"This is why I weep and my eyes overflow with tears.
No one is near to comfort me, no one to restore my spirit.
My children are destitute because the enemy has prevailed."
Lamentations 1:16 (NIV)

February 1–2, 1968

1968 was the Year of the Monkey—the ninth animal in the 12-year zodiac cycle. Born in 1920, my father was the only member of our family celebrated as a monkey. According to the stars, monkeys were smart and quick witted, compassionate, and stubborn. That characterized my father perfectly.

By the second day of Tết I had collected about 800 dong. I carried the Vietnamese currency under my clothing during the day and put it under my pillow at night. It was a hefty amount of money for that time and could have fed my family of eight for several days. I had yet to imagine what I might spend it on, as there was still one more day to collect.

Our nanny and cook had three days off to visit their families and celebrate the New Year with them, but the work of their hands was evident everywhere. The trees were bursting with fruit—mangos, jackfruit, and terracotta oranges with thick, bright green skins. The piglet had been ordered, butchered, and roasted to perfection.

Special foods, like pickles and sticky cake known as *bánh chung*, were available in the pantry.

Friends and family dropped by both day and night to celebrate with us and exchange small red envelopes. My siblings and I were dressed in new holiday outfits of white with a touch of red. We answered the door and provided refreshments while my mother directed the proceedings. Not one to do any physical labor herself, she was quite gifted at pointing her finger and giving directions.

While we all made merry, the enemy living in our midst prepared for attack. Wrapped up in the Tết celebrations, Saigon was unaware of the dangerously close proximity of the enemy though more than half a million refugees had recently crowded into shantytowns surrounding Saigon to escape the communists who had already invaded the countryside.

In the months leading up to Tết, General Võ Nguyên Giáp the North Vietnamese Defense Minister, strategically directed a massive buildup of communist troops in South Vietnam. Both Vietcong guerillas and members of the People's Army of North Vietnam (PAVN) began pouring into South Vietnam from points along the Ho Chi Minh Trail, which runs parallel to South Vietnam's western boarder through Laos and Cambodia. At the beginning of 1968, American intelligence had identified seven North Vietnamese divisions hiding in South Vietnam totaling around 55,000 soldiers. Unlike the Vietcong, the PAVN were trained military personnel and were armed with modern weapons from China and the Soviet Union.[3] These weapons had been smuggled into targeted areas across South Vietnam in such things as flower carts and vegetables trucks. North Vietnamese sympathizers living in the south hid both the weapons and the communists who transported them.

On the first evening of the three-day holiday, North Vietnamese troops attacked main cities and administrative centers in the northern part of the country. This was just a distraction to turn the focus away from Saigon, the base of American operations. On the second evening of the three-day holiday, the PAVN and Vietcong launched the Tết Offensive, which was comprised of simultaneous attacks in major cities throughout South Vietnam and on politically important targets such as the Presidential Palace, the airport, the radio station, and the newly constructed U.S embassy in Saigon. The attacks came as a total surprise.

I am guessing that it was around 2:00 a.m. when I was shocked out of a sound sleep by a loud blast. A moment later, my bed started to shake, and I wondered if we were experiencing an earthquake. Confused, I laid perfectly still. I could hear gunfire and yelling outside, but I wasn't able to make out the words. Suddenly my father appeared crawling along the floor of my bedroom. He reached up and grabbed my arm, pulling me off the bed. Putting his hand over my mouth, he indicated to me that I was not to talk. Instinctively, I reached for my five-year-old sister, Chau, and pulled her onto the floor with us. She didn't say a word.

Together the three of us crawled to the spare room at the end of the hall. This room had a window that looked out onto our garden and provided a pleasant breeze. There was only one piece of furniture in this room—a wooden platform that served as a small bed. It sat about two feet off the ground. We crawled under it. My brothers Thanh and Dan were already there, lying feet to feet and pressed against the wall. My sister and I pushed up against them, and my father shielded us on the outside. I tried to hold my breath thinking it would stop the loud pounding of my heart, which to me was as loud as the gunfire outside. For a brief moment I wondered where my mother and two other brothers were. I quickly let the concern go, assuming my father had hid them elsewhere in the house.

From my vantage point, I could see sparks of light ricocheting off the walls as a result of gunshots, bombs, or fires. Screams and painful laments of *"Trời ơi!"* (Oh my God!) could be heard from the men and women witnessing the horror outside. With the constant rat-a-tat-tat of gunfire and explosions, the noise was deafening and chaotic. Shouts of *"Lui ra! Lui ra!"* (Pull out! Withdraw!) filled the air, but I didn't know whether they came from the enemy or our allies.

Then I heard the arrival of a helicopter with its distinctive thrum of whirling wings whipping through the air. Suddenly there was a whiz, and a frightening explosion shook the earth. I heard stones fall and imagined the wall around our home crumbling in defeat. There were more blasts to follow, and I braced myself each time

I heard the whiz from above knowing it would end in a frightful explosion.

I feared the worst—the ceiling crashing in, the walls tumbling down, and my entire family dying in a pile of rubble. My fears started to become reality when a huge explosion, which literally brought pain to my ears, rocked our home. I watched in shock as the wall across from our hiding place crumbled before my eyes, rocketing shards of cement across the room and creating a wall of dust. When it cleared, I had an unobstructed view of the garden.

It was much worse than I had imagined. This was hell. Fires were blazing in a sea of smoke. Bodies were lying in awkward poses among our trees and bushes. Men I did not recognize were in our yard. Some had rifles and were shooting at people on the ground. Others had shoulder-fired missiles aimed at the helicopter overhead. I recognized the shooters' language, but not the accent. These were not my people.

I heard the helicopter fly away, and the shooting on the ground suddenly stopped. A uniformed soldier, probably a member of the PAVN, came walking along what was left of our garden path. He peered into the room in which we were hiding and started to climb over the fallen debris. My father, my siblings, and I tried to make ourselves small and invisible while in plain sight of the enemy. It was no use. He saw us. Keeping his gun pointed downward, he motioned for us to come out of hiding. We had no choice but to do as he ordered.

Protectively, my father gathered us children to himself like a mother hen with baby chicks. Stepping over the rubble, we made our way outside and fell in line with the other captives, several of whom I recognized as neighbors. There were about 30 of us in total, of all ages. My father pushed us behind him, using his body as a shield. Thanh, who was a year younger than me, stood solemnly off Dad's right shoulder. I stood directly behind my father holding Chau's right hand and Dan's left. And we waited as the enemy soldiers used intimidation tactics to demonstrate their power and keep us in line.

Starting at the far end, the soldier in charge began his interrogation. I could see his lips moving as he spoke to the first woman in the lineup, but I couldn't hear what he asked. She responded with a desperate plea for mercy. He had none. I heard the shot and watched her fall to the ground.

The soldier moved on to the next person, and the interrogation continued. It appeared to me that children were not being shot because I could hear them crying long after their parents fell. I remember thinking that the soldier conducting the interrogation was a very powerful man because he got to decide who would live and who would die. He held our future in his hands.

I must have been in shock because I don't remember feeling anything as the horror moved toward us. I simply watched. Some people were shot; others were not. From what I could tell, several adults were let go based on their responses. *What had they said? Who were these people?* The soldier was obviously looking for specific information. I desperately hoped that my father would have the right answer when it was his turn to speak.

I heard crying. It was Dan and Chau. Lost in time and space, I had forgotten that they were with me, holding onto my hands. I turned away from the killings playing out to my left and focused my attention on my young brother and only sister. I tried to comfort them by saying, "It will be OK." I had no idea if my words would prove true.

And then it was our turn. The soldier stood before us. He told my father to kneel. Dad knelt. I think he asked my father his name, but I'm not sure. I do remember him asking, "Are these your children?"

"Yes," my father answered. Then he added, "They are harmless."

The soldier smiled cynically before responding, "That's what *you* say!"

Did my father answer correctly? Would we be spared? I looked up at the soldier, and we locked eyes. I didn't look away. I held his gaze the way Mademoiselle Laurentin had taught me. Predictably, he engaged me in a conversation. He asked, "Do you love your father?"

I hesitated. I wanted to shout: *Yes!* But was "yes" the right answer? Or would "yes" get us shot? The word was in my head and in my heart, but I couldn't form it on my lips. I loved my father with my whole being, and I wanted him to know it. Yet surrounded by hate, I feared that "yes" to love might get us all killed. I shifted my gaze to my dad, thus ending the conversation with the soldier. I needed my father's help, but he was frozen like me. We simply stared at each other. There was a sadness in his eyes I will never forget.

I don't think the soldier appreciated my silence. With a flick of his head, he said, "You can go back to your home."

Did we hear him correctly? My father attempted to confirm what he heard. Slowly he said, "If you let us, we will."

"You can go," the soldier said again. Affirming his decision.

Cautiously, Dad began to rise from his knees. We instinctively huddled around him, falsely assuming we were free, but the soldier had no intention of letting us walk away. Our ordeal was just beginning. Tauntingly, he said, "Let's see how fast you and your children can run to your home." This wasn't going to be a clean execution. It was to be a hunt.

I remember my father turning to us and saying that we had to run as fast as we could back to the house. I was a fast runner—the best at Saint Paul Catholic School. But the landscape before me was nothing like the track I was used to; it was covered with rubble and dead bodies. I looked down at my beautiful five-year-old sister and handsome seven-year-old brother clinging to my hands. All my skill as a relay runner had not equipped me for this race.

"We can't run very fast!" I pleaded.

"I will help you," Dad replied as he scooped Dan into his arms. I followed his lead and picked up Chau. Thanh took off, and we followed. We all ran for our lives.

I'm pretty sure my father expected to die. As we began running, he yelled out, "God help us!" This was the first and only time I had ever heard my father call on God. It was also the first time since the destruction and slayings started that God had entered my own thoughts. *Where was He?* I wondered. *Did He see what was happening?*

A shot rang out; we kept on running. "I've almost got you!" the soldier yelled, as if we were playing a friendly game of tag.

My brother Thanh was in the lead. I watched him jump over the rubble of the demolished wall, my Dad and Dan right behind him. The gun fired again. My Dad fell, taking Dan down with him. As Dan stood up, the gun went off again. I watched his little body fall like a rag doll.

By now I had made it back to the house with Chau, but in order to get inside, I had to set her down to climb over the rubble. I thought she would follow. Instead, she turned toward my father's body and became the perfect target. The gun fired again, and Chau fell. I had failed to protect her. Disoriented, I went after her lifeless body.

Suddenly, shots rang out in all directions. Someone shouted, *"Lui ra! Bọn nó trở lại!"* (Pull out! They're coming back!) I could hear the American helicopter in the distance. It was returning. People started screaming and running in all directions, soldiers and civilians alike. There was mass confusion.

Our assassin was momentarily distracted. Before giving up the chase though, he turned his gun toward me and pulled the trigger. I had been in the process of rolling Chau's body under the bed when I heard the whiz from the helicopter overhead. Seconds later, the blast rocked our home, and the ceiling caved in.

CHAPTER 4

*Religion that God our Father accepts as pure and faultless is
this: to look after orphans and widows in their distress and
to keep oneself from being polluted by the world.*
James 1:27 (NIV)

February 1968

When the dust settled, I surveyed the situation. Chau was
dead in my arms. All I could see of Dan was his little foot
sticking out of a pile of rubble, and I knew we had lost him too.
Miraculously, Thanh and I were still alive, though our arms and
legs were covered in cuts and burns. I crawled over to my Dad. He
was still breathing, though barely. I did what the nuns had taught
me to do in situations where someone was near death. I asked him,
"Dad, do you want me to baptize you?"

With great effort, he whispered in a gravelly voice, "You have
to take care of your brothers."

"No! I can't!" I pleaded. I needed him.

"You can do it Minh Phuong. You're a big girl now."

I did not want to be a big girl. I wanted to be my father's little
girl. This shouldn't be happening! It wasn't fair. Acutely aware of
the seriousness of his injuries, I asked him again, "Do you want
me to baptize you?"

"But I already have God with me," he said.

What was he saying? I looked around. I couldn't see God anywhere in this horrific and hopeless situation. My father squeezed my arm to get my attention. Struggling to speak, Dad said to me, "You're very special. You're *my* special girl. You can do it." His breathing slowed, and with one finale exhale, he died.

I don't remember how long I remained kneeling over my father's lifeless body. Time seemed to stand still. My Dad had given me my marching orders, and even in death I would obey. In due course, I pulled Thanh out from under the bed, and together we crawled into the interior of the house in search of our mother.

We found her with my brothers: Duc, age 9, and Giang, age 3. They were all hiding under the covers of her big bed. I find it ironic that Dad had crawled under a bed for protection and Mom had crawled into one. She gasped when she saw Thanh and me and pulled us into her cocoon. "Oh my God! You're bleeding!" she said.

I looked down and saw that I was covered in blood. The little flowers on my white satin pajamas were barely visible through the red stains that appeared to be growing before my eyes. *Was I bleeding? From where?* With an urgency I had never before witnessed in my mother, she sprang out of bed and headed toward the bathroom where the bandages were kept. As soon as she opened the door there was a loud crash, and the bathroom ceiling caved in.

My mother immediately jumped back into the bed and gathered her four living children to her bosom. Then she began to pray. I remember her praying for a long time, begging God to save us. It was both awkward and soothing. At some point, she turned to me and asked, "Where is your father?" I told her he was dead. A genuine look of sadness mixed with shock crossed my mother's face. Despite all their arguments, I felt my mother was truly grieved to hear of his death.

God must have heard my mother's prayers because help arrived in the form of friends and neighbors. They came looking for us, banging on the front door, calling out my mother's name. They could see what we could not from under the covers of the big bed. Our home was in shambles and surrounded by fire. It was only a matter of moments before it would all cave in or burn up.

My mother ushered us out of the house, cautiously stepping over broken furnishings and debris. We made our way to the front door, a large metal plate on rollers. Mom slid it open and pushed us outside. That's when she finally counted her brood, a routine she had perfected over the years. *One, two, three, four...* A look of panic crept across her face. Looking directly at me, she asked, "Where are Dan and Chau?"

"They died with Dad," I answered.

The words sounded surreal coming out of my mouth. I can't imagine what my mother must have felt at this moment. Two of her children were dead. Though she bore them, she hardly knew them. Her husband of twelve years was dead. Though they fought practically every day, he had provided her with a high standard of living. Her fine home had been obliterated by war, and she had lost everything except the clothes on her back and four young children. Nothing would ever be the same again.

Without saying another word, my mother pushed us forward, out of the yard and toward the road. I turned one last time to look at what remained of my home. It was engulfed in flames, a mere shell of its former glory. And somewhere in that wreckage were the lifeless bodies of my beloved father, my little brother, and my only sister. I watched as all my treasures and memories savagely went up in smoke.

Directly across the street from our house was a beautiful botanical garden. It had been a magical place on warm afternoons, and we were privileged to have such direct access to it. With war raging all around us, I believe my mother thought the gardens would be the perfect place to take refuge. We soon learned that there is no sanctuary in war.

Ahead of me was a sea of dead bodies. Mom, whose strongest quality was giving directions, told us to step on them and get to the garden. Vietnamese culture teaches us to respect the dead, so this order conflicted me. I tried my best not to step on anyone, but that was impossible—there were so many bodies! Each time I placed my foot on one, I apologized. "I am so sorry," I would say. I was sure these people would one day come back to haunt me for my disrespectful actions.

As we approached the perimeter of the gardens, gunshots that were too close for comfort rang out. Mom pushed us to the ground, and together we crawled behind a tree for protection. Several minutes passed before two American MPs came crawling toward us. One of the MPs was black. I had never been so close to a black person before, and I was surprised by how white his teeth were in the morning light. This man saw that I was bleeding from my head and asked my mother for permission to check my skull. She nodded her approval. I held very still while he inspected the source of my bleeding.

The MP told my mother that I had been shot and that I needed medical attention. Because he spoke in English, my mother had to translate what was being said. I was surprised to learn that a bullet had grazed my skull; I did not feel a thing. The MP asked my mother if he could take me back to some vehicle where there were medical supplies. When my mother told me to go with the MP, I responded, *"Con không đi đâu với người da đen này!"* (I am NOT going anywhere with this black man!)

Luckily, the MP did not speak Vietnamese and, therefore, was not offended by my racial response. However, when he realized that I had no intention of going anywhere with him, he pulled a bandage roll out of his bag and wrapped my head as best he could under the circumstances. Then he told us to follow him, and together we crawled out of the garden and away from sniper fire.

Today when I think of this MP's face, I see an angel of God. He appeared at dawn in the smoke of disaster, bandaged my wounds, and led us to safety. He could have ignored us. Instead, he chose to have compassion on a Vietnamese widow and her young children. I never learned his name, but he played a significant role in my life, for I am sure that I would have bled to death had he not attended to my wound.

As the sun rose, the gunfire began to subside and the smoke began to dissipate. I was horrified by what I saw. Saigon was in shambles. I barely recognized my city. People appeared out of nowhere like shadows, gray and lifeless. We folded in with this displaced crowd, moving with uncertainty down battered roads in search of something we could recognize. No one was left unscathed. We all had wounds; some were just more visible than others.

Whatever my mother felt towards me faded into the background as she directed our broken family on an unseen route toward the hospital. Apparently my wound was severe, and she was not about to lose another child.

The walk was long and difficult, and we were hungry and weary by the time we arrived. My brothers began to cry for food and water. My mother told them to stop crying; she had no money. But I did. The 800 dong I had collected during Tết was tucked in my pajama pocket. It really was lucky money.

The five of us spent the entire day waiting to see a doctor, the line growing longer and longer as evening approached. The injured just kept coming. At first I couldn't help but stare at them and their injuries. After awhile though, they became commonplace, and I became immune to their cries of pain.

Finally, it was my turn to see a doctor. He unwrapped the bloody bandage from my head and announced that I was in desperate need of stitches. The wound was still bleeding and would not close without them. Unfortunately, the hospital was out of anesthetic. The doctor asked my mother what she wanted him to do, and she said, "Just stitch her!"

Lucky for me, the doctor was a sympathetic man, and he warned me that what he was about to do would hurt. I nodded to him that I understood. He cleaned my wound and began stitching. Halfway through the procedure, he ran out of thread and finished the job with a staple. He was right. It did hurt. A lot. But I never cried. I remember the doctor telling me that I was very brave. All I could think was that my father would have been proud of me.

With no home to return to, we began the long trek to my mother's hometown of Chợ Lớn on the southwest side of Saigon where several of her siblings and her father still lived. Unbeknownst to us, the Vietcong had captured Chợ Lớn and had taken control of the Phú Thọ Racetrack where my grandfather often placed bets. The racetrack was a city landmark and strategic in that it could serve as a landing zone for helicopters. With night closing in, the fighting seemed to renew, making our journey a dangerous one. Luckily, a mother and her children were not what the Vietcong were targeting, so we kept moving.

We hadn't walked far when a Good Samaritan offered us a ride in his car. My mother graciously accepted, which provided us with a clear view of the devastation of war as we rode down roads littered with dead bodies and destroyed buildings. What affected me the most were the children. Injured. Crying. Alone. No parent in sight. I wondered where they would sleep that night. Little Giang sat on my mother's lap in the front seat, seemingly unaware of the tragedy before us, while Thanh, Duc, and I huddled together in the back seat in futile consolation. It was now my responsibility to take care of them, and I would try my best to fulfill my father's dying command.

There was great rejoicing at my Auntie Ubon's house when we arrived, followed by deep anguish over the loss of my dad and two siblings. As far as I could tell, no one from my mother's side of the family had been killed, though the whereabouts of several family members conscripted with the South Vietnamese military were unknown at the time.

My aunt's house was tiny in comparison to my former home, but it was safe. My mother, brothers, and I were given a single room in which to live and sleep. It felt odd to be in proximity to my mother for any extended period of time. I desperately hoped that living in these cramped quarters would be a balm for all of us and that we might bond through our shared horror. Instead, the remnant of my family began to unravel like an old blanket.

Because the streets were unsafe, we children were forbidden to leave my aunt's house. My mother, however, ventured out daily. Where she went, I do not know, but I feared for her life. I couldn't imagine what might happen to my brothers and me if she were killed. My uncle warned me to keep my brothers quiet and not to answer the door. I obeyed faithfully. We played silently in our room and spoke in hushed whispers. Fear was my constant companion.

The fighting in Chợ Lớn would continue for more than a week as American troops moved in, reclaimed the racetrack, and systematically cleared the area of Vietcong, building by building and house by house.[4] Because my mother's family was Catholic and most of her siblings worked alongside the allies in one way or another, we were safe as long as the Americans were in control. Our survival depended on it.

The Têt celebration of 1968 would forever be known to the world as the Têt Offensive, when New Year joy was replaced by unimaginable grief. The attacks left families homeless and children fatherless. Though the Vietcong and North Vietnamese casualties greatly outnumbered the American and South Vietnamese figures, the offensive served as a psychological victory for the communists.[5] News reports in both Vietnam and the United States questioned whether the war was winnable, and if not, worth it.

The men may have been on the frontlines, but it was the women and children who took the greatest hit. My mother found a job in the port city of Nha Trang, which was about nine hours away by bus. She would be gone for several days at a time, and she always took Giang with her because he was too little to leave in my care. I had no reason to question her decision, though it left Thanh, Duc, and me to fend for ourselves, and we were little too.

As I look back on this period, I can't help but wonder what exactly my mother was really doing to eke out a living for my siblings and me. She told me that her limited command of the English language had secured her a position buying and selling items, such as blankets, to and from American soldiers there. Surely the American soldiers were all issued the standard uniform and equipment, including blankets. So, what was she really selling, and to whom?

Nha Trang, I have since learned, had around 100 brothels that catered to roughly 20,000 U.S. servicemen during the Vietnam War. Though prostitution was illegal, there was no easy way to stop it, and opportunities for women to earn a living during the war years were limited. It is estimated that by the end of the war in 1975, some 500,000 women in South Vietnam earned a living through prostitution. The average salary of a prostitute in Nha Trang rivaled the salary of then-president Nguyễn Văn Thiệu.[6]

Despite the overwhelming possibility that my mother may have been operating in this despicable line of business, I prefer to believe that she was working covertly for the American military. After all, her brothers had been trained by the Americans and served in the South Vietnamese military, and her sister worked at the United Nations office in Saigon. She did have connections. Nha Trang was far enough away for my mother to have assumed a different identity, one that would have separated her from her brothers and her Catholic upbringing. In Nha Trang with my baby brother at her side, she could have posed as a widow with no allegiance to any side in order to gain valuable information for the allies. This scenario, too, seems plausible to me.

I will never know the truth; but it doesn't matter. During times of war, people do what they need to do to survive. What really matters is that my mother had protected us and brought us safely to Chợ Lớn. I don't know whether she was driven by love or duty. Whatever the case, I am grateful that she did not leave me bleeding on the side of the road.

CHAPTER 5

O LORD, how long shall I cry for help, and you will not listen?
Or cry to you "Violence!" and you will not save?
Habakkuk 1:2 (NRSV)

1968

M y mother's father was a mean-spirited man. He drank a lot and gambled often. We rarely visited him growing up, and that was all right by me. When we did visit, Ông ngoại would make me sit on his lap while he quizzed me about what I was learning in school. If my responses did not meet his approval, he would pinch me on the inside of my arm or leg, right on the tendon where it would hurt the most and leave a black-and-blue reminder of my stupidity. He apparently knew everything, and everyone else knew nothing. My father never accompanied us on these rare visits to Ông ngoại's house. If he had, I'm sure he wouldn't have allowed such behavior to occur. As it was, my mother looked the other way.

Living at my Auntie Ubon's house now put us in close proximity to Ông ngoại—just a ten-minute walk down the road. Four of his eleven children still lived at home with him. First there was Auntie Khanh, the breadwinner of the family. She had a prestigious job working as a secretary at the UN. Such a position provided her with certain perks, like easy access to nylon stockings. Next was my Uncle Toan who had a mean streak like his father. He attended university by day and was quite the playboy by night. Then there was my Uncle Vinh; he was my age, but all boy—rough and tough. The youngest child was my Auntie Linh. She was my grandfather's favorite. Auntie Linh had a wickedly mischievous streak, and though she was only nine years old, she would often crawl out the attic window at night to party with friends. My grandmother (her mother) had died a year earlier, which might be the reason why Auntie Linh was able to be such a wild child.

Now that the Americans had resumed control of Chợ Lớn and the fighting had subsided, life could return to some semblance of normal. With my mother rarely present, other family members decided that it would be better for me to earn my keep under my grandfather's roof. There I would be expected to clean the house, do the laundry, and put supper on the table for my grandfather, two aunts, and two uncles. I had no experience in any of these areas, but my grandfather said he would teach me. I braced myself for the insults and pinches that undoubtedly lay ahead. I never aspired to be a maid and voiced my complaints to Auntie Ubon. She told me that any job should be considered a gift in wartime. Unfortunately, the position I was walking into more closely resembled slavery, for I was never paid for my services.

When I asked whether my Uncle Vinh and Auntie Linh would be helping me, I was informed that they would be busy attending school. That's how I discovered that my education had come to an end. I do not know why my aunts and brothers were allowed to continue going to school while I was not. My gut feeling is that my mother did not think I would amount to much. Therefore, education would be wasted on me.

After breakfast each morning, when my two younger brothers headed out to school, I headed to Ông ngoại's house to work. My chores kept me busy from sunup to sundown. Each day began with a trip to the market to buy food. My grandfather or Uncle Toan would provide the grocery list, which I was ordered to follow explicitly. Ông ngoại had several favorite vegetables: carrots because they gave color to the meal and were good for the eyes, spinach to put iron into our bodies, and green peppers because they were a source of vitamin C. (At least my grandfather taught me something.)

I was instructed to purchase only fresh seafood, which meant fish that were still alive. At first I was frightened to buy a fish that was still moving, let alone kill it. But over time, I learned how to properly decapitate, descale, and debone a whole fish. I would make a soup from its head and tail, and I would cook the fillets on hot coals outside to serve over rice with a side of fish sauce.

As much as I hated killing a fish, my most stressful cooking memory involves a live chicken. The proper way to kill a chicken is to chop its head off with one, quick swing. This seemed barbaric to me and likely affected the speed with which I brought the knife down on the chicken's neck the first time I attempted to kill one. The blade did not sever the head from the body, and in the struggle that followed I let go of the chicken's legs. It started to run around the kitchen, dripping blood from its neck as its head hung limp against its chest. Two thoughts ran through my head. The first was that my grandfather was going to pinch me bloody if dinner wasn't ready by the time he got home. The second was that the chicken would seek revenge on me in the afterworld and somehow kill me for what I had done to it.

Try as I might, I could not catch the mutilated bird. How it managed to stay one step ahead of me made no sense in light of the fact that it was half dead and clearly couldn't see where it was going! With blood splattering everywhere, I left the house and went to ask a neighbor for help. She was a kind woman who came right over, caught the chicken with one swoop of her hand, and finished it off properly. Then she showed me how to pluck the feathers and cook the bird over hot coals. She even gave me directions for dividing the meat after it cooked. This neighbor saved dinner and my skin.

Each meal had four components: vegetables, rice, a soup, and a protein. They could be cooked quickly as a stir-fry or slowly over low heat throughout the day to create a stew. In the beginning, Ông ngoại would scream out directions at me, call me names or pinch me, but after a few short months, I was able to do all the cooking myself. As I worked, I would recite the prayers I had learned at boarding school; then I would ask God to help me get through the day without making any mistakes. My prayers ranged from, *"Please God, help me not to burn the rice today,"* to *"Please God, don't let there be an explosion while I'm cooking."* My grandfather had warned me that if I changed the bottled gas on the two-burner stove before all the gas had been used up, there would be an explosion. I now know that this is not true. He purposely lied to me to ensure that I didn't waste his precious fuel.

Some days God honored my prayers, and my meals were deemed a success. Other times I was convinced that God was just tired of listening to me.

As the lowest ranking member of the family, I was the last to eat. All the food would be placed on the table; then each person would fill their plate according to their rank. This meant my grandfather went first, followed by Auntie Khanh, Uncle Toan, Uncle Vinh, Auntie Linh, and finally me. Yes, even my Auntie Linh, who was two years younger than me, was served before me because she ranked above me.

With so many mouths to feed, there was little left by the time I was allowed to scoop food into my bowl. My meals usually consisted of rice with a little sauce. Sometimes my grandfather would direct one of his children, usually Auntie Linh, to take a second helping before I was allowed to take my first. He did it just to be mean and to validate my low position in his household. It was his way of telling me that I was no longer the honored child my father had raised me to be and that my life of privilege was over.

The lack of food increased my incentive to bargain better at the market the next day in order to purchase something sweet for myself with the leftover coins. My preferred treats were sticky rice balls or dumplings with a bean center covered in caramel sauce. I didn't make these selfish purchases to be malicious. I did it because I was hungry.

Fighting dust was a daily battle at Ông ngoại's house; I was forever sweeping the floors and wiping off the furniture. Even though shoes were not worn inside but rather left at the front door, the dry weather of Vietnam ensured that dust would settle everywhere, continually, throughout the day. Once the floors were swept, they had to be washed, which I did on my hands and knees. Thankfully, the floors were tile and relatively easy to clean.

Laundry was a tedious and labor-intensive chore. Every other day I would soak the clothes and sheets in large buckets overnight. In the morning, I would scrub each item and hang them from a rope on the attic verandah to dry. Luckily, there was running water at the house, so I didn't have to cart water from a community pump like many of the neighbors did.

Ironing was one of the more difficult chores. Not only was the electric iron heavy for me to handle, ironing on top of the flat, wooden dining table proved problematic. Without the benefit of padded edges, like those found on European ironing boards, extra creases appeared in the most unlikely of places. My ironing skills angered Uncle Toan who would yell at me when his trousers had more than one neat crease down the center of each leg. He acted as if his success with girls depended on the number and crispness of his creases.

My favorite chore—if there could be such a thing—was washing the dinner dishes because once they were clean, I was allowed to return to my aunt's house to sleep. By this point in the evening, I would be exhausted. Looking back, it's no wonder! I was only eleven years old. The walk home each night in the dark took a psychological toll on me, for I greatly feared being attacked by the Vietcong who secretly lived among us. Upon reaching Auntie Ubon's house, I would collapse onto my sleeping mat next to my brothers and fall asleep within minutes. Mornings always came too soon.

I could tell by the way my grandfather walked toward the house each evening whether he had won at the horse races or not. If he had lost, nothing I had done that day was good enough. Clothes would need to be rewashed, and floors would have to be re-swept. Everything I cooked would be questioned and criticized. Though he never hit me, I was fearful that he would. I had once witnessed him punch my uncle in the face so hard that blood spewed out of his mouth and across the room. I didn't want that to happen to me.

Not to say that my uncles didn't deserve a good beating every now and then. My Uncle Vinh had a nasty streak, as evidenced by the fact that he would use his slingshot to shoot me with paper bullets just for laughs. Other times he would force me to play hide-and-seek with him, a game I absolutely detested. When he would discover my hiding place, he would scream and yell like he had won a trophy. It was so humiliating! When the roles were reversed, and I discovered my uncle's hiding place, he became a sore loser. One time when I found him, he bit my nose till he drew blood.

Hide-and-seek was even worse when my Uncle Toan played with us. If he found me first, he would stick his hands under my clothes and touch my private parts. I hated the feel of his hands on my skin. I always fought him, but I never yelled out. Between my uncle and the former gardener I came to believe that my body was not my own and that there was no purpose in screaming for help. There was no one to come to my rescue.

The abuse increased the day my grandfather decided that it would be best for me to move into his house permanently. His reasoning was for my own good, or so he said: I wasn't getting enough sleep, and it wasn't safe for me to walk the streets at night. I believe the real reason was because my Auntie Ubon and her husband did not appreciate me scavenging for food at their house. My fear of being attacked by the Vietcong paled in comparison to my fear of living with my grandfather and uncle.

Now that we all lived under the same roof, I was required to sleep with my two aunts, my two uncles, and my grandfather in the attic room. Everyone slept on roll-up mats that were placed one right next to the other. Uncle Toan always wanted to sleep next to me. Try as I might to position myself at least one mat away from him, it was not always possible. Without proper adult guidance, I assumed I had to respect my elders and, therefore, I was not at liberty to push his hands away in the middle of the night when he groped my breasts and later reached between my legs. Occasionally I would ask my grandfather for permission to visit my brothers at the end of a long day, hoping to spend the night with them where it was safe. Ông ngoại would shake off my request as ridiculous. "Why do you want to go over there?" he'd ask. "You don't need to go. They're OK."

Eventually I stopped asking, believing my fate rested in my grandfather's hands; he had the power to keep me or kick me out. I didn't want to end up like the homeless children I had seen on the streets of the city. Their eyes were vacant, and many were naked. To me, homelessness would have been a fate worse than death. So I put up with the abuse, pouring all my energy into performing my daily tasks with diligence. I worked in such a way as to not draw attention to myself. My goal was to simply fade into the background, to be invisible. Perhaps, if I wasn't seen, I couldn't be abused.

Sundays were considered a day of rest for everyone except for me. I still had meals to prepare and floors to sweep, but laundry and ironing were suspended till Monday. As Catholics, my grandfather insisted that we all attend church, though he was often too busy gambling and drinking to attend himself.

The Catholic Church was within walking distance, and several pews were designated for children only. This provided my brothers and me special time to sit together, apart from the adults. Spending extended time with my siblings was the highlight of my week. Prior to the mass, my brothers and I would all go to confession. One by one we would enter the small stall at the back of the church and confess our sins to a priest who sat behind a lattice wall. Penance was issued depending on the severity of our sins. The lattice wall was supposed to protect the sinner's identity, but I remember the priest once calling me by name. "Minh Phuong," he said, "what did you do this week?"

Shocked, I was convicted to tell all. First, I responded with the required prayer, "Bless me father, for I have sinned…" Then I went on to confess my worst atrocities. I hadn't washed the vegetables completely before cooking them because I wanted my grandfather to eat dirt. And I hadn't changed the water in the laundry tub overnight, which meant my uncle's clothes were soaking in yesterday's dirty water.

Did the priest laugh? I don't know. He did hesitate before announcing my penance. It was always the same—three or four rounds on the rosary, which would take about an hour to complete.

I remember one particular Sunday when I missed church altogether because I had haggled too long at the market. I knew if my grandfather found out, he'd pinch me raw. A neighbor was outside when I got back to the house, and she told me about another church in town that met an hour later. I grabbed one of the bicycles and took off. When I saw a crowd of people entering a building, I figured I had found the right place. I folded into the crowd and looked for the confessional booths. There weren't any. Then I noticed the empty cross at the front of the church with no crucified Christ hanging on it. I thought it must be a fashion statement of some sort. I looked around to see if there was a special children's section, but all the boys and girls were sitting with their parents. In an effort to blend in, I sat next to a young girl who was about my age.

The priest was dressed in a robe not unlike the one worn by the priest at my Catholic Church. And though the format of the ceremony was slightly different, there were enough similarities to keep me in the pew, such as the traditional call and response, corporate prayers, and a mix of standing and sitting. I was, however, quite pleased by the absence of kneeling. I followed the crowd and participated fully in the service. It wasn't until I was leaving that I discovered that I was not in a Catholic Church. The giveaway was its name, which didn't include the name of a saint. All the way home I apologized to God for my error and pleaded with him to protect me from my grandfather's wrath. Since I hadn't been able to go to confession, I gave myself a penance of four rosaries to be said at a later date.

When I got back to Ông ngoại's house, he asked, "Did you go to church today?"

"Yes, I did!" I answered. When he asked me nothing more, I knew I was safe, and I decided to forgo the penance I had assigned myself.

Although I was diligent in attending mass each Sunday, I cannot say that I fully grasped an understanding of what it meant to be a Christian. Nor would I have been able to defend my beliefs. I operated on rote principles, rote prayers, and rote participation. I believe it was no accident that I ended up visiting a church that was not Catholic. God had blessed me that day by allowing me to sit with a family, as if I belonged there. Blending into this Protestant congregation made me feel strangely welcomed and safe. Also, the unfamiliar surroundings of this church required me to pay closer attention to the prayers and the message from the pastor. Through this experience, I was able to see how wide God could spread his arms—wide enough to envelop the whole world, wide enough to grasp people who were not Catholic, and wide enough to include me.

CHAPTER 6

But Jesus called the children to him and said,
"Let the little children come to me, and do not hinder them,
for the kingdom of God belongs to such as these."
Luke 18:16 (NIV)

Late 1968–1970

N o one had mentioned my father since that fateful night. He was forgotten, invisible like me. So I could hardly believe what I was hearing when my mother showed up at my grandfather's house and instructed me to finish my chores quickly because we were going to visit Dad. I had never witnessed his funeral or burial; maybe there hadn't been one. Perhaps neighbors had pulled him from the rubble and nursed him back to life. My heart leapt in my chest at the prospect that my father might still be alive—like Jesus, raised from the dead. I completed my tasks quickly, dressed in my Sunday best, and purchased some peach hydrangeas at the market before running to Auntie Ubon's house to join my brothers for the journey.

Memories of my father that I had buried deep in my heart came bursting into my consciousness like spring crocuses breaking through the winter snow. His warm laugh. The way he held my hand as we walked through the garden. Our visits to his cousins' house. Playing hooky to indulge in ice cream. I could barely contain my excitement on the bus ride; my expectations were so high!

Then we pulled up to a cemetery, and my hopes of a physical reunion with Dad died. He had been laid to rest inside the family crypt alongside Dan and Chau. The dates of his birth and death were chiseled into the stone below his picture. The span between the years was too short. I looked at his photo and sobbed silently as tears cascaded in a slow and steady stream down my cheeks. I had never grieved my father's passing; there hadn't been an opportunity to do so. Now the pain overtook me. I tried to focus on his picture, but it kept fading in and out of view with each wave of tears. My father's death was permanent. I would never again feel his touch or hear his gentle words—words full of love, affirmation, and encouragement. He was gone. Gone. Truly gone.

"What do you want to say to your father?" my mother prodded.

So many things flooded through my head, but they were a jumbled mess. Instead of speaking, I laid the bouquet of hydrangeas below his picture. As I did so, my mother spoke, "Your daughter brought you the flowers you hate the most!"

I gasped. "You didn't tell me Dad didn't like this flower!"

Mom didn't respond. I started to wail. Whether the tears were for him or for me, I don't know. Maybe both. She had a way of making me feel so worthless; so empty. Everything good in my life had been stripped away, and all that remained was loss. I fell to my knees, unable to bear the weight of the pain. My mother let me be and said nothing more.

Once I was able to compose myself, I whispered softly to my father so my mother wouldn't hear, "I am so sorry that I didn't bring you flowers that you like. I didn't know."

In the silence that followed I felt a quiet and redeeming peace wash over me. It was as if I was being swaddled in a warm blanket. In that moment I knew that Dad wasn't upset with me. He loved me. Even in death, he loved me. I whispered softly, "Tomorrow I will look for a star, and each time I find one, I will think of you."

I never had the opportunity to visit my father's grave again. As promised though, I always think of him when I look to the night sky and see the heavenly points of light. It's then that Dad and I are reunited. His memory has helped sustain me during some of the most difficult periods of my life. In fact, there were times when I felt closer to him in death than to anyone who was living.

The life I now lived was a mere shadow of what I once had. I no longer was the privileged child with a Catholic education and an engraved pencil case. Now I was a maid, tending to the needs of others with no hope of escape. Thoughts of a better future did not enter my mind; I was simply not capable of envisioning anything beyond the next load of laundry.

I was a lost soul, just another nameless victim in a war-torn country. I wasn't even sure what the fight was all about. What I do remember is hearing rumors that American troops might be pulled out of South Vietnam if Richard Nixon won the presidency. Though this speculation alarmed my grandfather, it sounded like a good thing to me. Surely the North Vietnamese would stop the killings and my country could begin to heal once the Americans left. Or so I thought.

Sometime after my 12th birthday, my mother announced that she was taking her children and moving to the highland city of Dalat, about 150 miles northeast of Saigon. She had saved enough money to rent a small apartment there, which would give her the opportunity to start a new life.

My grandfather was reluctant to let me go; I had served him and his household well enough to be missed. My mother, however, insisted that she needed me to take care of the boys while she continued to work. I was excited to reunite with my brothers and escape my grandfather's demands and my uncle's abuse. God had heard my prayers after all.

My hopes were high as we boarded the bus to leave Chợ Lớn. Perhaps I should have felt ill will toward my uncles, aunts, or grandfather, but I did not. I was naïve enough to presume that the life I had with them was normal. I did, however, wonder how they would all get on without me.

The apartment we moved into was a two-room extension off a single-family home. One room was the sleeping room and the other was the living room, equipped with a little stove and a sink with running water. It was small, but I loved it because we were all together. The house was also situated close to a public Catholic School, and my mother enrolled all three of us in classes. I was overjoyed to learn that I would be able to resume my education alongside my brothers.

While my mother was away, Thanh, Duc, and I attended school six days a week. The nuns taught the girls while the priests taught the boys. On Sundays we went to confession followed by Catholic mass. The idea of skipping class, confession, or mass never entered my mind, and my brothers obediently did as they were told. When my mother came home to visit, she would ask the nuns and the priest about our attendance; it was always perfect. I wish I could say the same about my rank.

Lessons were taught in Vietnamese, not French. Since I had never been taught how to read or write in my native language, I struggled with my studies. Missing several years of schooling did not help either, and the stress of taking care of my brothers made studying and learning practically impossible. Today I understand clearly why children who live under economic hardship perform poorly on academic tests.

Each evening when our studies were complete, I would assign my brothers to various chores, such as sweeping or laundry. All the cooking fell on my shoulders, but years of practice made this a relatively easy task for me. Omelets were my specialty, and my brothers were always grateful for whatever I dished out.

My youngest brother, Giang, did not attend school with my brothers and me. He continued to accompany my mother on work detail. I have often wondered what he remembers from this period, but I've never asked. That would be his story to tell, not mine. From what I gathered, my mother stayed with friends or with American soldiers on the ships that docked at Cam Ranh, some 50 miles east of Dalat. Whenever she visited us, she would bring goodies that were not available in the Vietnamese markets. Things like Wrigley's Chewing Gum, M&Ms, or a military-issued blanket.

On one of her visits, Mom painted for me a pleasant picture of the inside of the American ships, saying the beds were small but comfortable, and the food was delicious. In the same breath she told me that I would do well to marry an American serviceman. She asked, "Would you like to come to Cam Ranh and learn my business?"

I remember this conversation clearly as well as the sick feeling it created in the pit of my stomach. I wasn't entirely clear on what might be required of me if I said yes, but I was sure that my mother's intentions were not in my best interest. I was devastated. I declined her offer saying that I did not feel right about leaving my brothers to fend for themselves. She accepted my excuse and never raised the subject with me again.

I hated the American servicemen and blamed them entirely for the misery in my life. Because of them, my mother was not able to live at home with her children. Because of them, my country was a mess. And because of them, my father was dead. My classmates would run after the American soldiers hoping to score a piece of gum or a pack of M&Ms. They would save the wrappers and press them flat between the pages of their books like prize tokens. I told Thanh and Duc that I would beat their bottoms raw if I caught either one of them with a piece of American candy, let alone a candy wrapper. They needed to have more pride in themselves and in our country. It was honorable for us to hold on to our identity. I told my brothers I would rather die than ask an American soldier for candy, and I expected them to feel the same way.

Thanh, Duc, and I had happy times together, just the three of us. In our free moments we hung out in the front yard playing hopscotch or just talking. Though our talks were nothing deep, the camaraderie was rich. When we were together, the wounds of our past seemed as far away as my grandfather. We lived a relatively peaceful existence with little outside influence for about a year. Then things began to change.

One day, my brothers and I were playing outside when two men showed up with Bibles in their hands. They were not Catholic; they were missionaries from another denomination. My pleasant memories of the church service I had once accidentally attended provoked me to honor their request to speak with us. They all spoke English with an Australian dialect, and one of them could speak a little Vietnamese. Since I was interested in learning the English language, I encouraged the men to visit again.

Our meetings were sporadic at first but became more frequent over time. Eventually, we set a regular meeting time for English lessons. Our conversations always began socially in Vietnamese with questions about school and chores. They would ask, "Can we help you with anything around the house?" or "Do you need anything at the market?" Then we would discuss daily life over a snack, which they often provided, or a cup of tea, which I provided. Gradually the conversation would turn spiritual, and our time together would end with one of them reading a Bible passage.

The first Bible story I remember learning in English was from the book of Matthew: *And whoso shall receive one such little child in my name receiveth me. But whoso shall offend one of these little ones which believe in me, it were better for him that a millstone were hanged about his neck, and that he were drowned in the depth of the sea.*[7]

I loved hearing that Jesus was a friend of children. I had never heard this in all my years of Catholic school, and the picture these missionaries painted of Jesus intrigued me. The God I knew was judgmental and full of wrath; He required confessions and penance. These missionaries spoke of Jesus, God's son, who was gentle and full of love; He desired a relationship with His people. He desired a relationship with me. I wasn't sure what that looked like however. Religion was something I *did* at school and at church on Sundays; it was not something I *lived* at home or in the world.

Somewhere along the way, a Vietnamese man who lived in Dalat began joining the two missionaries on their visits. They had been mentoring this local man in the hopes that he would continue to do the work they had started after they returned to their homeland. That meant they expected him to mentor me in both English and Christianity when they left. This man's name was Nhu. Nhu was reasonably good looking and dressed properly in the dark green uniform of a soldier with the South Vietnamese Army. I could not find any fault in his appearance, which told me his ironing skills were much better than mine. Nhu had a gentle and inviting manner.

I liked him. He was nothing like my uncles, and I was grateful for his frequent presence.

One day I invited Nhu and the missionaries to a full meal with my brothers and me. It was a bold move on my part, but my intentions were pure. I merely wanted to acknowledge them as friends before they returned to Australia. They accepted my invitation and even helped me with the cooking. The evening turned out to be a huge success.

After the missionaries left Vietnam, Nhu began visiting me more frequently on his own. Sometimes he would take me to the market on his motorcycle. Though this cut down considerably on the time I spent away from home, it also prompted the neighbors to start talking. Or rather, teasing. They thought Nhu and I were becoming a couple. Yes, he was attractive and kind, but I was not interested in him—he was old! Nhu was 25, and I was not yet 13.

On my mother's next visit home, I told her (and the neighbors did too) about Nhu. She seemed shocked to learn that I had been spending considerable time with an older man. Perhaps my mother feared that I would follow the same crooked path she had taken. Perhaps she wanted to protect me from the hardships she had experienced in her early years of dating. Or perhaps she was resolute in stopping me from bringing shame to the family, knowing that nothing good could come of it.

You see, when my mother was 20 years old, she fell in love with one of her teachers who was several years older than her. My grandparents did not approve of this relationship, but my mother was in love and felt trapped under her father's roof. (I could understand why.) She left home and moved in with this man, bringing great shame and dishonor to the family. Things did not work out as planned, and after a year she left him. Since she was no longer welcome in her father's house, she moved into an apartment with a girlfriend. That's when she met my dad.

My father lived just down the street from my mother and her girlfriend, and he would often see them waiting at the bus stop on their way to work. One day he offered them a ride. It was just like my father to extend kindness to a stranger. Soon he was driving both women back and forth to work. At the time, my father was a widower caring for two young boys. I believe he must have fallen hard for my mother because he asked her to marry him soon after they met. She was 14 years his junior. My dad allegedly told my mother that he knew she deserved better than an old widower, but he promised to be a good provider.

Though she didn't love him, Mom said yes to his proposal. Then Dad did the chivalrous thing and went to my grandfather to ask for his permission to marry my mother, which my grandfather happily gave. After all, she was damaged goods and lucky to be wanted by such a respectable man. Six months after meeting, my parents married. It is obvious to me now that my mother chose money over love. I knew none of this, however, when I told Mom about Nhu.

On schedule, Nhu visited that evening. I introduced him to my mother who looked him up and down thoroughly and asked him a lot of questions. What did he do for a living? (He worked in provisions for the military.) Had he been married before? (No.) Why was he visiting her daughter so often? (To teach her about the Bible and Jesus as well as the English language.) Where did he live? (With his mother and sister across town.) Nhu answered all my mother's questions politely, and she seemed pleased. They talked some more, but I didn't pay all that much attention to their conversation.

Mom returned to Cam Ranh the next day. Nhu continued to visit me, though not as frequently. I was sure that was my mother's doing. I would often see him on his motorbike heading out of town. I did not view Nhu as a love interest, but I missed his visits. As time passed, I soon found I didn't miss him as much as I missed the rides he gave me to the market.

When my mother showed up at the apartment again, she announced that she had purchased her own place in Cam Ranh and could no longer afford to pay for the apartment in Dalat. Therefore, my brothers and I would have to move in with Nhu and his family. The news stunned me, especially in light of the fact that I hadn't seen Nhu in weeks.

"Why can't we all move to Cam Ranh with you?" I asked.

My mother responded, "It will be good for you to have an adult watching over you."

Wasn't she an adult? Couldn't she watch over us? What was wrong with my caregiving? I had been cooking and cleaning for several years and raising my brothers without her help. Couldn't I continue to do this in Cam Ranh? But the discussion was closed. Thanh, Duc, and I packed our bags and moved in with Nhu and his family that very day.

Nhu lived on the poorer side of town with his mentally ill mother and mentally ill, physically handicapped sister in a dilapidated house with no running water or indoor stove. The lower floor served as the living or common room; the upstairs was the sleeping room where all six of us were expected to sleep on roll-up mats, one right next to the other. The sleeping arrangements reminded me of nights at my grandfather's house, and I suddenly found myself feeling nauseous and afraid. For the life of me, I could not understand why my mother would choose to place three of her living children in such dire conditions. Was this really a better choice than taking us with her to Cam Ranh?

My mother now expected me to earn our room and board by assisting with household chores and the care of Nhu's sister. So, once again my education came to a halt. The amount of work I was expected to do far surpassed the workload I carried at Ông ngoại's house. Without the benefit of running water, a daily excursion to the community well — located about a quarter mile down the road — was required. Experienced Vietnamese women are able to carry two buckets of water at a time balanced on a bamboo pole across their shoulders. I was not an experienced Vietnamese woman and could only carry one bucket successfully. Gratefully, my brothers often offered to tackle this chore when they got home from school.

All meals had to be cooked outside over hot coals. Every afternoon, when it was time to light the coals, Nhu's mother would start yelling directions. "Prepare the fire. Prep the food. Wash the rice." Other than this afternoon ranting ritual, she rarely interacted with my brothers and me.

Nhu was hardly ever home anymore, reneging on his promise to the missionaries that he would give me English and Bible lessons. I didn't know where he went, and quite honestly, I didn't care. When he was home, he treated me kindly and even assisted with the chores. Though thankful for his help, I found myself harboring ill feelings toward him because of my situation.

When I turned 13, I became old enough to participate in continuing education classes that were offered during the evenings at the French school. My mother was gracious enough to pay for a French language course that met five nights a week, providing it didn't interfere with my household duties.

After the lessons, I would hang out at the school with the cool girls who pushed the boundaries of respectable behavior. Without any strong female role models in my life, I had fallen in with a racy and popular clique that easily influenced me. They introduced me to miniskirts, cigarettes, alcohol, and the International Pen Pal Club. The ad read: *Want to have friends from all over the world?* I did! So I filled out the application and paid my annual fee using money I had skimmed from my purchases at the market.

Several weeks later I received a list of men along with their credentials and addresses. I wrote to several of them in Germany, France, Austria, Canada, and Algeria—anywhere that French was spoken. Some wrote back and sent me their picture. I reciprocated in like fashion. All the girls at the French school had several pen pals, and I did my best to keep up with them. Sometimes we would skip class and just read our letters aloud to each other as we smoked and drank alcohol straight from the bottle. What began as a half-hearted attempt for acceptance among my peers soon became my lifeline. The letters I received each week from men overseas helped me escape the harsh realities of my life and fed my empty soul.

My favorite pen pal was Hubert from Switzerland. He was a college student about six years my senior. Not only was he smart, he was compassionate. His letters conveyed a gentleness that I had never experienced in a male before, not even Nhu. He was the only pen pal of mine who seemed truly interested in knowing the real me, and he asked questions I had never been asked before. Questions I had never pondered. *What is your favorite color? What makes you smile? What kind of music do you like?* I cherished Hubert's letters.

Looking back, I can see how incredibly naïve I was. First, I thought nothing of the fact that all my pen pals were male and much older than me. Second, I had turned a blind eye to acknowledging my mother's true occupation. And third, I trusted Nhu and often put my bedroll down next to his—until one night when he reached for me the way my Uncle Toan had.

I awoke abruptly when I felt Nhu's hand on my waist. First I froze. Then I responded in the same way I had always responded to my uncle: I pretended to be asleep. Nhu's hand moved up toward my breasts. I coughed and rolled over. He took the hint and went back to his own mat.

The next night, I made sure Thanh slept between us. Nhu had never before exhibited any of the qualities found in Uncle Toan, so I gave him the benefit of the doubt. I told myself that he was probably not fully aware that he had been touching me in his sleep.

Several months went by before I found my mat next to his again. That night, I awoke suddenly when I felt his hand between my legs. I rolled away, but this didn't stop him. I tried to fight him off without waking anyone; he held me tight. What could I do? This was his house, and he was my elder and captor.

Over the next several months, Nhu fondled me while I slept. Though we never had sexual intercourse, the damage was done. It would be hard to reverse my belief in the life lessons I had learned through experience: love was conditional, circumstances can change in the blink of an eye, and men could not be trusted.

CHAPTER 7

Flee from sexual immorality.
All other sins a person commits are outside the body,
but whoever sins sexually, sins against their own body.
Do you not know that your bodies are temples of the Holy Spirit,
who is in you, whom you have received from God?
You are not your own; you were bought with a price.
Therefore, honor God with your bodies.
1 Corinthians 6:18-20 (NIV)

September 1970–May 1974

E very family has a black sheep. Even dysfunctional families like mine have a black sheep. That role belonged to my mother. She had brought shame to the family many years before, and she was about to do it again.

My mother's visits to Nhu's house suddenly became more frequent. I had a creepy feeling that she was checking to see how Nhu and I were getting along. I considered telling her what Nhu sometimes did to me at night, but I couldn't bring myself to do it. Such behavior would have reflected poorly on me, and I did not want to embarrass my mother.

I was not considered a pretty girl, and without my father, it was up to my mother to find me a husband. Though young by Vietnamese standards, I was old enough to be betrothed for marriage at a later date. I prayed my mother did not have her mind set on Nhu. I did not want to marry him or any man, for that matter. Marriage frightened me. Every married couple I had known was profoundly contentious and critical of one another.

On one particular visit I noticed that my mother was addressing Nhu differently. In the Vietnamese language, you can address individuals casually, formally, or familiarly. I addressed Nhu casually and with respect, as I would address an older brother. My mother addressed him familiarly, as if she knew him well. Nhu addressed her in like fashion even though he was much younger than she. It would have made more sense for him to address my mother with the same kind of respect one would afford an elder. I asked her about this, and she said, "We are friends."

Mom decided to throw a party at Nhu's house. There were around 20 guests in attendance, mostly Nhu's extended family. Either none of my mother's relatives were invited or no one chose to show up.

Halfway through the night, my mother asked if she could have everyone's attention. All eyes turned to her as she began to tell the story of how she met Nhu and how they had gotten to know each other. *What was going on?* My heart pounded like a drum in my chest. Something was not right. As my mother spoke, she coyly smiled at Nhu. Their glances suggested something more than friendship. Then she dropped the bomb.

"I have fallen in love with Nhu," she said, looking at the crowd, "and I would like your permission to marry him." She was practically giddy.

I was in shock, unable to move my feet or my lips. Frozen. My mother turned her gaze away from Nhu toward my brothers and me. Smiling sweetly she said, "I want to marry Nhu so you will have the benefit of a father to care for you."

This man was no father figure! He was a snake in disguise. He had not only tricked me, he had tricked my mother. Something inside me snapped. After years of silent obedience, I suddenly found my voice.

"I DO NOT NEED ANOTHER FATHER," I screamed. "IF YOU MARRY THIS MAN, I WILL LEAVE THIS HOUSE!"

I will never forget the look that crossed my mother's face. She was mortified. Her humiliation quickly turned to anger. I ran up the stairs, away from her and the crowd; but she followed me, screaming and scolding my behavior. How dare I embarrass her! How could I insult her in front of all these people? After all that she had done for me! After all that Nhu had done for me! Who did I think I was? I was a disgrace!

I lost it. "YOU DIDN'T EVEN ASK ME HOW I FELT ABOUT YOU MARRYNG NHU!" I shouted. "I DON'T NEED A FATHER!"

The slap was unexpected and shocking, delivered with anger and force. My left cheek burned with pain, but the pain in my heart was greater. Unable to keep it in any more, I shrieked, "THAT MAN TOUCHES ME AT NIGHT!"

My mother became deathly quiet. I had caught her off guard. She stared at me for a moment as if she didn't recognize me. Then she turned and yelled for Nhu to come upstairs. Cautiously, he entered the room.

My mother looked directly at him and said, "Minh Phuong says you play around with her at night. Is that true?"

He denied it. Without missing a beat. The snake lied, and mom believed him. Just like Eve believed the serpent: because she wanted to, not because it was the truth.

My mother slowly turned to me and, with a tone of disgust that I can still hear clearly, asked, "How could you lie to me like that?"

I realized in that moment that I meant nothing to her. I never had and never would. I was my father's daughter, and she hated me for it. I was unloved and unwanted, alone in this world, no luckier than the orphans I had seen begging on the streets. My mother would not protect me. She would choose Nhu over me.

I hated her.

At age 13, it would have been more acceptable for me to be engaged to Nhu than for my mother to marry him. Marrying a much younger man is improper in the Asian culture and brings shame to both families. My mother's family, therefore, could not in good conscience attend her wedding.

I, too, had no intention of attending. Nor did I plan to remain living under Nhu's roof once they were married, but I had nowhere else to go. Luckily, my Auntie Khanh stepped forward and ordered my mother to send me back to my grandfather's house in Chợ Lớn saying it was no longer appropriate for me to live in Nhu's house. My mother agreed. Sexual impropriety never figured into the equation.

A few days before the wedding, I packed my small suitcase with the few clothing items I possessed and my treasured pen pal letters. Through tears, I said goodbye to my brothers. My mother walked me to the bus station in silence. There really was nothing more to say. Before placing me on the bus, she shoved some money into my hands. I couldn't tell whether the money was meant as a parting gift or as a bribe to keep quiet. Whatever it's purpose, it made me feel cheap.

My mother finally got what she wanted—a man she loved and a Roman Catholic Church wedding—for the low cost of her daughter. Meanwhile, I resumed my role as a maid in my grandfather's house. The workload was the same, but I had changed. I was stronger. My anger toward my mother had somehow strengthened me.

My two uncles and two aunts who were still living with Ông ngoại seemed to treat me differently now. I would not venture so far as to call it respect, but they did view me more like an adult than a child.

In my absence, Uncle Toan—ever the playboy—had acquired a girlfriend. With his attentions turned elsewhere, I could sleep in peace—at least for a while.

Uncle Vinh had mellowed, thanks to his deep passion for music and his skill at playing the guitar. I enjoyed singing duets with him when he would let me, and the music transported me to a world that was safe and predictable. I was particularly drawn to the folk melodies of Simon and Garfunkel. When I was alone at the house I would often sing *The Sound of Silence*. "Hello darkness, my old friend. I've come to talk with you again." For some reason, the lyrics brought me solace.

Auntie Linh was still a wild child, but she was also an academic wonder, continually ranking in the top of her class without ever studying. She would often come home after school and pack a bag with play clothes, then turn around and head out to meet up with friends. Before leaving, she would instruct me, "Tell my father I went to a friend's house to study." Her worldliness intrigued me, but I did not aspire to be like her.

Auntie Khanh still worked as a secretary for the United Nations. She was probably the person I looked up to the most. She was not elegant like my mother or outgoing like Auntie Linh, rather she was levelheaded and courageous. Upon my return to Chợ Lớn, Auntie Khanh said to me, "You know, the only future you have is to marry a foreigner." I didn't want to believe her, but I had to admit that without an education, my options were limited.

Within the year, my Auntie Khanh asked me to accompany her to an American nightclub that she frequented on weekend nights. I agreed. When we arrived, she greeted many of the servicemen by name. As she introduced me around, the men looked me up and down, which made me feel like a fish for sale at the market. I was out of my comfort zone. I felt awkward and probably looked like a fish out of water. These men all spoke in English, and I had to depend on my aunt for translation. In an effort to make me more desirable, Auntie Khanh told them that I was a singer.

"Minh Phuong knows a song!" she announced.

This was a painful moment for me as I realized her purpose was to pawn me off to an American. How I wished I could just disappear. I didn't know what the men were saying, but they were obviously begging me to sing. Though I protested, my pleas were ignored as the men pouted and stroked my arms. I wanted them to stop, so I launched into a rendition of *Love is Blue*, which I often sang in English with Uncle Vinh. The only words I understood were "love" and "blue." Because blue was my favorite color, I assumed the song had a positive message. The haunting melody should have given me a clue, but I hadn't given it that much thought.

"Blue, blue, my world is blue," I sang sheepishly, "blue is my world since I'm without you."

My pronunciation of the English words was probably terrible, but the men knew the song well enough to overlook this. They all laughed and clapped. They wanted more. It was humiliating. The night couldn't end quickly enough.

On the way home, Auntie Khanh warned me that because I was not a pretty girl and Vietnam was in the midst of war, my only hope of stability was to marry an American. The thought repulsed me. Who in her right mind would marry a man who laughed at her when she sang? Besides, we didn't even speak the same language!

The next week, Auntie Khanh invited me to accompany her to the nightclub again. When I declined, she reminded me once more that I was not very attractive and that it was in my best interest to seek an American husband. So, against my better judgment, I consented. Auntie Khanh spent a great deal of time that week prepping me on how to dress, how to act, how to tip my head, and how to smile with my eyes. I found the lessons quite disturbing.

Friday arrived, and off we headed to the American nightclub. We only stayed for about an hour; then we headed to an apartment where a party was taking place. I soon realized this was no regular party. Girls were hooking up with men and disappearing into rooms. Auntie Khanh introduced me to some of the guys; then left me to fend for myself. One man tried his best to communicate with me in Vietnamese, but I was so troubled by what was taking place around me that I could barely maintain focus, let alone smile at him with my eyes.

On the way home, Auntie Khanh voiced her frustration with my inability to connect with a man. She told me I would have to work harder, but I told her I had no intention of ever going back to that nightclub. I didn't have it in me to flirt with a man in whom I had no interest. Auntie Khanh said it was not my choice. It was my mother's. "Your mother asked me to groom you to be an escort to American men," she said.

I couldn't breathe. *Was this really how little my mother thought of me?* My aunt was not on a mission to find me a husband; she was on a mission to sell me. My 14-year-old brain did not fully comprehend the meaning of the word "escort," but I knew it made me feel sick to my stomach.

How I missed my father. Had he lived, he would never have allowed my mother to put me in this position. Without his protection, I would have to stand up for myself. I told Auntie Khanh that I would never marry an American, so there was no reason for her to invest any more precious time into grooming me. It simply wouldn't pay off.

Even if I had taken Auntie Khanh's lessons to heart, my chances of marrying an American soon dwindled. The last U.S. troops were pulled out of Vietnam and sent home in March of 1973, and South Vietnamese President Nguyễn Văn was forced to assume control of the war strategy against communism on his own.

During the transition, the United Nations offered to relocate many of its employees. Auntie Khanh took advantage of the offer and submitted paperwork claiming that her siblings, Vinh and Linh, were actually her children. Since I was the same age as Uncle Vinh and just a couple years older than Auntie Linh, I begged Auntie Khanh to claim that I was her child too. She refused. She explained that it was already dangerous for her to request passage for two younger siblings who were clearly not her children. Adding a third child to the list might disqualify her from going altogether.

I panicked. I dreaded the possibility of being the only female left in my grandfather's house, catering to the whims of my male relatives. Nor did I want to become an old maid, cooking and cleaning for the rest of my life. And I most certainly did not want to end up as an escort looking for an American husband as a last resort. With no family members willing to help me, I turned to the only respectable institution I knew: the Catholic Church.

The nuns in Chợ Lớn helped me secure a job as a teacher's aide in a Catholic orphanage. Though I wasn't skilled enough to be a teacher, the children called me *cô giáo,* a respectable title for teacher assistant. The pay was low, but it gave me a sense of purpose and got me out of my grandfather's house six days a week. This forced Ông ngoại to redistribute the chores. My aunts and uncles were now required to pull their own weight, which meant we all took turns purchasing the household food, cooking meals, and doing laundry.

The children at the orphanage were all half American, or Amerasians—the product of short-lived relationships or one-night stands between Vietnamese women and American soldiers. I felt incredibly sorry for these little ones who weren't wanted by their mothers. In many ways, they were no different than me. We each hungered for love and a safe place to call home. These orphans were a daily reminder of the destruction the Americans were leaving behind. I especially saw this in the children who had dark skin. Blacks were considered most undesirable in the Vietnamese culture, and Black-Asian orphans would be viewed as outcasts all their lives. Caring for these little ones made me loathe the Americans even more.

My main responsibility was reading to the children and teaching them the Vietnamese alphabet. The work helped me refine my own reading and writing abilities. As my grasp of the Vietnamese alphabet took root, I began to compose short stories about children whose hearts had been broken by circumstance. Though fictitious in nature, the stories were based heavily on my own experiences.

The local newspaper held a short story contest every month for children, and I decided to submit one of my own creations. To my surprise, my story was selected for publication. Being selected was an honor, and I found myself wondering what my mother would think of my accomplishment. I imagined her reading the paper, smiling at my story, and announcing that she was proud of me.

I hadn't seen my mother in almost two years, long enough for the hate in my heart to dissipate. I wondered if we could start over. For some reason, which I cannot explain, I still yearned for her approval. Perhaps the passage of time and my gift for writing would be the link to a new relationship. As a published author, I could prove to her that I had the potential to be a woman of substance, or at least something more than an escort.

During our time apart, my mother had given birth to two more children whom I had never met. My grandfather had directed her to focus on her new family and to leave me alone. She had. But now I had done something worthy of praise, and I wanted my mother to know it. Like an abused dog expectantly waiting for its master's affection, I sent my mother a letter and waited for her response.

Her answer arrived via a neighbor woman. My mother had read my story and wanted to see me. I was thrilled and nervous. My grandfather would never approve of our meeting, so I had to sneak and lie to see my own mother. We met on a street corner where vendors sold various treats. She looked radiant and younger than I remembered her. Happy even. In comparison, I had gained a lot of weight and now wore thick glasses. *Beauty and the beast,* I thought. One would never have suspected that we were related.

"Did you read my story in the paper?" I asked her.

"Yes. You wrote a very good story," she stated matter-of-factly, "but why is it so sad?"

I wanted to say, *"Because my life is sad!"* Instead, I shrugged and said nothing. What was the point? My mother hadn't changed. She saw only what she wanted to see.

"Would you like a treat?" she asked.

I told her I did, so she bought me a sweet bean drink mixed with coconut milk. Nothing more was said about my story. I still remember how I felt after finishing that delicious drink: my stomach was full and my heart was empty.

Every six months or so, my mother and I would meet in secret. I looked forward to our get-togethers like a young teen exploring the possibilities of a new friendship—not sure if I would make the right impression, but wanting desperately to try. When the neighbor woman would relay the rendezvous location and meeting time, my heart would skip a beat.

Discussions between my mother and myself were never deep or encouraging. She would ask about my work and about her siblings. Then she would offer advice, which I usually interpreted as criticism. Much of her criticism revolved around my clothing—it was too modern, too revealing, or too short. Like any teenager, the more she put me down, the more I wanted to act out, which resulted in even shorter skirts and more revealing necklines. I think it was my way of showing her that I was in charge of my decisions, not her. Though still bothered by the knowledge that she had asked her sister to groom me to be an escort, the topic was never raised or discussed between us, but it festered like an open wound whenever she judged my attire.

Over the next few years, several of my stories were printed in the local paper. I continued to work at the orphanage, and I enrolled in an accounting course two nights a week to further my studies. Classes sometimes ran late, which meant I would get home late. Late arrivals did not sit well with my grandfather who assumed I was up to no good like my mother before me. He would be waiting at the door to interrogate me upon arrival.

"Tell me which boy you were seeing tonight!" he would yell over and over. "You tell me which boy!"

I would try to explain that I had been studying or asking the teacher questions, but Ông ngoại never believed me, even though I was telling the truth. To teach me a lesson, he would hit me with the bamboo handle of the feather duster.

Bamboo is known for its durability and strength. It does not break easily under extreme force. I always had welts and black-and-blue marks on my skin as a result of the beatings. The bruises just added to my already unattractive appearance. Though I liberally applied tiger balm and prayed for the marks to disappear, the pain would often last for weeks.

I truly couldn't understand why my grandfather assumed I was involved with a boy. I didn't think I was capable of attracting one. For as long as I could remember, my family spoke of me as ugly, overweight, and unintelligent. They had given me several nicknames: moon face, piglet, ugly duckling, and elephant, to name a few. Without my father's positive influence, I came to believe that everything my family said about me was true.

Needless to say, I never finished accounting school. Not only did I hate the late night beatings, I hated accounting! I can honestly say it was the most boring subject I ever tried to learn.

The day finally arrived when the thing I had been dreading most came to pass: Auntie Khanh received word that she and Auntie Linh had been approved for "holiday" in Australia. Auntie Khanh's request to take Uncle Vinh, however, had been denied.

I cried terribly the day my aunts left. Their holiday would be permanent, and I was sure my life was about to become more miserable as the lone woman left in my grandfather's house. I was quickly proved right.

Uncle Toan began to abuse me again. I had no emotional strength to fight him. I learned that the sooner he got his way, the sooner it would be over. So when he reached for me at night, I just lay there and allowed him to run his wicked hands all over the most private parts of my body. Even though I gave him no encouragement, he was always able to find satisfaction with one hand on me and the other hand on himself.

Shortly after my aunts left the country, Ông ngoại went into the hospital. Though he had become quite thin and pale over the last year, I had every expectation that he would come home within a few days. He didn't. My grandfather had advanced leukemia, and his late diagnosis was a death sentence. He died several days after entering the hospital. His passing was both a blessing and a curse.

I did not mourn my grandfather. I certainly wasn't going to miss him, but I dreaded the fact that Uncle Toan would now be in charge of the house. I didn't make enough money to afford an apartment of my own, so I was stuck cleaning and serving my abuser. My stomach was constantly in knots, and I searched for a way out.

One day I left my chores and walked down the street to my Auntie Ubon's house. She had five young children and more work than she could handle. I made her an offer: I would help with the household chores, including the cooking, if she would allow me to move in. It would be a tight squeeze to fit me into her already cramped house, but my offer was too good to pass up. I packed my bag and moved that very day.

As a token of my appreciation, I purchased my aunt a small box of chocolates with the money I made at the orphanage. Many years later, she reminded me of this small gesture, which unbeknownst to me had made a big impact. "You bought me candy out of the little you had," she said, "instead of your excess."

I would one day read a similar story in the Bible about a poor widow who put everything she had into the temple coffers.[8] I didn't see the similarity at the time, but looking back I see that both the widow and I were desperate for a change in circumstance. I think God used this moment to prove to me that he had heard my pleas. He was guiding me. Refining me. Shaping me. He was taking what was bruised and unattractive, unloved and abused, and turning it into a masterpiece for His kingdom's purposes.

CHAPTER 8

Our God, will you not judge them?
For we have no power to face this vast army that is attacking us.
We do not know what to do, but our eyes are on you.
2 Chronicles 20:12 (NIV)

Early 1975–May 1, 1975

Because of the chaos in my own life, I wasn't aware of the chaos in the world around me. It was early 1975, and Vietnam was at the peak of political turmoil. My pen pal, Hubert, wrote and asked me what my plans were if Vietnam were to fall into the hands of the communists. I had to admit to him that I had no idea. Until his letter arrived, I hadn't given much thought to the communists. I had been too focused on merely making it through another day. When I wrote back to Hubert, I asked for his advice.

Come to Switzerland as my fiancé, he wrote. His offer was taking our friendship to a whole new level, one I had never considered. Now 17, the prospect of marriage did not frighten me like it had before, but I wasn't sure if I was ready to be married. Though I had never met Hubert, his letters conveyed a warmth and concern that spoke to my soul. While other pen pals had dropped off, Hubert continued to write to me faithfully. If I had to marry, Hubert seemed like my best choice. At least he wasn't an American.

Whether Hubert would really marry me or not, I did not know. It was clear, however, that he was offering me a chance at a whole new life, far away from war and my dysfunctional family. Perhaps Hubert was my ticket out. Perhaps I could have a future after all. I decided to make Hubert my fallback plan if the communists took control of Saigon. Cautiously, I wrote, *yes*.

As promised, Hubert composed a letter to the Swiss embassy in Vietnam requesting that I be awarded asylum in Switzerland as his bride-to-be. In a separate letter to me, Hubert sent a copy of the paperwork along with 100 Swiss francs. His letter instructed me to go to the Swiss Embassy at once to present the papers and warned me not to risk waiting until Saigon fell.

When I called the embassy later that day, the woman who answered the phone said the staff was in the process of packing. This was a bad sign. I needed to get to the embassy immediately, but since it was already getting dark, it was too late for me to start the journey. I rose early the next morning and boarded a bus to downtown Saigon with the papers from Hubert in hand.

As bleak as my life was, I was fearful of the unknown that lay ahead. I knew how to navigate the terrain in Vietnam, but I knew nothing about Switzerland and very little about Hubert really. I questioned whether he really had my best interests at heart or whether it would be wiser for me to remain in Vietnam where I spoke the language and understood the culture. Somewhat conflicted, I walked through the gates at the Swiss Embassy only to discover that the choice was no longer available. The embassy was closed, and no one was there to process the paperwork.

During the month of March 1975, the North Vietnamese military attacked key areas in the northern-most provinces of South Vietnam. Encountering very little resistance, troops were able to take control of half the country, from Hue in the north to Cam Ranh Bay in the south. South Vietnamese citizens flooded into Saigon for protection. My mother and Nhu were forced to abandon their home and take refuge in the city as well.

The North Vietnamese Politburo had originally planned to launch a final offensive on Saigon in early 1976, but given the quick collapse of South Vietnam's military resistance, the North Vietnamese military and Vietcong immediately began their rapid advance down the coast. By early April of 1975, communist forces were only 60 miles from Saigon.[9] The news was all over the air-waves. It was only a matter of time before the enemy showed up again in my backyard. Flashbacks of the Tết Offensive six years earlier began to haunt my thoughts and dreams.

Weeks later, on April 21, South Vietnamese President Nguyễn Văn Thiệu resigned in a TV and radio speech to the people. Amid tears he condemned the Paris Peace Accords, stating that former Secretary of State Henry Kissinger had betrayed South Vietnam. Calling the United States untrustworthy, he accused former President Richard Nixon of breaking his promises.

Five days later, Nguyễn Văn Thiệu was ushered into exile in Taiwan. Before leaving, he nominated his aged vice president, Trần Văn Hương, as his successor. On April 27, enemy rockets exploded in Saigon, and Trần Văn Hương resigned. The presidency was then handed over to Captain Dương Văn Minh, who at six feet tall was affectionately known as Big Minh. My uncles were overwrought by the most recent change in power. It was common knowledge that Big Minh had contacts in the communist regime and, according to my uncles, Big Minh would side with the enemy just as readily as talk peace with them.

During the course of that week when South Vietnam blew through three different presidents, thousands of Americans and Vietnamese were evacuated on overloaded planes and helicopters. My uncles, who had all served in the South Vietnamese military, feared for their lives when they were unable to secure themselves and their families seats on any aircraft.

Then North Vietnamese rocket fire destroyed a United States Air Force C-130 at Tan Son Nhut Air Base, just north of Saigon. This put a stop to the use of all fixed-wing aircraft for evacuations.[10] It was just too dangerous. In response, American President Gerald Ford issued orders for Operation Frequent Wind to take effect— the helicopter evacuation of Saigon. My Uncle Hoang, who was a high-ranking intelligence officer with the Vietnam Air Force, called all the family together—including my mother and Nhu. Given the circumstances, it was no longer appropriate to shun her.

Uncle Hoang told us that it was time to leave the country. "A helicopter will be taking off from the American Embassy," he said, "and we can be on it if we leave now."

Within the hour, a group of about twenty of us was en route to the embassy with little more than the clothes on our backs. The date was April 29, 1975. I stayed close to my brothers and mother as we struggled to make our way amid a sea of panic-stricken people. I was under the impression that my uncle had secured us seats on the chopper, but that was not the case. My family joined the growing swarm of frightened people pushing, yelling, and elbowing their way toward a single aircraft. I stayed the course, weaving my way through the crowd till I was positioned just feet from the helicopter's door. I knew without a doubt that I was going to make it. Freedom was in my grasp. Instinctively, I turned around to make sure my family was with me. My mother, with her 2-year old daughter wrapped tightly around her neck, was several feet behind.

"*Mẹ, Mẹ,*" (Mama! Mama!) I screamed. Like a duckling, fearful of being separated from its mother, I pushed against the mob, relinquishing my position at the front of the flock. She yelled at me, but I couldn't make out what she was saying over the pulsing noise of the helicopter blades and the din of the crowd. I pressed on, straining to hear her.

"*Đi trở lại máy bay trực thăng!*" (Go back! Get on that helicopter!)

With great difficulty, confused and crushed from all sides, I turned back toward the aircraft only to see it lifting off the ground. I watched as a serviceman inside accepted the last passenger—an infant child.

I had missed my opportunity.

I have often wondered what became of that child and the parent who gave him—or her—away. Had I made it onto the helicopter, I wonder if I would have had the privilege of holding that baby during the flight. As orphans, we could have comforted each other on the long trip to freedom. Instead, I was with my mother who chastised me on the long walk back to my aunt's house.

Our decision to head home rather than wait for the possibility of another helicopter saved us from the tear-gas bombs launched later that day by U.S. soldiers in an attempt to stop a stampede at the embassy. Over the course of 19 hours, some 81 helicopters carried more than 1,000 Americans and 6,000 Vietnamese to aircraft carriers off the shore of Vietnam. The last helicopter left the U.S. Embassy at 7:53 a.m. the next morning.[11] Later that day, North Vietnamese tanks

73

crashed through the gates of the Presidential Palace in Saigon, and Big Minh surrendered the country to communist rule.

The name of the city was immediately changed to Ho Chi Minh City in honor of the former revolutionary leader who spent most of his life fighting for the reunification of Vietnam. April 30, 1975, is marked in history as "The Fall of Saigon." It is also the day that the Vietnam War officially ended. To me, the date marks the death of my beloved country.

For those of us who were left behind, the future was not only uncertain, it was terrifying. Because of my family's association with the American and South Vietnamese military, our very lives were in danger. We could not rest. We had to keep moving.

"The only other way to escape is by sea," my Uncle Hoang told us. "American ships are in international waters just off the coast, waiting to rescue us."

My family listened intently to my uncle's assessment of the situation and clung desperately to his every word. The communists had set up checkpoints throughout the city, he said, to prevent the escape of any American sympathizers. It would not be safe for us all to travel together. We had to split up.

Uncle Hoang proceeded to separate us into small groups of two or three. We were assigned to take different busses out of the city that were heading to the coastline. I was paired with my brother, Thanh. My mother and Nhu were to travel with the rest of her children.

My uncle ordered us to destroy any evidence of our identities by burning our birth certificates and family photos. If we were stopped and asked to provide information about our relatives' jobs, we were to play dumb. If asked whether a family member worked for the South Vietnamese government, we were to state that the women were homemakers and the men were farmers. To avoid suspicion, we were instructed not to take any luggage with us. Instead, we were to wear two sets of clothing, one on top of the other. Any valuables we planned to take needed to be small enough to conceal beneath our undergarments.

In the days preceding the fall of Saigon, the adults in my family had prepared for the worst by converting gold jewelry into thin sheets that could be used as currency. Once the North Vietnamese had established power, the South Vietnamese dong would be as useless as a two-legged stool. My mother now handed me eight gold sheets, thin as construction paper that measured roughly three-by-six inches. Her instructions were, "Use this to pay for you and your brother to get out of Vietnam."

I had bargained enough at the market to know that my mother had handed me a generous amount of gold, but I had no way of knowing whether it was enough to purchase freedom for Thanh and me. I put the gold in my bra along with the small amount of Vietnamese money I had in my possession and prayed for the best.

My mother also handed me a little piece of paper with an address written on it for her Uncle Cuong who lived in France. Until that moment, I was unaware that I had an uncle in France. Apparently, he was my grandfather's brother. On the same sheet of paper, I scribbled Hubert's address in Switzerland. I couldn't take his letters with me, but I vowed to write to him when I was able.

Less than 24 hours after concocting the plan to escape by sea, my family was on the run. Before boarding the busses out of Saigon, Mom gave Thanh and me one more direction: *Tiếp tục đi. Đừng quay lại,* which translates as "Keep going! Don't turn back!" She probably told me this to ensure that I would not behave as I had when I neared the helicopter. This time I heard her loud and clear. I was to press forward, no matter what, because there was no place to go back to.

Thanh and I boarded the first bus; my mother and the rest of her brood boarded the bus behind ours. As my uncle had predicted, we encountered a communist checkpoint near the edge of the city. My bus was waved through, but my mother's bus was ordered to turn back to Saigon. Thanh and I were now on our own, headed to the seaside resort town of Vũng Tàu. I had never been to this town and did not know what to expect. However, my mother's words rang resolutely through my head: *Tiếp tục đi.*

Suddenly the world before Thanh and me felt very big, and I remember thinking it would swallow us up if we weren't careful.

CHAPTER 9

*Two are better than one because they have a
good reward for their toil.
For if they fall, one will lift up the other;
but woe to the one who is alone and falls
and does not have another to help.
Ecclesiastes 4:9-10 (NRSV)*

May 1–3, 1975

It was early evening when Thanh and I got off the bus. Everywhere we looked there were Vietcong soldiers with guns who appeared to be watching everyone very closely. We kept our eyes down and went in search of a boat that would take us out to sea. Neither of us knew what we were doing, of course. My only experience with the sea had been beheading and frying fish.

For strength, I prayed the prayers I had been taught in Catholic school over and over again in my head. My grandfather used to pinch me back into reality when he caught me mouthing the rote prayers in church while my mind was a million miles away. Out here, however, in the middle of enemy territory, my mind was very much in the present moment. I leaned into the words, and the rhythm of the prayers provided courage with every step.

With its sandy beaches and numerous resort hotels, Vũng Tàu seemed like the perfect place to get lost among the tourists. The streets were crowded, but I had to wonder whether any of the people were actually vacationing. Vietnam was in the middle of a government takeover. Who would take a vacation under such conditions? Perhaps we were all pretending.

A great number of boats bobbed in the water, some quite a ways off shore. Which ones were ready to cruise out into international waters was a mystery, and it seemed too risky to approach any of the men we saw along the water's edge and ask. Who could we trust? Thanh and I decided that it would be wise to rest and make our move in the morning.

We scoped out a cheap hotel, and thanks to my years of bargaining experience at the market, I was able to negotiate a low room rate using Vietnamese money. Meanwhile, Thanh purchased us some street food with the few Vietnamese coins I gave him. While eating our meager supper, Thanh shared the story he heard from the concierge about the reason why I was able to secure a relatively cheap rental price with the hotel. Apparently, a prostitute had recently committed suicide in our room. Thanh found the story captivating. I found it gruesome.

That night, I could not sleep. In my head, I kept seeing a dead woman staring down at me as she hung by her neck from the ceiling above the bed. We checked out early the next morning.

Our plan was simple: we would walk close to the sea and look for suspicious activity that might indicate an escape route. We didn't know what suspicious activity might look like exactly, so I prayed for God to make it clear.

The beach at Vũng Tàu was literally lined with hotels—one right next to the other. One hotel in particular seemed to be busier than the rest. Thanh and I planted ourselves outside the entrance and spent the day observing the facility's comings and goings. I was in a state of hyper vigilance, aware of both hotel guests and armed soldiers walking the beach. For the most part, the soldiers kept to themselves and did not enter any of the hotels. I, therefore, determined that we would be safer inside than outside. As evening approached, we left our post and found another cheap hotel in which to spend the night.

The next day we returned to our spot outside the busy hotel to resume our surveillance. This time we noticed that the parking lot had a lot more cars than spaces. It seemed to me that people were coming, but they weren't leaving—or maybe they were leaving by another route. It was time to take the next step. Thanh decided that I should go inside to investigate further. I told my brother to move on if I didn't return within the hour. For all we knew, this busy hotel could be a communist hub where people were being arrested on the inside.

When I entered the hotel, the lobby was empty except for a lone receptionist standing behind the desk. *Where were all the people?* I approached the receptionist and chose my words carefully in case she was a North Vietnamese sympathizer. No one could be trusted. I knew that anything I said could be used against me if spoken to the enemy.

"I'm wondering if you have a service to help people who are lost find their way," I said.

"Why do you ask?" she replied.

"Because I'm lost."

"Where are your parents?"

"I don't know," I said. "I need help to find them."

She hesitated before replying, "Maybe I know someone who knows. Come back later. Around 2:00 a.m."

I thanked the receptionist and left, my heart pounding like a jackhammer in my chest. *Was this the way out?* I sincerely hoped so.

When I told my brother about the conversation, he feared it was a trap. I did not agree. I was aware of the possibility that we could be caught and jailed—or even killed; but I was tired of living in fear and longed to be free, like a bird.

At the appointed time, we headed back to the hotel. The street was silent and no soldiers were in sight, though I easily imagined them lurking behind every building. Thanh hid himself in some bushes about a block away while I continued on. I entered the hotel lobby and found it completely empty. My legs were shaking terribly, so I forced myself to sit down on one of the benches to wait. Several minutes went by before I heard footsteps. Then a man appeared behind the desk. He did not look very friendly, nor did he acknowledge my presence. Cautiously I got up and approached him.

"I came in earlier today," I said. "Can anyone help me?"

If he was expecting me, he didn't act like it. In fact, he ignored me. He ruffled through the papers on the desk in front of him, pretending I wasn't there. Unfazed, I continued. "I talked to a woman here today, but I don't know her name."

This caught his attention. He looked up at me and asked, "Did she talk to you?"

I immediately recognized the importance of our conversation. He was choosing his words as carefully as I was choosing mine. Conversations about escape routes from Vietnam could be considered illegal depending on what side you were on. I had no way of knowing where this man's allegiance lay. I had heard stories that the Vietcong were using children to do their dirty work. Perhaps he suspected me of being a communist spy. This meant he was just as afraid of me as I was afraid of him.

I asked again, "Do you know anyone who can help me?"

"Maybe," he answered. I took that as my cue to offer him some money.

Bribing someone is an art in the Vietnamese culture. The key is to provide a payment that appears as a gift. In this way, the bribe doesn't offend the receiver and benefits the provider. Both of my parents had perfected this form of communication. I had learned from the best.

"I suppose you may have to travel far to find someone to help me," I acknowledged. "Can I contribute to your bus fare?"

He took the bait. "Well, it's true!" he replied. "I'll have to catch the bus or use my car, which needs gas."

"I would like to help pay for your gas," I said politely, slipping him some Vietnamese money. He nodded with appreciation and left his post.

I remained standing at the desk and used the time to pray. Looking back, I realize that during these tense situations, prayer was my stabilizer as I breathed the memorized words in and out like oxygen.

After what seemed like an eternity, the man returned. "I contacted someone," he told me. "That person can see you now. Follow me."

He turned and began walking toward the back of the hotel. Panic washed over me. "But I can't come now!" I blurted out.

He froze. "Why?" he asked slowly.

"I have a brother."

He looked at me questioningly.

"I really do!" I insisted. "He's waiting for me."

"How far away is he?"

"Not far," I told him. "I'll go get him. I promise to bring him right back!"

The night clerk blocked my way, insisting that he go with me. So we walked down the quiet street together. When I pointed to the place where Thanh was hiding, the man put his hand on my arm, restricting me from going any further. Then he told me to call for my brother.

"Thanh," I whispered loudly into the dark.

Thanh poked his head out from behind the bush. The clerk gave an audible sigh of relief, and together the three of us returned to the hotel. There we were led through a maze of hallways—down a long corridor, around corners, weaving left-right-left-right through the building. *If he abandons us now,* I thought, *we will never find our way out.* But there was no turning back. We had to keep going, no matter what. *Tiếp tục đi. Đừng quay lại.* My mother's words echoed in my head.

Eventually, we found ourselves at the rear entrance of the hotel where the night clerk led us to a parked van. Without warning, he opened the back doors and pushed us inside. The door closed behind us. "We're dead!" my brother whimpered. "Thanks to you, we're going to die!"

To my great surprise, I felt calm. I was sure that the man from the hotel and whoever was driving the van were merely taking precautions. I told Thanh to be quiet. "Sit there, and don't make a noise!"

The ride was quite dreadful as we bumped along unpaved roads with our bottoms bouncing against the hard metal floor. Thankfully, it was short and ended before major bruising occurred. The back door suddenly flew open, and someone—maybe the driver—told us to get out and go through the door of the office building in front of us. We did as we were told and were greeted by a woman who instructed us follow her. After winding down several passageways, we were directed to go through a door at the far end of a hallway. I moved forward confidently with my brother cowering behind me. As he braced himself for something terrible, I opened the door with great hope.

Where my confidence came from, I do not know. I simply did not feel like we were in any danger. I had seen more of life than my brother had and was, perhaps, better prepared to accept whatever lay ahead.

The room we entered was full of Vietnamese people who were huddled together in familial groups. They were whispering softly to each other while their eyes darted around the room in high alert. They reminded me of caged animals. Thanh and I fit right in. A weathered man, whose age was impossible to guess, was sitting at a small table in the very center of the room. It was apparent that he was the man in charge. I boldly approached him. The time for polite bribery was over.

"Are you arranging for people to get out of the country?" I asked.

"Where do you want to go?" he asked me.

"France," I told him.

Cocking his head he said, "I'm not sure we can get you there, but we can get you out to international waters."

"OK," I said.

He looked me up and down as if he were examining a pig for purchase. "It will cost you."

"How much?" I asked.

"Six sheets of gold," he replied. I offered him two-and-a-half. He demanded four, and I agreed. Something told me he had reached his limit and I wouldn't be able to bargain for less.

Once this man had negotiated a price with every family in the room, he announced details of the plan. We would all be returned to the hotels from which we came. The next day, we were to act like tourists by checking out the shops and the beach while purchasing enough food to get us through several days at sea. He warned us that there would be no guarantees. If a ship from another country didn't pick us up after a week, we would return to land.

The man walked from group to group assigning different rendezvous points. Our separation would safeguard the others if one group got caught. We were all instructed to scan the horizon in the early morning hours when the tide was at its lowest; we needed to be looking for a boat that displayed two lit lanterns. That would be the signal for us to swim out and board the boat.

Swim? That one word drained me of my newfound confidence. "I can't swim," I announced.

"Well, you'll need to learn quickly," the man responded.

Was that even possible? How would I learn? Had I just paid for my death? I kept my fears to myself and prayed for a miracle.

Once everyone confirmed their understanding of the escape plan, we were loaded into the van and taken back to our pickup spots. When Thanh and I got out, it was broad daylight. We had been up all night. We walked around the town as inconspicuously as possible. Using what Vietnamese currency I had left, we purchased crackers and dried meats sealed in plastic. Much of the day, however, was spent walking the beach in an attempt to physically and mentally prepare for the trip ahead. In less than 24 hours, we would be swimming for our lives. In an effort to divert my attention away from drowning, I tried to imagine what life would be like once we were out of Vietnam, but I couldn't. I knew no other life.

As the sun began to set, Thanh and I casually made our way to the rocks that had been designated as our rendezvous spot. There we waited. All that we owned was on our bodies. It wasn't much, but it was enough to weigh me down in the water. My confidence began to ebb. I couldn't swim, and wearing two layers of clothing and four sheets of gold wasn't going to help. Death seemed imminent. Imagining what it would be like to drown, I started to cry.

"What's wrong?" my brother asked.

"I can't swim." I sobbed.

"Don't worry," Thanh said. "I will help you."

"Can you swim?" I asked him, unable to fathom where he might have learned this skill.

"I can!" he told me. "You can too. Just paddle like a dog."

I had never seen a dog paddle. Thanh tried to model it for me as he waved his hands in the air and kicked his feet in the sand. Under other circumstances I might have laughed at his imitation; but in this situation, I listened intently, knowing my life depended on it.

The sun slipped below the horizon, and the air turned cool. I leaned into Thanh to keep warm. The thought of wading into the cold water chilled me to the bone and fear slipped in like a slow leak. To pass the time we munched on crackers and talked of all the things we would miss in Vietnam. We watched the tide go out, the beach becoming wider as the water slipped further into the distance. All was quiet. All was dark. Time moved slowly as we huddled together on the hard rocks scanning the waters for the light of two lanterns.

I remember asking Thanh if he thought we would make it out of Vietnam alive. His answer came quickly. "No," he said. I was stunned. If Thanh had no hope of our success, surely we would fail. I needed his faith to carry me to the boat. I tried to reason with him, to point out the logic of our escape to international waters, to encourage him. If we had made it this far, surely we would make it all the way. God had provided us with a route. Then I asked Thanh the question again. "Do you think we will make it out of Vietnam alive?"

His answer was the same.

I had nothing more to give. I was empty and scared. I didn't mean to cry, but the tears came freely, running down my cheeks in waves as salty as the water that would surely take Thanh's life and mine.

CHAPTER 10

Save me, O God, for the waters have come up to my neck.
I sink in deep mire, where there is no foothold;
I have come into deep waters, and the flood sweeps over me.
I am weary with my crying; my throat is parched.
My eyes grow dim with waiting for my God.
Psalm 69:1-3 (NRSV)

May 4–11, 1975

It was completely dark when Thanh shook me awake and pointed out to sea. Two shimmering lights were bobbing on a small boat in the distance. I remember arguing with Thanh over whether the boat was the right one or not. Looking back, I think it was just my way of stalling the inevitable. Thanh would have none of it. He had been awake all night, watching as lights appeared on the water. I had missed the signal. Thanh informed me that we had to move quickly or we would miss the boat too.

I hesitated. If only my father were here to guide us. I looked up into the sky in search of a sign from my dad that everything was going to be all right. The sky was pitch black and yielded no encouragement.

"It looks so far," I said. "We can't do it."

"Yes we can," Thanh said as he moved toward the water and valiantly stepped into the surf. Apprehensively, I joined him.

I was grateful that my uncle had paired me with my brother for this journey. I couldn't have asked for a better partner. In my weakness, he became strong. He led, and I followed.

The water was freezing cold! I gave a little squeal, shocked by the frigid temperature that met my ankles. "Don't make any noise!" Thanh whispered harshly.

I shut my mouth and walked with him further into the sea. It was then that I looked up and saw the stars. They hadn't been there minutes earlier, but now they were impossible to miss. There were thousands of them. I felt my father walking with us into the surf, and a renewed feeling of determination washed over me.

I was chubby and barely five-feet tall; Thanh was skinny as a rail, just like our father, and quite a bit taller than me. Before I knew it, the water was at my chin and my feet were having a hard time touching the ground. Panicked, I started to inhale and choked on the seawater. I remember Thanh saying, "Let me hold you," but I don't think he did. Instead, I think I held onto his shoulder as he paddled like a dog with me kicking violently beside him. The memory is rather blurry, though I do recall being on my stomach as we moved through the water. I also remember that when I relinquished control to Thanh, I stopped choking.

I'm not sure how long it took us to get to the boat; it seemed like an eternity. Considering the fact that neither Thanh nor I had ever swum before, and we were each wearing two layers of clothing as well as shoes, our success was surely a miracle.

The boat had a small rope ladder that Thanh and I used to pull ourselves up out of what could have been our watery grave. A number of people were already on board, yet no one offered us help. It was every man—woman or child—for himself. Only two more people boarded after us. Once the captain counted heads, the motor was engaged and off we went.

Most of the passengers were wearing dry clothes; I later learned that these people had paid for another boat to row them out. I'm pretty sure I would have paid for this service myself had I known of it. Apparently God had other plans for me—other lessons for me to learn.

That night we motored away from the coast into an expansive black mass of nothingness. Our escape vessel was a small, diesel-powered fishing boat. I was shivering cold, and the smell of fuel made me nauseous. Though the seas were relatively calm, I got quite sick, vomiting over the side of the boat until I was overtaken with dry heaves. Even so, I was grateful that the sea had not swallowed us up. Thanh and I were still very much alive.

When the sun began to rise, the morning light revealed that we were still within sight of land. I did not see this as a problem, but several other passengers did. They became angry and demanded that the captain explain why we were still so close to shore. Our captain told everyone to calm down. He reassured us that we were already in international waters; therefore, there was no need to venture any further. All we had to do was wait. Nauseous as I was, waiting was a strenuous exercise.

By day two, I was lightheaded and weak. I didn't even have the strength to scratch my skin, which had become irritated by the saltwater as it dried into my clothes. I wasn't the only one suffering, but at least I kept my complaints to myself—unlike another woman on the boat who whined so much that the other passengers begged the captain to get rid of her.

On day three, the captain had finally had enough of the whiny woman. Instead of pushing her overboard, he headed back to shore—four days short of his promise to stay at sea for a week. He warned us that, if stopped by a police vessel, we were to act like tourists returning from a pleasure ride. However, after three days at sea in an open fishing boat, none of us would pass as a tourist out for pleasure. That's probably why we were stopped.

The patrol that pulled alongside our boat with guns drawn asked a lot of questions, none of which I can remember. Our answers must not have been very convincing because we were all escorted back to shore and stuffed into a police van. Frightened, I asked one of the passengers what would happen next. He seemed to know the routine. "Just pay them," he said.

It was a short ride to the jail where we were all ushered into a holding room. Being on solid ground calmed my stomach and gave me the strength to respond to the commanding officer who called us forward for questioning.

"Where are you going?" he asked.

"I'm looking for my parents," I answered.

"Why did you get on a boat?"

"It seemed like the quickest way to find them."

"Where are your parents?"

"I don't know."

I couldn't have made a lot of sense, but the officer seemed fine with it. Then he asked me, "How much did you pay?"

I told him the truth: that I had paid for my brother and me with four sheets of gold. At a minimum, he learned that I had paid the least amount of money for passage and, therefore, he wasn't going to make much off of me.

After everyone in the holding room had been interrogated, the officer addressed all of us at once saying, "There is a penalty for what you have done because you are traveling without permission. You will have to pay a fine. Anyone who is ready to pay can talk to me."

Then he sat himself at the far end of the room and waited. One by one, in orderly fashion, we approached the officer. Following customary rules of respect, the eldest among us went first. As the youngest, my brother and I went last.

"How much is the fine?" I asked. "I don't have any money."

It was the truth. All of the Vietnamese money I had brought with me had gone to pay for hotel rooms, food, and a bribe.

"Don't worry," he answered. "We don't want money. There are other ways to pay."

His words filled me with horror. I was sure he wanted my body, but I was wrong. The officer looked directly at me and said, "You can pay the fine the way you paid for the boat." He wanted gold — the only currency that was worth anything.

"I only have one sheet left," I lied. "Is that OK?"

He said it was good enough.

Though everyone had paid the fine, we all had to spend the night in the holding room. This didn't bother me. After relinquishing a precious sheet of gold, I figured I deserved a safe place to sleep.

Keeping us overnight was probably meant to deter anyone from attempting to escape again, but it had the opposite effect on me. I had now learned firsthand how corrupt Vietnamese officials could be. The country I loved no longer existed, and I was more determined than ever to escape its hold.

When the police released us the next morning, Thanh and I quickly went in search of another hotel that seemed to engage in more than just housing overnight guests. It didn't take long to find one. Unlike the previous hotel with quiet patrons, this hotel had numerous people milling about in its lobby blatantly talking about escape. They didn't even bother to whisper.

I approached a woman who was not much older than my mother and said, "I overheard you talking about plans to go away." She said nothing, so I continued.

"My brother and I also want to go away, but we don't know how to do it."

I told her that our whole family had already left, that we wanted to reunite with them, and that we were willing to pay for help. She listened sympathetically, but said nothing. Finally I asked her pointblank, "Can you help us?"

She thought for a moment before stating that she would speak with someone on my behalf. I wasn't scared, and I wasn't anxious. I waited patiently while the woman was out of the room. Three sheets of gold were still tucked under my clothes. Hopefully, that was enough to get Thanh and me on another boat to freedom.

The woman soon returned and said that the leader of her group was still looking to fill a few spots. "Do you want to talk to him?" she asked.

"Yes!" I responded emphatically.

She took my hand as if I were her friend and led me to a room off the lobby that was filled with people. We approached a smug-looking man who was sitting on a couch in the very middle of the room sipping dark coffee from a little cup. He sized me up as I stood before him. I couldn't tell if he was an ally or an enemy. Whatever the case, he made me nervous. I hoped the woman would speak on my behalf, but she had already walked away. For a moment, this man and I simply stared at each other. Then he asked the obvious, "So, you want to escape?"

If he was a communist, I was trapped. He waited while I thought of an appropriate response. Finally, I whispered, "Not really."

His eyebrows shot up. "Well then, what do you want to talk about?"

I looked around. Unfamiliar faces surrounded me. I felt trapped. Choosing my words carefully, I said, "My brother and I want to go away and look for our family."

"You mean . . . ESCAPE," the man insisted. His eyes opened wide, taunting me to challenge his intelligence. I took my chances.

"If you are going to put it that way," I said, "then, yes." He could challenge me all he wanted, but I would not say the word "escape" out loud.

"Let's make a deal," he said, putting his little cup on the seat next to him. Leaning forward, he informed me that the cost of passage for two would be eight sheets of gold. Since I only had three sheets left, I offered him all I had. The man said nothing. After a moment, he let out a sigh and slowly leaned back into the couch. Then he picked up his coffee and looked around the room, acting as if I were invisible. He was done with me, but I was not done with him.

Tired and weary, I began to beg and plead in the hopes of playing on his sympathies. I told him that I would be extremely grateful if he would allow Thanh and me to travel at a reduced rate, and since he had a lot of customers who looked like they had plenty of money, he wasn't going to lose much by accepting a lower price from me. Besides, helping two children find their parents would demonstrate his generosity.

I honestly don't think I convinced him to feel sorry for me. I think, rather, I annoyed him. Like the persistent widow in the Book of Luke,[12] I wore him down. In the end, he agreed to three sheets of gold to cover the cost of passage for Thanh and me. Reaching into my bra, I gave the man all I had left knowing that if we were caught again, we would be in serious trouble.

It had been less than 48 hours since Thanh and I were last at sea. The quick turnaround worried me, but it was too late to go back on the deal. We were now out of funds and had no other options.

The boat was scheduled to leave early the next morning in broad daylight. Vietnam's coast is lined with hundreds of small islands that make sightseeing a relatively common water activity. But there is nothing common about tourism in the aftermath of war. That's why we were instructed to bring no luggage and to act as if we were merely going on a joyride.

Thanh and I and the other 15 passengers played our parts perfectly. No one tried to stop us or question us as we walked out the back of the hotel and down a small pier toward a waiting boat. The boat we boarded was about 50 feet in length with a cream colored canopy running down the center for shade. There was no distinctive smell of diesel fuel, and the seats were cushioned. As I took a seat along the railing I thought to myself, *I have spent our money wisely this time. We are traveling in style!*

We were at sea for only two days when the North Vietnamese police boarded our boat. Because we truly looked like tourists, I thought we would be excused to continue our cruise. With focused purpose, the police interviewed each and every person onboard. Most people, including the captain, had traveling papers and were allowed to stay on the boat. Eight of us did not. We were moved onto the police boat and taken to shore.

Deep fear overtook me as I climbed into the police van. Thanh sat down next to me. Filled with guilt and regret, I couldn't look him in the eye. I had failed him. Having heard stories of South Vietnamese boys being taken against their will and trained as Vietcong soldiers on the front lines of combat, and of South Vietnamese girls being raped by Vietcong soldiers before being shot, I worried about my brother's emotional and physical safety as well as my own.

I regretted my decision to board another boat so quickly. I regretted trusting a man who had made me nervous. I should have listened to my instincts. I had exhibited poor judgment, and now Thanh and I would have to pay dearly for my mistake.

We were taken to a different police station this time, but the drill was the same. After waiting for several hours in a holding room, we were interrogated and asked to pay a fine. When I told the officer I didn't have any money left, he coldly responded, "Well then, you will have to go to jail." And with a flick of his thumb, another officer came forward and took us away.

I had never been inside a prison before. I looked to the adults around me for reassurance that everything would be all right, but they looked just as scared as I felt.

When we arrived at the prison, the men were separated from the women. My heart tore in two when Thanh and the other male prisoners were directed through an exit door on the other side of the room.

"Can't my brother come with me?" I cried.

"He will go somewhere else," an officer answered as he pulled me toward the opposite door.

"Where are you taking him?" I pleaded. Thanh was my strength and my responsibility. How could I persevere or protect him if we weren't together?

The officer answered coldly, "His cell will not be that far from yours."

I yelled across the room to my brother, "*Thanh, mạnh mẽ lên em!*" (Thanh, stay strong!) These words of encouragement were wailed for my own benefit as much as Thanh's.

Thanh yelled back, "*Đừng lo chị.*" (Don't worry, sister.) Then he disappeared from my sight.

CHAPTER 11

Remember those who are in prison, as though you were in prison
with them; those who are being tortured,
as though you yourselves were being tortured.
Hebrews 13:3 (NRSV)

May 12–16, 1975

I was put into a small cell approximately five meters long and
three meters wide. The door that shut behind me was made of
solid wood with a small, barred window at shoulder height that
allowed the guards to peer in whenever they desired. Another tiny,
barred window was carved into the far wall near the top. It provided
the cell with minimal light by day and a view of the skies at night.

Two cement benches ran down the length of the room on the
opposite walls. The benches served as beds, and the space between
them was only as wide as one of the benches. The hardness of the
cement was buffered by a little blanket—an American blanket. I
recognized it immediately as one of the items my mother often
had in her possession. The North Vietnamese probably issued us
the blankets to demonstrate their superiority over the Americans. I
cursed America when I saw it. However, when the night air turned
cool later that evening, I was grateful for the warmth the blanket
provided.

My cellmate was probably in her late twenties but, having been deeply weathered by life's storms, she looked much older. She was tough as nails and blatantly acerbic, yet strangely protective of me, somewhat like a big sister. During my time at the prison, I never learned why Mai had been locked up. Her response when I asked was, "You know how things work. If anything doesn't go well for *them*, you get put in jail. That's communism!"

Having never been in jail before, I bombarded my cellmate with questions. Mai was incredibly willing to provide answers, as well as advice. "There's a simple rule," she told me. "You just do exactly what they want."

I told Mai that I thought I could do that. After all, I had had a lot of practice obeying orders in my grandfather's house.

"What do we do for activity here?" I asked.

She responded with a question, "Do you like to get dirty?"

"Not really," I said, though my clothes did not support my claim. My mother would have been appalled to see me in this condition. I looked down at the dusty, dirty rags hanging from my body and saw nothing but gray.

My cellmate smirked at my ignorance. "Well, you will learn to be dirty in this place."

The true meaning of her sentence was lost on me.

"Do we have to cook?" I asked.

Mai looked at me sideways, as if she was inspecting an alien from another planet. "No, we'll be treated very nicely," she said sarcastically. "Somebody else will cook for us. And wait till you taste the food!"

Each woman was provided with a small metal bowl and cup to use in the dining hall. Meals were served twice a day. Breakfast was porridge, and dinner was soup. The thickness or thinness of the meal depended on how the cook felt that day. We had two choices: take it or leave it.

The first couple days of prison life were relatively non-eventful. There were designated meal times, chore times, bathroom times, and shower times. Because all the guards were male, we showered with our clothes on. I found this to be a unique and efficient way of washing clothing, though the water was quite cold. There were no towels; so we literally drip-dried.

As one of the newest prisoners, I was assigned to cleaning duty around the facility, from officers' toilets to hallway floors. Meanwhile, all the seasoned prisoners were ushered out to labor in the cornfields or rice paddies. Because their workday was longer than mine, I sat for hours in my small cell with nothing to do, eagerly awaiting Mai's return. When she would arrive, I would bombard her with questions: What had she done all day? How far was it to the fields? How many people worked in the field? Could she talk while she worked? Did the workers get breaks? Did she work with any of the male prisoners? Did she have a good day?

Mai would graciously, yet sarcastically, provide me with answers. "If you think getting sunburned while straining your back equates to a good day, then mine was great!"

I wondered why I hadn't yet been assigned to work in the fields; I didn't have to wonder for long. New prisoners were required to undergo an interrogation before being assigned to manual labor. My interrogation came on day three.

I was summoned from my cell shortly after Mai and the other women left the prison building. An officer ushered me into the interrogation room just as another officer was escorting a male prisoner out. The prisoner I saw appeared defeated; his eyes were empty, as if he had been stripped of his soul. I knew at once that I was entering a place of darkness. A huge lump formed in my throat, and I found it hard to breathe. "Oh God," I prayed, "please be with me."

The interrogation room was rather large. A non-descript middle-aged officer sat in the chair behind the desk in the center of the room. Two assistant officers stood nearby. Upon entering, I was instructed to sit in the lone chair situated in front of the desk. As I did so, I caught sight of a long, wooden bench behind the desk laden with tools and buckets. The array reminded me of items one might find in a carpenter's shed.

"Why did you try to leave Vietnam?" the officer asked. He spoke slowly, softly, and deliberately.

My chest tightened, and my heart began to pound in my ears. "I was looking for my family," I told him, perhaps a little too quickly.

He considered my answer before responding. "We found you with people trying to escape from the country."

I explained to him that I did not know who those people were and that I was searching for my parents who had gone overseas. "I just wanted to be with my family," I said.

"What do your parents do?" he asked.

I was prepared for this question. I told the officer that my mother was a homemaker and that I didn't know what kind of business my stepfather was in. I tried my best to explain that I had been in boarding school and hadn't spent much time with my new stepfather. I didn't know him well. In other words, I lied.

"Do you have uncles and aunts?" he asked.

I told him I did.

"What do they do?"

This question unnerved me. My Uncle Hoang had warned me about questions such as this, questions that could bring death to a family member if answered truthfully. A huge lump formed in my throat as I thought of the uncle who had flown jets for the South Vietnamese Air Force, and another uncle who had risen to the rank of Army Captain, and yet another uncle who had worked as a magistrate in the South Vietnamese government.

If I shared any of this, my life and theirs could be in danger. Perhaps I could tell him something about my aunt who had a prestigious job as a U.N. secretary. Since she no longer lived in Vietnam, retaliation would not be possible—unless, of course, they chose to take out their vengeance on me instead. I had to be careful.

"My aunts are homemakers, and my uncles work for the government," I said.

"What do they do for the government?" he asked. "What are their jobs?"

"I don't really know," I lied.

I began to wonder whether my relatives were dead or alive, whether they were locked away in prisons or sitting at home, or whether they were cruising on boats bound for safer countries. It didn't matter though. I had to protect them. I had to protect Thanh and myself.

After several grueling minutes of questioning that led to nowhere, the officer sadly admitted, "You didn't tell us much." I knew by the tone of his voice that he wasn't happy with me. He then beckoned the two assistants to come forward.

The assistants took hold of my arms and led me to another chair directly behind the officer's desk. As I got closer to the chair I realized that the items on the bench were not carpenters' tools for restoration or creation; they were sadists' tools for ruin and destruction. These were tools of torture. Something very bad was about to happen to me.

"Let's see how much more you really know," the officer stated. His tone was fiendish, and it sent a chill up my spine.

My forearms were bound to the chair's arms with rope; my back faced the bench so I could not see what tools were selected. Convinced that I was about to die, I closed my eyes and silently confessed my sins so that I would not be turned away at the gates of Heaven. I distinctly remember asking God to take care of Thanh, wherever he was.

Then I heard the sound of a welding torch being lit, and I smelled the scent of burning fuel. *What were they going to do to me?* Overwhelming fear gripped every fiber of my body. I struggled to breathe normally, but I could not. I searched my brain for the words to any prayer, but they were lost from memory.

The officer looked down on me and asked, "Have you ever been hurt?"

"Yes," I answered quickly.

"What happened?" he asked.

Panic gripped me unlike any terror I had ever known. *What does he want me to say? What kind of pain is he interested in hearing about?* Physically, I had been shot, whipped, pinched, and practically drowned. Emotionally, I had experienced intense grief, severe loss, and prolonged abuse. *Is there a right answer?* My breaths came in short spurts. He waited. Finally, I said, "My mother slapped me."

"Huh!" he grunted with disgust. "That's what you call hurt?"

He reached out his hand; his assistant placed a long metal poker in it. The end was red hot. I knew he was going to use it on my body. *Where? Where? Where?* Seeing the implement of torture did not make the inevitable any easier to accept. I wanted to close my eyes, but I couldn't.

Holding up the burning poker, he asked, "Where would you like me to put this?"

I have a choice? My mind whirled. "My leg?" I asked, as if I was a contestant on a game show.

"No," he shook his head insidiously. "I don't think the leg is good. I will give it to you somewhere to remind you of our conversation. Stick out your tongue."

I don't know why I did it. Perhaps I was afraid he would burn my lips if I didn't offer him my tongue willingly. So I stuck it out as far as I could. The pain was unimaginable, and I will never forget the smell of my own burning flesh. The effect was immediate.

When he asked me again about my family, I screamed out everything I knew. My uncle was in the Air Force; my other uncle was in the army; another uncle had been a South Vietnamese magistrate; my aunt worked for the United Nations in Australia; I had tried to escape from Vietnam twice. On and on I went, but nothing I said made much sense. My tongue was so badly burned that I could not pronounce my words properly. Everything I said came out garbled.

I vaguely remember the assistants suggesting to the officer that he allow me to go and rest for a few hours before continuing with the interrogation. The officer took their advice, and I was led back to my prison cell, screaming and ranting the entire way, like a lunatic.

I stayed in my cell that evening instead of going to dinner. I couldn't have eaten anything anyway. After a fitful night of sleep, I was led back to the torture chamber in the morning. Overnight I had developed a defiant attitude. My tongue was extremely swollen and searing with pain, yet my mind was steady, and my heart had hardened. Fear had turned to anger, and I was determined not to be broken.

When the door opened, I walked directly to the torture chair behind the desk and sat down. I placed my forearms on the chair arms, offering them to be tied. Unfazed, the officer slowly got up from his desk and walked over to me.

"You're ready to start, huh?" he asked mockingly.

With much difficulty I responded, "I think my tongue is a little bit tougher today."

I was challenging him. In retrospect, that was quite stupid since he held all the cards. The officer gave me a wicked smile and waited a beat before stating, "We don't want your tongue today."

And just like that, the world slipped out from under me.

The fearlessness I possessed when I entered this godforsaken room immediately vanished. I was ready to face the burning poker, but I was not prepared to face a torturous unknown. *What was he going to do to me now?*

I stiffened when I heard the sound of water being poured into a tin vessel behind me. Suddenly, one of the assistants pulled me to my feet and tied my hands behind my back. He then forced me to kneel in front of a large metal tub filled with water. Water scared me. My torturer knew it. I shudder to think how he discovered my weakness.

With a sinister sweetness, the officer touched the back of my hair and said, "Let's see if you can take this." Then he violently pushed my head under the water. I fought his hold, but he had a tight grip on my hair and my hands were tied. After several seconds, he yanked my head out and asked, "Are you ready to talk now?"

I wanted to die. I shook my head no, and he shoved my face back into the tub.

This deadly dance went on for some time. He would ask me for information about my family, and I would refuse to provide it. Then my head would be shoved under water. I remember once responding to his interrogation this way: "You can ask me the question as many times as you want, but you will not get an answer."

The agony of breathing water into your lungs cannot be compared to the agony of having your tongue burned with a red-hot iron rod. Both are horrifically painful. Stripped of my dignity and strength, I succumbed to the process and focused on the end. I had given up and was ready to die. When I began having difficulty breathing even when my head was not submerged, I presumed my death was imminent. Silently, I asked God to take me. That's when one of the assistants suggested, "Maybe we should stop. It doesn't look like she has much to tell us."

My torturer considered his words and ended the proceedings. He didn't really want me dead, I discovered. His joy came in watching others suffer, not die.

I was lifted off the floor and dragged back to my cell where I collapsed on the floor, still struggling for air. Death seemed so sweet, but it was not my day to die. God, I thought, had abandoned me.

It was many years later that I learned of other atrocities the North Vietnamese had inflicted on the South Vietnamese people that made my ordeal pale in comparison. Following the takeover, former military, government, and business leaders were rounded up by the new communist regime and shipped to camps in North Vietnam for "re-education." There they were forced to do manual labor under horrendous conditions with little food or water. Medical care was purposely denied, and torture was a common—if not daily—occurrence for many.

I heard of prisoners being locked in metal storage boxes where temperatures soared above 100 degrees, of prisoners having their hands and feet tied together and swung from a rope while being beaten with bamboo, and of prisoners having their limbs shackled in painful positions for weeks at a time. It is estimated that nearly a million people were imprisoned in these camps following the fall of Saigon and thousands died of malnutrition, poor sanitation, disease, and torture.[13]

Some might say that my Uncle Hoang was lucky to have made it out of a North Vietnamese re-education camp alive. I don't agree. Death would have been more humane. I'll never know what my uncle experienced at the hands of his captors, but he was not "re-educated." Following his release, he did everything he could to get the rest of my family out of Vietnam before he attempted to escape himself. Along with tens of thousands of South Vietnamese, he took his chances on the open seas rather than succumb to communist rule. Unfortunately, he did not get far before he was captured and sent to a North Vietnamese prison where he labored for several years. Near death, he was finally released.

I thank the Lord that he was able to experience two full weeks of real freedom in Australia before passing away from respiratory complications.

The North Vietnamese thought they could break the spirits of their prisoners. They were wrong. Following my two days of torture, I had experienced enough evil to last a lifetime. Like my uncle, all I could think about was escape. Vietnam was hell on earth. How I wished I had been born elsewhere. Even America.

CHAPTER 12

Having hope will give you courage.
You will be protected and will rest in safety.
You will lie down unafraid, and many will look to you for help.
Job 11:18-19 (NLT)

May 18–Late May 1975

"What day is it?" I asked my cellmate. After two days of torture, I was unaware of how long I had slept.

"Sunday," Mai said.

I wanted to go to church. I wanted to participate in the calming practice of rote prayer and ritual among a body of believers. I wanted to be in a place where I knew what was coming next. I wanted to feel safe.

My tongue, still swollen to twice its normal size, hurt when I tried to speak. And coughing through the night in an attempt to empty my lungs of water had left my throat raw. Still, my desire to attend mass was stronger than the pain. I lay on the hard stone and prayed for God's forgiveness. Surely, I surmised, I was a sinful creature to have received such punishment. I begged God to have mercy on my soul and protect me from further assaults.

As I prayed, a peace descended on me that I remember to this day. Some might say I was delirious. I say it was God's holy presence that enveloped me, more tangible than the American blanket in which I was wrapped. God had heard my prayer.

I have come to realize that God is present even when we don't see Him. He was with me in prison in the midst of the pain and atrocities. He kept me from death and protected my family. As bad as things were, they could have been worse had God not intervened. I'm sure my torturer would have killed me if his assistant hadn't suggested that he stop. And third degree burns on my tongue prevented me from speaking clearly and implicating family members during my interrogation. I don't profess to understand why I had to suffer in this way—or why anyone has to suffer at all—but I do know that God is good, and I believe that he grieved alongside me. I also believe that God blessed me the next morning by allowing me to go to the rice fields. This signaled the end of my torture and recovery period.

Planting rice plugs is easy, but it's backbreaking work. It involves standing barefoot in about 10-inches of water from sunup to sundown while pushing plugs of rice plants into the mud below. Whenever breaks were allowed, I would stand tall and reach to the sky. How I wished I could fly away over the fields, weaving in and out among the trees, unscathed by mans' wars.

Though grateful to have spent the day outdoors, my entire body felt stiff and numb at the end of the shift. And to make matters worse, my feet were covered with leeches. I wasn't a large person and feared that the vampire-like worms would suck me dry. Luckily, a woman showed me how to get rid of them swiftly. With one hand I would slide my finger over my skin toward the sucker to push it out while the other hand pulled the slimy leech off. I managed to become quite proficient with this maneuver.

Near the end of my first week in prison, I was moved from the rice paddies to the cornfields. This was a definite improvement. I didn't have to bend over all day, and there were no leeches to contend with. As my cellmate and I picked the corn off the stalks, some kernels fell to the ground. Mai picked them up, handed them to me, and told me to put them in my pocket. Naively I asked, "Are we supposed to collect these too?"

"No!" she said. "Just save them for tonight."

This memory calls to mind a passage in the book of Leviticus that reads: *When you harvest the crops of your land, do not harvest the grain along the edges of your field, and do not pick what the harvesters drop. Leave them for the poor and the foreigners living among you. I am the Lord your God.*[14]

That evening, when we were served our watery soup, Mai reminded me about the corn kernels in my pocket and instructed me to put them in my bowl. I thought the raw kernels would taste awful, but they were actually quite sweet. I looked around and noticed that all the women had yellow kernels floating in their bowls, even the women who had worked in the rice paddies all day. Our ability to survive was entirely dependent on our willingness to care for each other. We shared what little we had with those around us, and God blessed us for it. Those little specks of yellow corn brought sunshine into our gray lives and ignited a strong flame of kinship among us.

With the aid of these women, the prison routine became manageable. After dinner each evening, there were chores to do, such as mopping the kitchen floor, carting water from the well pump, and sweeping the hallways. Some women were selected to prepare meals for the officers. Given my disdain for cooking, I was grateful not to be assigned to this work crew.

My favorite assignment, if there could be such a thing, was fetching water. On my way to the water pump I was able to view the men's prison through the barbed wire fence. I always looked for my brother. Always. Though unable to make out any of the faces, I imagined Thanh was looking for me too.

One evening, as I was settling in for the night, I heard a cell door open across the hall. Peeking through the small opening in the door, I witnessed a prison guard removing a woman from her bed. When they were out of earshot, I whispered to Mai, "I think they're going to kill her!"

She laughed. "No," she said. "She's on her way to having a good night's sleep." When I asked her to explain, she told me that some girls were selected to spend the night with an officer. Those lucky girls received a good meal and got to sleep in the officer's comfortable bed.

I thought this over. I had lost a great deal of weight on the prison meal plan, and my jail cell often felt as if it was closing in on me like a coffin. I must have been under a great deal of stress at the time because sleeping with an officer seemed like a reasonable exchange for a good meal and a comfortable bed.

"What do you have to do to get picked?" I asked.

"You have to be very good!" Mai said.

The next day, I was very good. I worked hard and performed each task with great enthusiasm. I desperately hoped for a complete meal and a soft place to lay my head. That night, I got picked.

When I got called to follow the prison guard out of my cell and down the corridor, I felt more excited than afraid. I remember thinking that Thanh would have been appalled if he knew the depths to which I was willing to sink for a good meal and a comfortable bed. I pushed Thanh's face out of my mind though and brazenly lined up with several other women. Each one met my gaze with a warm welcome as if I had just been initiated into an elite sorority.

"Oh, you got picked too!" one woman said cheerfully.

Another woman, who recognized that this was my first time, tried to make me look more attractive by smoothing my hair and pinching my cheeks to make them rosy. I asked her, "Where are we going?"

"We'll all be in different places," she replied. "Make sure you are polite, no matter what they say. Please them! And never say no."

I took this advice to heart though I couldn't imagine what I might be asked to do. I just hoped I would not be asked to sing any American songs, for I didn't have it in me to perform for anyone.

Once all the chosen women had been assembled, we were led to the showers. For the first time since my arrival, I was given a towel and a bar of soap. I was elated! We were ordered to remove our clothes, shower thoroughly, and put on the clean garments that our jailors provided. Our old clothes were placed in brown paper bags that we carried with us into the night.

The officers' living quarters were located near the perimeter of the prison grounds—cabins situated one right after another. The guards were familiar with the drill and delivered designated women to their assigned cabins. I watched as our group got smaller and the cabins got larger. Some women went into cabins alone; others entered cabins in pairs. Several men were always waiting at the cabin doors. Finally, I was the only one left. The guard told me to wait while he confirmed my arrival at the last cabin. I couldn't help but think that I was in some way special.

The guard came back and said to me, "Captain Quan is ready to see you now."

I walked tentatively to the door and entered the cabin alone. He was sitting in a chair just inside the room. His black hair was cut short and his dark eyes met mine. Dressed in the traditional North Vietnamese military uniform, he appeared to be slim and just slightly taller than me. He was older, but not ancient. I had never seen Captain Quan on the prison grounds before, nor had I ever heard his name mentioned, so I did not know what to expect.

"Close the door," he said. His voice was kind, not authoritative or chauvinistic. I closed the door. He gestured to the seat in the chair opposite his. When I hesitated, he said, "Don't be scared."

It wasn't an order. It was an invitation. In that moment, I decided I liked Captain Quan. He asked me when I had arrived at the prison. I hesitated while my brain tried to calculate the correct answer. There had been waiting days, then two days of torture; this was followed by rice paddy days and eventually cornfield days. "Two weeks?" I responded, more like a question than an answer.

Captain Quan nodded in acceptance, not confirmation. Then he asked me how I was doing. My head went down, and I could feel the tears welling up in my eyes. Not because prison life was unbearable, but because I could not remember a time since my father's passing when someone had asked me how I was. I found I could not speak.

"Would you like something to drink?" he offered. Getting up, he presented me with a choice between a local soda or a Coca-Cola. I pointed to the Coca-Cola. "I expected you to choose this one," he said kindly, referring to the American brand.

"Yes," I replied. "It's the best."

He popped the top and handed me the bottle before settling back into his chair with a Vietnamese beer in hand. Captain Quan continued the conversation by asking me to explain why I had tried to leave Vietnam. I did a quick look around the room; seeing no evident tools of torture, I decided to tell him the truth.

I told the captain that when the North Vietnamese captured Saigon, my family said it wasn't good to be under communist rule and we had to escape. In the process, I had been separated from my mother and my siblings. I told him that I was just trying to reunite with them.

Captain Quan listened intently, as if he really cared about what I had to say. He encouraged me to go on, so I did. I told him that the Vietcong had killed my father years earlier during Tết and that I had been shot trying to seek refuge.

Captain Quan looked down at the floor. He seemed almost embarrassed to hear this. "We're not all bad," he said.

I found myself saying, "I believe you, but I also have to believe my family."

There was a knock on the door. A guard had arrived with the dinner delivery. A proper dinner. My tongue was still healing, so I couldn't chew very well. However, I did manage to eat all of the soft items on my plate. Captain Quan never asked me about my tongue, my torture, or my impression of prison. Though he never asked, I suspect he knew something about my treatment. I tried to imagine Captain Quan participating in torture tactics, but I couldn't. He was too nice.

Captain Quan went from drinking beer to scotch whiskey. My grandfather also drank whiskey, and to this day I am reminded of both men whenever I catch a whiff of it. In my mind's eye I can still picture Captain Quan relaxed in his chair, sipping from a small glass, and asking me thoughtful questions. He listened intently as I rambled on about everything from geography to the French language. Captain Quan seemed especially interested in my educational experience in the Catholic schools. His fascination with all I had to say provided the impetus for me to keep talking, lending credence to the aphorism that more flies can be caught with honey than with vinegar. I willingly provided personal details about my siblings and spoke fondly of Thanh as the brother I was closest to.

"Where is your brother?" Captain Quan asked.

"I don't know," I told him. "He was taken to the men's jail. I believe he's still there."

I wondered whether I had talked too much, shared too much. If so, the damage was done, and I didn't regret it. It was the first time in a very long time that I felt human, and I was grateful to Captain Quan for providing me with that privilege.

After talking late into the night, Captain Quan then politely stated, "We have to go to sleep now." It seemed like the appropriate thing to do. He walked me to the bedroom where I saw a double bed that was not unlike the one my mother and father used to sleep in. My heart began to race. Now that my stomach was full, I no longer felt special to have been selected to sleep with a man. I thought of my Uncle Toan and Nhu probing my body as I slept. I knew how to lie perfectly still and pretend to be asleep, but I had never experienced intercourse and wasn't sure about what I was supposed to do.

Captain Quan went into another room to change out of his uniform. I crawled into the bed wearing all my borrowed clothes. Pulling the blanket up to my chin, I waited.

Captain Quan returned wearing simple pajamas like the ones my father used to wear. He slipped in beneath the covers and drew me gently to him, hugging me as a father would hug his child. At first it felt awkward. I could tell that he wanted more than a hug, but he didn't push himself on me. He let my lack of response dictate his next move. He fell asleep.

Though it was probably wrong to feel this way, I felt protected in that big bed. I fell asleep in Captain Quan's arms, my head on his shoulder.

"You have to go back to your cell now," he said, gently waking me the next morning.

At his instruction, I quickly changed back into my dirty, old clothes and put my clean, borrowed clothes in the same paper bag. Then I looked around, unsure of what I was supposed to do with it.

"Would you like me to hold onto those clothes for you?" he asked.

"Yes, I would like that!" I said, handing him the bag. "I have to work in the fields."

Captain Quan smiled and nodded. His tenderness touched my heart. Just as he took the bag from my hand, there was a knock on the door. It was the guard, ready to collect me for my daily activities.

I remember experiencing a certain joy that day as I picked cobs of corn off the stalks. I know that sounds strange, but it's true. Captain Quan had kept my clothes, so I knew I would be seeing him again. He had given me something to look forward to.

That night, after all my chores were complete, a prison guard came for me. I was ready and waiting. When I arrived at Captain Quan's cabin, I willingly entered, closing the door behind me. The captain welcomed me warmly, like an old friend. Once again, there was food and drink and deep conversation. That night, I lost my virginity.

Suffice it to say that Captain Quan and I settled into a comfortable routine, meeting together each night. Though I had been stripped of all rights and imprisoned, I felt alive and free when I was with him. My father would have been unnerved to know that his favored daughter was content playing the role of mistress to the enemy. I didn't see it that way.

After a childhood fraught with anger, abuse, and manipulation, Captain Quan's gentleness brought healing to my soul. I can't profess to understand God's ways, for His ways are mysterious; but I do believe that God, in His mercy, used my enemy to sustain me during this time. God alone knew I desperately needed compassion lest I lose all sight of hope. And without hope, my soul would have been lost.

CHAPTER 13

How long will you defend the unjust and
show partiality to the wicked?
Defend the weak and fatherless;
uphold the cause of the poor and the oppressed.
Rescue the weak and the needy;
deliver them from the hand of the wicked.
Psalm 82:2-4 (NIV)

Late May–June 1975

Several weeks into our arrangement, Captain Quan asked, "Are you happy with me?"

"Yes!" I replied rather emphatically.

"Aren't you interested in finding your family?" he asked.

"I don't know where to look," I answered honestly. Nor, *could* I look. I was in prison, after all.

"But if you had the opportunity to find them, would you want to?"

It was a question I hadn't contemplated, and it triggered something in the pit of my stomach. How could I tell Captain Quan that I was happier being imprisoned with him than living with my family? And why had he asked me that question anyway? I had to wonder whether he was rejecting me, thinking of releasing me, or just making conversation. Was it possible that he had been using me to get information about my family in order to arrest them? I just couldn't tell.

Since Captain Quan had come into my life, I hadn't thought much about my mother or extended family. The only person I had any concern for was Thanh.

"Can you find out if my brother is OK?" I asked.

He told me he could.

The next night, Captain Quan informed me that Thanh was fine and that there was nothing to worry about. Though the news was reassuring, it reminded me that I was responsible for his welfare. My father had told me to look after my brothers. My mother had given me the same charge. I could not in good conscience leave Thanh to rot in a prison cell while I ate good food and slept in a comfortable bed each night. Mustering up the courage, I asked the captain, "Can you help us escape?"

"No," was his first reply. I hadn't expected him to say yes, but I must have felt it was within his power to assist with a jailbreak if he wanted to because I continued to ask the same question night after night.

Several days later, Captain Quan's response turned into, "I don't know." Then one night he said, "I suppose." But he wanted to know what was in it for him if he helped me. After considerable thought, I promised to send money to his family in South Vietnam once I was safely out of the country and earning an income. In essence, I promised to send him the equivalent of a year's wages.

He thought long and hard about my offer, yet he said nothing. He did acknowledge that if he agreed to the terms, he would be taking a big risk since there was no guarantee that I would make it out of the country once I was out of prison. He was right. My chances were slim.

A week passed, maybe two. Then one night the captain held me a little tighter than usual while he stared at the ceiling. Time seemed to stand still. I knew this was the turning point. Finally, he let go of me, rolled onto his elbow, and looking directly into my eyes announced, "I'm going to do this. I'll plan your escape."

Whether this was his plan all along, I'll never know. Perhaps he had helped young women before me escape. If he did, he didn't let on. Nevertheless, I believe in my heart that I was the first and only person he assisted in a jailbreak. I truly cared for him, and I believe Captain Quan really cared for me. What we had was the closest thing I had ever experienced to a love relationship, but we both knew there could be no future for us. I was a prisoner, and the greatest gift he could give me was to set me free.

We spent the next several nights hammering out the details of the plan. Before my eyes, Captain Quan transformed from my loving protector into a military strategist. Affections gave way to mediation. I had to convince him over and over again that I would be true to my word and send money to his family as soon as I was able. I considered myself to be a good negotiator, but he was better. In the details, it became clear how my lover had risen to the rank of captain.

As the plan came together, I began to realize that Thanh was not part of it. I told Captain Quan, "I only have my brother. I cannot leave him behind. I will double what I've agreed to pay your family if you can find a way to release him too." Tentatively, the captain agreed to my offer.

The day of the break finally arrived. We reviewed the plan hours before it was to be executed. At an appointed time of the night, the captain would wake me. Then I would head to the outhouses—the third one from the right to be exact, where the toilet could easily be pulled off the floor. I would then crawl through the latrine hole and the accompanying tunnel, which reportedly emptied outside the prison fence.

Meanwhile, Thanh would escape in a similar fashion via the men's latrines. Once he and I were reunited, we were to run as fast as possible away from the prison grounds.

"You need to remember," Captain Quan told me, "that your chances of being caught are very high." I was keenly aware of this. If someone entered the third stall shortly after I had disappeared, my capture would be inevitable.

"If you get caught," he told me, "I will be the one to shoot you." Captain Quan couldn't take the chance that under torture I might implicate him in my escape.

I accepted his conditions. Surely, it was better to die by a bullet to the head than by torture.

As planned, Captain Quan woke me up in the middle of the night. I put on the clean clothes provided by the prison, and I made my way to the third outhouse. There were no drawn out goodbyes. No tears were shed. No words of encouragement were offered. I simply left.

I had two small sheets of paper tucked inside my bra—one contained the addresses of my uncle in France and my pen pal Hubert in Switzerland; the other contained Captain Quan's home address. The Captain knew where to find this paper on my body so he could destroy the evidence in case he had to shoot me.

When Captain Quan had given me his family's address, I was stunned to see that their house was located in South Vietnam, not North Vietnam. This meant that either he—the enemy—had been living among us for some time, or his family had recently moved to the area to acquire land. Either way, the revelation was upsetting. There was so much I did not know about him or the war in my own country.

I entered the outhouse where the toilet easily separated itself from the floor. The hard part was lowering my body down through the small opening, feet first. The tunnel, however, was larger than I had expected. Crawling on my hands and knees through excrement was not all that difficult, though it was certainly disgusting. Thankfully, it wasn't a very long tunnel, and I soon found myself on the other side of the prison fence.

My first thought when I breathed in the fresh air and looked around was, *I've been cheated,* because my brother was nowhere in sight. I started to cry, certain that death was just moments away. I did then what I had been taught to do—I confessed my sins. I began with the sin of the flesh. I confessed each sexual encounter with Captain Quan, trying my best to explain that I had little choice in the matter. I remember crying out to God, "I want my brother." And practically on cue, I turned around to find him standing next to me.

Grabbing his hand, we began to run. I don't know whether it was out of fear or joy, but I couldn't stop talking. Thanh told me several times to be quiet, but I just couldn't contain myself. Suddenly, he stopped running, and in exasperation he yelled, "SHUT UP and smell the air!"

"I smell crap," I said.

Thanh replied, "I smell water."

We looked at each other and started to laugh. Soon we were running again, and before we knew it, we saw it—the beautiful South China Sea. We ran into the surf, letting the waves wash over us, carrying the evidence and smell of prison life out to sea. The water was freezing cold. We didn't care because it was life giving.

We waded a ways down the coast and eventually took refuge behind some large rocks. It was pitch black except for a scattering of stars in the sky. I was sure our dad was watching over us. Sitting perfectly still, we listened to see if anyone was on our trail. All we heard was the sound of the waves crashing against the shore. After several tense minutes, we began to relax. We were free—truly free!

Thanh found a large piece of cardboard that we used as a shield against the cool evening breeze. We huddled beneath it, and in a matter of minutes, we were asleep in each other's arms.

The morning light shed clarity on our situation. Thanh and I were safe and completely lost. Nothing about this beach looked familiar. Whether we were south or north of where we had first been captured, we had no idea. Luckily, any trace of our footsteps had been swept away with the waves; so even passersby had no clue about our jailbreak.

It was discomforting to find ourselves penniless in an unknown location surrounded by strangers with nothing more than the clothes on our backs. I thanked God and Captain Quan that I was not alone. Thanh's presence beside me was priceless. I fully intended to pay Captain Quan back for his merciful act as soon as I was able.

Thanh and I spent most of the day scavenging for food in garbage cans outside the nearby hotels and shops. Unfortunately, we didn't find much. As stores began to close, our hopes of finding suitable sustenance faded. Hungry and exhausted, Thanh boldly began to approach merchants directly to ask them for food. A few took pity on us and provided enough morsels to calm our aching bellies. It was impossible to go on living like this.

From our vantage point, we had two options: return to Saigon or look for another way out of Vietnam. Thanh cast his vote for the first option; I voted for the second. My mother had made it clear that we were not to return home under any circumstances. Besides, I did not want to live in a country that tortured its own people. Nor did I want to return to Saigon and live at the mercy of my extended family members. I could not tell Thanh of the oppression and abuse I had suffered at their hands, so I merely reminded him of our mother's instruction to keep going and not turn back.

Thanh relented and gave me one more chance to find a vessel that would take us out to sea. I'm sure he thought I would fail since we had no money with which to pay for passage. Such details did not deter me.

Dire situations call for desperate measures. I selected a hotel and walked directly up to the receptionist and asked, "Do you know of anyone who can help my brother and me find my parents? We don't know where they are, but we think they may have boarded a boat."

The woman responded without hesitation, "I think I know someone who could help you." She wrote a name on a slip of paper. Then she walked me to the door of the hotel and pointed to a house about two blocks away. It seemed too easy, yet perhaps it was.

"Is it safe for me to knock on the door?" I asked.

She assured me that it was, saying, "You'll be fine. He's a real fisherman."

My luck with tourism companies had not proved successful. Maybe I would have better luck with a fisherman. I had nothing to lose—literally and figuratively. Thanh reluctantly tailed me to the house, which was built right on the edge of the road. It was a cheap structure in critical need of repair. Though uninviting, it did not strike me as a communist hub.

A young girl answered the door when we knocked. I asked for Mr. Khoa as the hotel receptionist had instructed. Thanh and I were waved inside and ushered into a small living room packed with many other would-be escapees. I found I was no longer shocked by the number of people congregating in rooms across the coastline attempting to book seats on vessels heading out to sea. Despite the fact that Thanh and I had just come from a stint in prison, crawled through a sewer, bathed in seawater, and spent the night on the beach, we seemed to blend right in. The only significant difference between them and us was that we carried no personal belongings or, I suspected, currency.

I took a seat on a worn sofa next to an older woman. We chatted briefly, but mostly we sat in silence, waiting. I used this time to pray for God's favor; it was a one-sentence request for success that I repeated over and over again, like a mantra. Who in their right mind would take two destitute teenagers seriously? God was my only hope.

I smelled the fisherman before I saw him, and his looks rivaled his scent. He was probably about 60 years old, though he looked much older. His little goatee was not sufficient to mask the weathered lines in his face from years at sea. His long white hair was secured in a ponytail with a tattered piece of string, and he was dressed in faded brown workpants and a shirt so thin that it was see-through.

Despite his looks, Mr. Khoa entered the room with authority. And why shouldn't he? It was his house, and his boat. Looking around, his eyes landed on me—the new person. He approached and asked, "Do you want to talk to me?"

I nodded. "My brother and I would like to talk to you."

I took note of his dried, cracked hands and dirty fingernails. I'm sure I didn't look much better, but I still had the air of an aristocrat and viewed him as my inferior.

Thanh and I followed Mr. Khoa into the next room where he offered us a seat on a bench. Now I became nervous and worried. Without anything to barter with, my hopes of getting onto this man's boat were precariously slim.

Mr. Khoa asked us where we wanted to go, and I told him, "To international waters where American ships are waiting to save us."

He seemed surprised. "Really?" he questioned with disbelief. I seemed to have something he didn't—knowledge. This was my bargaining chip.

"It's true!" I replied. "My uncle is in the Air Force, and he told us that U.S. ships would be waiting for us in international waters. We just have to get out there to meet them."

It was as if Mr. Khoa had been waiting for the assurance I provided. The next thing he said was, "The price for each of you is six sheets of gold."

"Can you give us a deal?" I asked. "We just got out of prison, and we don't have any money. We lost everything."

"You don't have *any* money?" Mr. Khoa asked. "How will you manage in another country?"

"I have family members overseas," I told him. "They will look after Thanh and me."

"Which country?" he asked.

"France," I answered proudly. "And I speak French."

Mr. Khoa seemed impressed. "Well, at least you have someone. I would like to live in another country, but I don't have anyone to go to."

The light bulb went on inside my head. "I can help you," I declared.

I told Mr. Khoa that France had a huge Vietnamese community and that he would fit right in. All he needed was someone to pose as his wife, and I was willing to do that. Since refugees were not required to have legal papers, there was no chance of us getting caught in a lie. Once we were rescued, I told him, he could accompany my brother and me to France where he could easily start a new life. I didn't know if any of this was true or not, but hope was the only thing I had to offer.

It was a tough sell, but eventually Mr. Khoa bought into my plan—hook, line, and sinker. He warned Thanh and me to tell no one about our agreement. We promised to keep it a secret and returned to the living room to await orders.

Mr. Khoa outlined his escape strategy to the group. Each family was assigned a rendezvous location and informed of the signal that would identify the escape boat. When the tide was low and we saw the signal, we were to swim out to the craft. Mr. Khoa warned that hiring another boat to row us out would not be tolerated, as this would draw unwanted attention.

To avoid excess weight, we were told not to bring any food or water. Mr. Khoa said he would provide what was needed for the journey. Having no money with which to purchase groceries, Thanh and I were most grateful for this provision. Then we were dismissed for the night with instructions to get some sleep and show up with only the clothes on our backs.

Thanh and I returned to the hotel down the street where I negotiated cleaning services in exchange for a place to sleep. In other words, Thanh and I were told we could have space in the storage room to lay our heads after we cleaned 30 toilets. I thought the deal was fair; Thanh thought it was stupid. By the time we finished cleaning all the toilets, we were only a couple of hours away from the rendezvous time. Afraid of missing the boat, we decided to leave the hotel and head to the beach.

I tried to barter for some of the canned foods I saw in the storage room, but the clerk refused my request. She did, however, give Thanh and me two small packets of crackers instead. It was probably for the best since we didn't have a can opener anyway.

Long before the sun rose, Thanh spotted the dragon lantern shining off the stern of a large fishing boat about 50 feet off shore. The dragon, a symbol of power and good luck for people who are worthy of it, seemed like a good omen. I prayed I was worthy enough to survive the journey and not get caught again. We watched as people began swimming out to the boat. More than half of the passengers were Chinese. *How odd*, I thought. Even the Chinese wanted to escape from Vietnam.

Thanh and I walked into the surf hand in hand. When the water got to my chin, I started paddling like a dog, copying the strokes of the other swimmers around me. I was doing fine until the water went up my nose. Memories of my water torture set in, and I began to panic. I reached out and grabbed Thanh's shirt, forcing him to pull me alongside him.

It was by God's grace alone that we made it to the boat where hands reached over the side and hauled us into the vessel. We had made it! Thanh and I fell into each other's arms and cried with relief.

The boat was not built to carry so many people (there were about 30 of us). To accommodate us all, Mr. Khoa strategically seated us along the sides and down the center in such a way as to keep it balanced. Thanh and I were seated together in the center along with two younger children. We were packed in tightly, like canned sardines. Our total body mass weighed heavily in the boat, lowering the hull deep into the water.

A simple railing ran around the boat's perimeter, and there was a small roof amidships that protected a ladder leading to the engine below. With no canopy of any sort, we were totally exposed to the elements. It was not going to be a comfortable ride, and if we ran into bad weather, our safety would certainly be jeopardized.

This vessel also smelled strongly of diesel fuel and fish. I feared nausea would soon set in, but at the moment I was high on adrenaline, elated to have another chance to leave Vietnam. A free chance, no less! I was sure Thanh and I would make it this time because God had provided a way where there was no way.

Once everyone was on board, the anchor was raised and the men used a long pole to quietly push us out to deeper waters. The motor was not activated at first. Silence was necessary to elude capture by the police patrolling the coast. I remember thinking that Mr. Khoa was wiser than the tour boat captains I had encountered.

I turned to Thanh and asked, "Do you think we will make it out of Vietnam this time?"

"Maybe," he answered. There was hope after all.

We drifted along for several hours, simply letting the tide carry us out to sea. It was a beautiful, starlit night. I leaned into Thanh, gazing at the sky and thinking of our dad. I prayed for his protection over us. The light breeze and the lapping of the waves against the sides of the boat soon lulled me to sleep.

CHAPTER 14

Do any of the worthless idols of the nations bring rain?
Do the skies themselves send down showers?
No, it is you, Lord our God.
Therefore our hope is in you,
for you are the one who does all this.
Jeremiah 14:22 (NIV)

June 1975

The sharp noise of the engine being engaged woke me from a sound sleep. I was shocked to discover that the sun was already high in the sky. In every direction, all I could see was water—beautiful, deep blue water, clear as crystal. I had never been out of the sight of land before, and it made me question whether my two previous journeys had been nothing more than crooked schemes between boat owners and the police to get desperate individuals onto vessels where they could be easily arrested and have their gold extorted. I wondered, but it no longer mattered. This time, Thanh and I were free.

Mr. Khoa was a most skillful captain, and I marveled at the way he navigated the open seas. With his binoculars close to his chest, he periodically scanned the horizon for other boats that might save us or pose a threat. He kept us on course by watching a compass by day and the stars by night.

Mr. Khoa ran a tight ship, rationing out the food and water at specific times throughout the day. I had total faith in his abilities to get us into international waters where we would surely be rescued. What I had less faith in was my ability to pretend to be Mr. Khoa's wife when the time came to do so.

Everyone on our boat was traveling in family groups except for one. Mr. Yen was an elderly man who aligned himself with Thanh and me, watching over us as a surrogate parent. I found his presence comforting, and I'm sure our presence gave him a sense of purpose. Mr. Yen kept us entertained for hours by telling us stories and providing spiritual advice. As a professed Buddhist, his words of wisdom went over my head, but I listened intently and respectfully. One thing I remember him telling me was to serve mankind with gratitude. I assured him I would, though I wasn't sure quite what that meant.

After several days at sea with plenty of time to reflect, I found myself feeling grateful for the time I had spent in jail. Though I will forever be scarred by the tortures inflicted upon me, I was thankful for the kindness shown to me by Captain Quan and the gentleness I experienced at his hands. I was grateful to have escaped from prison with my brother. I was grateful that we wound up in a fishing town with fishermen rather than tour boat guides. And I was sincerely grateful that Mr. Khoa had been willing to take Thanh and me on his boat for free.

Ironically, I realized, I had much to be thankful for. It had been a strange turn of events that led me to this place—one that God alone was capable of orchestrating. He had taken something evil and had turned it into something good. God was undoubtedly guiding my steps, changing my heart, and showing me that He was present in all situations.

The first three days passed uneventfully as we continued to motor further away from land under an unforgiving sun. Then on day four, Mr. Khoa turned off the motor. We sat silently in the middle of the sea, bobbing up and down like a leaf in the wind. Finally, someone asked, "Why aren't we moving?"

Mr. Khoa replied, "We're now in international waters. This is where the Americans are supposed to be, so we'll wait."

We didn't have to wait long before we saw a huge ship. As it approached our small boat, it sounded its horn, which practically shocked us out of the water. Mr. Khoa recognized the vessel as a Norwegian cargo ship. He sent up a flare to get the crew's attention, and we all started waving frantically. When the ship showed no sign of slowing, Mr. Khoa sent up two more flares. And then it was over. The ship had passed us by.

A few of the women started to cry. "Why didn't they stop for us?" they wailed. "What are we going to do now?"

I was distressed too, but not devastated. I fully expected the American Navy to appear at any time or die waiting. We were precariously low on food and dangerously low on water. *I* understood that there was a risk in taking to the open seas. Didn't *they*? There was no guarantee that any of us would survive.

We spent two more days drifting along the edge of international waters when another cargo ship was spotted in the distance. Though Mr. Khoa couldn't make out its flag and country of origin, he sent up three more flares to get its attention. Oddly, it too passed us by.

I now began to feel the true weight of our situation. We had run out of food and were about to run out of water. Surely the captains on those ships had seen us. What was preventing them from helping us? How could they purposely pass us by? And where was the American Navy?

"I think we are going to die on this boat," I confessed to Thanh. He assured me that we would be all right. We just had to maintain hope, he said.

I did my best to remain hopeful, which was difficult to do because I was quite weak from the lack of nutrition, lack of movement, and prolonged time in the sun. "Just close your eyes and sleep," Thanh would tell me. So I did.

I remember waking once when I heard the passengers whining for more food. I couldn't understand their complaints, as I had surpassed the point of feeling hunger in my stomach. Rather than praying for food, I prayed for God to block their cries from my ears.

It was during this time while curled up in a ball in the center of the boat that I experienced some of the most vivid dreams imaginable. In one of them I was floating in the air, surrounded by an expanse of food and water. My father was there along with my little sister and brother. We were all together in this peaceful place, eating and drinking to our hearts' content. Oh, what a happy time we were having when the sound of the engine and the awful smell of diesel fuel rudely awakened me.

"Where are we going?" someone asked. "Are we going back?"

"No," Mr. Khoa answered. "We're going forward."

Mr. Khoa wanted to leave Vietnam as much as the rest of us and was no longer content waiting in international waters for the Americans to show up while cargo ships passed us by. He decided to take matters into his own hands and move us deeper into the South China Sea in the hopes of locating a U.S. military ship. If they weren't coming for us, we would go to them.

Unbeknownst to any of us, the information I had shared with Mr. Khoa was outdated. The American government had pulled out of the South China Sea fifteen days after the fall of Saigon. There were no American ships waiting for us in international waters. In addition, many countries had instructed their cargo ships to look the other way if they saw a boat filled with Vietnamese boat people, as we were called. The odds of being rescued were stacked against us. We had a better chance of dying than surviving.

The strain of the situation was played out in spades: dehydration, sun exposure, and overall seasickness. Having gone without food for three days, everyone had finally lost the desire to eat. It was as if our stomachs had surrendered to starvation and simply stopped sending hunger signals to our brains.

With no food in my stomach, I became incredibly nauseous and convulsed with dry heaves. My lips were covered with blisters that hurt whenever I gagged or tried to speak. Exposure to the hot sun and salty air made my skin peel and itch. Sleeping was the only thing that brought me relief, so I slept a lot as my brain vacillated between dreams and hallucinations. Sometimes I would hear Thanh calling me. I would try to respond to reassure him that I was still alive, but this was often difficult to accomplish.

When I was awake, I would work my way to the side of the boat where I could hang my arm over the edge and feel the cool water slipping through my fingers. *Water, water everywhere, but not a drop to drink.* Though soothing to the touch, I supposed it was only a matter of time before I—before all of us—succumbed to its call for our lives.

Mr. Khoa seemed to handle our situation better than anyone. However, not even an experienced seaman can survive without water. We ran out somewhere around the one-week mark. At Mr. Khoa's insistence, we all began to pray for rain. He told us that if prayer didn't work, he would have to resort to Plan B. None of us knew what Plan B was, and he refused to divulge any details until it became necessary. In response, we all started praying. Thanh and I recited our rote Catholic prayers together while the Buddhists, including Mr. Yen, chanted over their prayer beads. Others called upon their ancestors for help. This was the first time I experienced what might resemble an interfaith prayer service. It was both moving and strange. With nothing else to occupy our minds, our prayers went on for hours.

And then a miracle happened. The raindrops came. God had heard us!

We laughed with joy as we opened our mouths wide to catch the pure water that fell like manna from Heaven. The precious drops quickly turned into pounding sheets, turning our joy into panic. As the seas turned rough, the boat began to pitch and turbulent waves crashed over the sides, filling the hull with seawater. It was all hands on deck as the men began to bail the water overboard using buckets, hats, and anything else they could find. The women joined the fight, soaking up the water with their clothing and wringing it out over the sides. It was a battle between humans and nature, and nature was winning.

In my delirious state, I remember feeling as if I were sitting in a warm bathtub. The persistent rocking transported me from one side of the vessel to the other in a matter of seconds. Fearing I might be swept overboard, Thanh found a piece of rope and tied one end around my wrist and the other to the railing. I started to cry, vaguely aware that Thanh could be washed overboard too. I would call out, "Thanh, are you there? Are you alright?" Then I would pray, "God, take me, but please don't let my brother die!"

The storm raged on for what seemed like hours before it ended as abruptly as it began. The clouds rolled away and a blue sky appeared. Thanh gently untied my wrist from the railing. Miraculously, no one was lost and the boat was not damaged. However, very little rainwater had been collected in the chaos. It was as if God was challenging us—providing us with just enough to get through another day and no more.

The clean rainwater had been rejuvenating. My mouth was no longer pasty, and my parched skin no longer itched. As night approached, we settled back into our assigned places and fell asleep.

The storm had been too much for my elderly friend. He was weak and delirious the next morning. I held his hand in mine to let him know that he was not alone. I remember his grip was weak yet sure. Sometime in the middle of the next night, he turned to me and whispered, "Make sure you do something good for mankind when you get through this." I promised him I would.

By morning, Mr. Yen was dead. Without ceremony, the men dumped his body overboard. Such a dishonorable treatment of such a wonderful man. This was a hard moment for me, and I cried like a baby.

Had it not been for Thanh, I might have willingly thrown myself into the sea with Mr. Yen's body. The vast blueness outside the boat was so inviting in comparison to the grayness inside. We were all going to perish on this little gray vessel, wasting away in our gray thoughts, unlike Mr. Yen who would spend eternity in the beautiful blue expanse where blue ocean water met blue summer sky. The color hypnotized me, and I yearned to fall into it. But I couldn't leave Thanh. An invisible thread tethered me to him.

Though we had no poles or bait, the men attempted to fish using line and hooks they found in the boat. Mr. Khoa suggested that something shiny be used as a lure, and one of the women offered her earring. Too weak to watch, I closed my eyes and nestled into the spot where Mr. Yen used to sleep.

Within minutes, I heard one of the men yell, "SHARK," and on reflex, I began to pray. The image I envisioned of being eaten by a shark was paralyzing. I was too weak to pull myself up to look, and fear kept me from trying. I thought of Mr. Yen's body being torn apart by this predatory animal before it turned on us. We were a floating banquet of human flesh. Mr. Khoa ordered the men to cut the fishing lines and hold perfectly still. Sharks, he said, could smell death. We reeked of it.

We sat in silence for quite some time while the men scanned the surface of the water looking for the telltale fin to resurface. It didn't take long. Soon strained whispers of "shark" resonated from several sections of the boat. I held my breath.

"That's not a shark," Mr. Khoa admonished. "It's a dolphin!"

Laughter and joyful gasps punctuated our profound relief. Mr. Khoa proved his expertise on the water yet again by explaining that sharks possess a straight-edged dorsal fin whereas a dolphin's fin is curved. Dolphins, he added, brought good luck.

We watched as the dolphin swam circles around our boat as if it were inviting us to come and play. Surely, its appearance was a sign of protection. I remember looking up at the clear blue sky and thanking God for this unwarranted blessing. I have since come to believe that blessings are always present in our lives if we just take the time to look for them.

The dolphin traveled with us for two days and then disappeared from sight. At roughly the same time, Mr. Khoa announced that he had to institute Plan B. He then asked each of us to pee into our cups. Peering into each one, he selected the clearest urine. Using a small piece of cloth, Mr. Khoa strained the selected urine into the water that remained from the storm. I stood resolute in my decision not to partake of this beverage, but the captain insisted that no one should perish from dehydration on his watch.

"I don't know what will happen," he said, "but we need to continue our course however we are able." In the end, I drank the water, and so did everyone else on the boat. It bought us a little more time.

We had been at sea for almost two weeks. At least six days had passed since our last bite of food, and now we had resorted to drinking our own urine. That wasn't the worst of it. We had not seen any type of ship in over a week. We were in the middle of nowhere, far from any sympathetic nation, and just days away from running out of fuel.

CHAPTER 15

Anyone who is captured will be cut down—
run through with a sword.
Their little children will be dashed to death before their eyes.
Their homes will be sacked, and their wives will be raped.
Isaiah 13:15-16 (NLT)

June 1975

The closest country that might offer us sanctuary was Cambodia. To get there, we would have to travel hundreds of miles westward around the southern tip of Vietnam, deep into the Gulf of Thailand. Mr. Khoa spoke frankly with the men about the dangers of heading into these pirate-infested seas.

Piracy is not unique to Asian waters, but in the years following the collapse of South Vietnam, it escalated to a whole new level. As hundreds of Vietnamese took to boats following the fall of Saigon, piracy on the surrounding seas increased, as did the savagery of the attacks.[15] Operating outside the parameters of international laws with no fear of retribution, pirates ruled the Gulf of Thailand with brash cruelty. They were known to board boats, steal the valuables, rape the women, abduct young children to use for prostitution, and kill the men in a variety of horrific manners.

It was too great a risk to attempt passage to Cambodia, so Mr. Khoa headed south instead, through the rough waters of the South

China Sea toward Malaysia. The longer route increased our odds of dying from dehydration and hunger, but it decreased the risk of a pirate attack. We all stood behind the decision, acknowledging that it would be better to die by natural disaster than at the hands of pirates.

"I don't know if we have enough fuel to make it," Mr. Khoa stated, "but we will try."

Out in the open expanse I contemplated what my life might look like if we survived the crossing, and I pondered the commission Mr. Yen had given me before he died: *Make sure you do something good for mankind when you get through this.*

As we drifted along under the scorching sun, I decided that, if I lived, I would become a nurse. I had never considered nursing before, and I had no idea how I would pursue such a profession, but it suddenly seemed so right for me. I prayed that God would keep us safe so I could achieve my first real goal in life.

Two more days into our journey we heard cries for help. Mr. Khoa scanned the horizon with his binoculars. *Who could possibly be more desperate than us?* I wondered.

I was in my usual position in the center of the boat fighting seasickness when I felt the engine pick up speed to respond to the call. Mr. Khoa was a compassionate man, not one to ignore a cry for help. That admirable character trait had secured my brother and me a seat on his vessel. Just as the cries were getting louder, I felt the boat jerk away from its intended target.

"Pirates," Mr. Khoa whispered. We had almost responded to cries of distress from a large pleasure cruiser that was under pirate assault. Being in no position to offer assistance, we fled. I prayed we would not be pursued.

Early the next day, Mr. Khoa announced that he was turning the boat around to go back to the scene of the pirate attack. He was sure that the pirates would have fled by then and that the abandoned ship might contain items that could help us with our voyage to Malaysia.

I don't know how he did it, but Mr. Khoa was able to locate the pleasure cruiser successfully even though we were miles apart. Through his binoculars, he confirmed that the large boat had indeed been abandoned. Slowly and cautiously, he approached it. Speaking with the other male passengers on our boat, Mr. Khoa selected four people to board the vessel: two men, Thanh, and me. The men would provide protection while Thanh and I searched the ship for food, water, and other valuable items. I was not pleased with this plan, but I understood the reasoning behind our selection. Since we had not paid for the trip and had no parents to plead for us, we were considered the most expendable.

My legs had grown weak from lack of use, making it extremely difficult to climb up the metal ladder at the stern of the vessel. Fear and nausea gripped my body in equal intensity as I prepared to board.

There was no comparison between Mr. Khoa's boat and this one, which was a private yacht—luxurious, quite large, and undeniably expensive. It was the perfect pirate target.

The ugliness of the pirate trade was revealed the minute I stepped on the main deck. Blood was smeared all across the landing and railings, and the smell of death rose from the stairway that led to the living quarters below.

While the two men walked the perimeter of the deck, Thanh and I headed down the ladder to look for supplies. At the bottom, we found a dead man slumped over a chair. He had been shot through the head and blood was dripping from his nose and mouth. Memories of my father flashed through my brain like a bad horror movie, and my stomach felt queasy. Turning away, we went in search of food.

Thanh hit the jackpot when he found a cabinet full of dried bananas and dates, crackers, and other snacks. We took it all, shoving it into a pillowcase. We also found canned goods, which we left behind because we had no way to open them.

Moving further down the passageway, I heard her before I saw her—a woman gasping for life. She was completely naked. Exposed. Spread eagle on a mattress and covered in blood. She had been slashed mercilessly, and the ghastly cuts had dried in a vulgar labyrinth across her body. Lying beside her was a dead child. A little boy. It is a horrifying image that I have never been able to erase from my mind.

"Help me," she whispered.

I didn't know what to do. Her wounds were beyond measure. "I'm going to call for help," I told her.

I went in search of the two men on deck. They ordered Thanh and me back to the boat with the supplies we had gathered. Then they descended the ladder to assess the situation below. We did as we were told, but I felt terrible that I had not taken the time to cover the woman with a blanket or towel before the men arrived.

Thanh and I were helped back onto our small boat with exclamations of joy for the food we had found. Caught in a web of bloody images streaming through my brain, I could not participate in the celebration. Something terribly evil had taken place on that ship, and no amount of praise or food would provide release.

Several minutes later, the men climbed back onto our boat carrying large plastic containers of water and fuel. They, too, were met with shouts of joy. Though there was a renewed sense of relief among the passengers as Mr. Khoa started the engine, I could not shake the distress I felt knowing we were leaving the injured woman behind. There was no room for her on our boat, nor were any of us capable of nursing her back to health, but to leave her in that dark room, next to her dead son as she gasped for breath, was too cruel to accept.

As we motored away, the two men spoke to Mr. Khoa in low voices. I moved closer to hear what they had to say. "There was a man, a woman, and a child. There were probably others, but the pirates must have taken them or thrown them overboard. The woman was still alive."

"What did you do?" Mr. Khoa asked.

One of the men responded, "We helped her join her family."

I was traveling with killers! These men appeared to me to be no better than the pirates. *Did they really have to finish her off? Wasn't there a more merciful way to help?* I had no answers, but death did not strike me as the solution. Confused and angry, I kept my distance from these two men, blaming them rather than the pirates for the woman's fatal end.

Looking back, however, I now realize that my shipmates did what they could under the circumstances. This woman was beyond saving, so they took the most humane route available at the time. They did not kill her; they ended her suffering.

What pains me the most is knowing that the woman had witnessed the death of her loved ones before she was sexually molested and left to die. She had been stripped of her clothing, her family, and her dignity. No one should ever have to endure such agony. No one. I think of her often.

Thanks to the gift of food, water, and fuel that we had salvaged from the yacht, we all were able to regain some of our energy and pinned our hopes on reaching Malaysia. For three days straight, the ocean kissed the sky, one plain sheet of blue canvas stretching as far as the eye could see. It was beautiful until day four.

With land still nowhere in sight, the sky turned gray, and rain started to fall down in buckets. This time the men were ready. They bailed water efficiently and collected what they could for drinking. I found the storm invigorating; it strengthened me, and I took it as a sign that we would reach our intended destination. I remember telling my brother, "I think the worst is over."

Later that evening we saw a piece of wood floating in the water, a sure sign of a shipwreck, probably as a result of the storm. A few minutes later, we heard a male voice yelling for help. Over the waves we saw a hand waving in the air. The hand belonged to a middle-aged man who was precariously balanced on top of a piece of wood; his other arm was wrapped around his four-year-old daughter.

Mr. Khoa eased our vessel alongside the duo so they could be pulled into our boat. The man repeated "thank you" over and over, non-stop, like a broken record. Then pointing out to sea, he informed Mr. Khoa that there were three more children somewhere out there. "Can you save them? They are my sons."

Mr. Khoa peered through his binoculars searching for evidence of the three boys. "How do you know your children are out there?" he asked.

"They're older and stronger," the man replied. "I know they're alive."

Mr. Khoa was a sympathetic man and would not willingly leave anyone to die. However, scouring the seas for three boys who may or may not be alive was not his top priority. Mr. Khoa was first and foremost committed to bringing his current load to safety.

"I want to help," he told the man. Then looking at us all sitting in our cramped spaces around the boat added, "But I can't risk the lives of all these people. We are at capacity. If we attempt to take three more bodies on board, I'm not sure any of us will survive."

"Please," the man begged. "Please don't leave them!" It was heartbreaking to hear. "Please don't leave my children!"

There truly was no room for three additional people on our boat. This man and his young daughter were already infringing on everyone's space. I'm sure it wasn't easy, but Mr. Khoa stood his ground.

"I cannot save your children," he said. "I can give you food and water and put you back in the sea, or you may come with us. I will not search for your sons because I cannot fit all of you on this boat. You will have to make a decision."

The man looked at his daughter and cried. Deep, gut wrenching cries. We all felt his pain. Finally, he looked up to Heaven and wailed, "Please God, forgive me." Turning to Mr. Khoa, he said, "Let's go."

Mr.Khoa revved the engine and turned the boat toward Malaysia. As we sailed away, the man yelled out across the water, "I will come back for you! Don't worry!" Then he crumpled into a ball and wept bitterly.

Many years later I had the strange privilege of reconnecting with this man that Mr. Khoa pulled from the sea. His daughter had grown up and moved away. She did not wish to have a relationship with her father who had become an alcoholic and suffered with depression. When I saw him, I said, "I am sorry we were not able to save your other children."

He replied, "That's the way life goes. I took care of myself, and now look at me. The one child I managed to save doesn't even want to know me."

I couldn't help but wonder if the man regretted the decision he made that day. Had he known how his life would turn out, would he have chosen to take the food and water offered to him and return to his floating piece of wood? Going back to the open sea would surely have been a death sentence for both him and his daughter. Perhaps death would have been preferable to the life he ended up living.

This is the conundrum of many refugees. We carry the pain of the past in our veins. True freedom is reserved for our offspring, not us. This father's sacrifice bought life for his daughter and her descendants. I pray some day she will realize that.

CHAPTER 16

I am sick at heart.
How long, O Lord, until you restore me?
Return, O Lord, and rescue me.
Save me because of your unfailing love.
For the dead do not remember you.
Who can praise you from the grave?
Psalm 6:3-5 (NLT)

Late June 1975

I was just one of thousands who had taken to the sea in boats too small to navigate properly, too ill-provisioned to complete the journey, and too crowded to maintain dignity or comfort.[16] Thanks to Mr. Khoa's expertise, food, water, and fuel were no longer an issue for us in the middle of the South China Sea. The real issue was whether we would be rescued before we died of grief, pirates, depression, storms, sickness, sharks, heat exhaustion, or a leak in the boat.

Not only were we physically weak, we were also mentally frail and prone to hallucinations. Keeping my eyes closed and dreaming of better days was the only way I could handle the oppressive monotony and intense heat. My dreams were consistently filled with oceanic thoughts, a vast desert of rolling water with no beginning or end. Sometimes the thought of sinking to the bottom of the sea, never to be found, seemed like a peaceful escape from our brutal reality.

Captain Khoa continued to push southward on heightened alert for the next danger looming on the horizon. Two more days passed without incident when suddenly he screamed with excitement. Through his binoculars he had spotted several large fishing boats—a sure sign that we were nearing a coastline.

As we closed in, we discovered the boats were actually a fleet of commercial fishing vessels. Mr. Khoa pulled alongside one of them to make contact. He yelled up to them in Vietnamese, *"Chào các ông. Thuyền trưởng của các ông đâu?"* (Hello. Where is your captain?)

None of the crew responded. Several turned away.

After a few tense moments, a man appeared on the quarterdeck that we presumed to be the captain. He yelled something down to us in a language I did not understand. Suddenly a loud cheer erupted among the Chinese passengers, and they all started hugging each other while the rest of us looked on. The captain was speaking their language. Acting as interpreters, our Chinese passengers informed us that the fishing fleet was from Taiwan, which was hundreds of nautical miles to the north. The Taiwanese captain was going to send a telegram inland asking for permission to bring us on board.

We all started screaming with joy and offering up individual prayers to our gods. We were about to be rescued—not by Americans, but by our Chinese neighbors fishing in waters near the Malaysian coast. Soon our ordeal would be over.

Several minutes later the captain came back and told us that the government had granted him permission to save all of the Chinese passengers—just the Chinese passengers.

Intense joy and devastating misery collided. Those of us who were Vietnamese watched in shock as our Chinese passengers gleefully climbed the ladder to board the fishing boat. I understood their excitement; I could taste it, but I couldn't partake of the feast. *Why should some be saved and not others?* It didn't make sense. It wasn't fair. We were all Vietnamese citizens. We were, literally, all in the same boat.

Relations between China and Vietnam had deteriorated rapidly following the fall of Saigon. Chinese businessmen who controlled much of the commerce in the city posed a threat to the new communist government.[17] In an effort to purge the Chinese and their "capitalist practices" from the Vietnamese culture, the new government began systematically confiscating Chinese businesses and property. While we were not personally responsible for how the Chinese were treated in Vietnam, the Taiwanese viewed us as the enemy. In truth, like our Chinese passengers, we were also victims of the new regime.

For the first time in my life I experienced injustice on a grand scale—denied equal rights because of my nationality. I may have been treated cruelly while serving in my grandfather's house, but I had never felt like a second-class citizen. Now I knew what it felt like to be discriminated against based on my ethnicity. It was demoralizing.

The Taiwanese captain demonstrated his appreciation for Mr. Khoa's services by offering him a substantial amount of food and water. Our former Chinese passengers who were now safely onboard the Taiwanese fishing vessel watched silently as supplies were lowered into our boat. Because we did not speak Chinese, we were not able to plead our case or even say "thank-you" for the provisions. We simply had to accept our fate.

It was too much for our Chinese friends to bear. What we couldn't do for ourselves, they did for us. In one voice, they pleaded for our rescue. They acknowledged the heroic efforts Mr. Khoa had exhibited on their behalf and described the hardships we had already encountered together on the South China Sea. They told the Taiwanese captain that it was not only heartless to force us back into unknown waters; it was a merciless act of murder.

We didn't ask them to advocate for us. They did it on their own. Their act of courage inspires me to this day whenever I have the choice between speaking up for what is right or turning a blind eye.

Looking down on us with pity, the Taiwanese captain asked Mr. Khoa if he could speak any Chinese. The question, of course, needed to be translated. Mr. Khoa responded with words that must have been Heaven-sent. "We can't, but we are willing to learn," he said.

There was a moment of silence during which the Taiwanese captain contemplated the idea. Finally, he stated his decision. "You must learn," he said. "Otherwise, I will be sent to jail for assisting fugitives against government orders."

We all cheered and showed ourselves eager to learn Chinese. Our trial at sea was finally over. We promptly boarded the fishing vessel, joining our Chinese friends. Mr. Khoa's boat was left to drift away, taking the last remnants of our flight from Vietnam with it.

Zǎo ān (Good morning). *Wǒ jiào* (My name is) *Minh Phuong*. *Nǐ hǎo ma* (How are you)? Day after day, Chinese words and phrases in the Mandarin dialect were taught, stated, and repeated in an effort to drill this foreign language into our brains so it would flow naturally off our tongues. The vice captain, who spoke a little Vietnamese, was our teacher. He would conduct language lessons for several hours each morning on the main deck while the rest of the crew worked the fishing nets. Chinese is a tonal language, which means pitch is as important as pronunciation. The same word can have four different meanings depending on where the speaker puts the emphasis. I was captivated with the lyrical intonations that made each sentence sound like a song. Learning Chinese gave purpose to my life, and I poured my whole heart into mastering the language.

Once morning lessons were over, the Vietnamese men would join the Taiwanese crew for chores while all the women retreated to the lower decks to rest or pray. My brother Thanh bounced energetically from the bridge to the bilge, running errands and cleaning the engine room. I believe the routine gave him a sense of meaning and stability like he had never known.

The men were allowed to roam the ship freely while the women were confined to certain areas. The top deck in particular was completely off limits to women. This was where the crewmen had set up a Buddhist shrine to their gods with little plaster idols and chanted over their Buddhist prayer beads. Women—Christians and Buddhists alike—were considered unclean due to their menstrual cycles; therefore, we were forbidden from entering this sacred area. As a Catholic, I was not the least bit interested in this pagan shrine, nor did I have any desire to spend additional time on the highest deck of the ship where the rocking was most extreme.

Only a handful of the Vietnamese women were Christian, and we met on a lower deck each day to pray together. Some women prayed aloud. Others, like me, prayed silently in our heads. Our prayers often centered on safe travel and success in learning the Chinese language quickly. We also prayed each other through the pain of menstrual cramps and seasickness. Our prayers were intentional, and there was much rejoicing whenever one was answered.

Prayer became a critical part of my day, and my prayer life blossomed with the tangible evidence of God's graces. Though I had spent close to three weeks on a boat in the middle of the South China Sea with these women, it wasn't until we were on the Taiwanese fishing boat that we bonded—through prayer. When I was not praying, I was often curled up in a ball in a bunk in the depths of the ship nursing my incessant seasickness, which only worsened when I menstruated.

One day, after Chinese lessons, I found an extra blanket lying on my bunk. I didn't know where it had come from or whether it was truly meant for me, but I clung to it like a small child clings to a beloved stuffed animal. Over the next several days, I continued to find thoughtful items on my bunk, such as a piece of fresh fruit or a small bar of soap. My favorite gift was a stack of paper towels that proved useful during menstruation.

The ship's cook eventually spilled the beans and told me that the gifts were from Jun, the brother of the vice captain. Jun was apparently providing me with tokens to express his interest in me, but his tactics were beyond my comprehension as I was unfamiliar with the subtleties associated with potential courtship. Though I was not attracted to Jun in the least, I sincerely wanted to express my appreciation for the thoughtful gifts. So, I worked extra hard on the tonal qualities of the Mandarin dialect hoping to one day be able to thank Jun in Chinese.

Unfortunately, my actions were construed as interest and resulted in an unintended consequence: the gift giving increased.

Jun had interpreted my perseverance to learn his language as a desire to fully communicate with him. Not knowing how to respond, I simply prayed over the situation, hoping that God would work it all out.

Occasionally we women were called upon to help the men sort through the fish. I was continually astonished by the abundance of sea creatures caught in the nets—tiny anchovies and large tuna, whiskered shrimp and spiny lobster, slippery eels, and the annoying jellyfish. After the net was emptied onto the platform, it was our job to throw the small or unmarketable sea creatures back into the ocean where they could continue to thrive or serve as bait. Once the sorting was complete, large trap doors in the deck fell open allowing the selected catch to fall into the hold below. It was amazing!

The first time we sat down for a meal, I thought I had died and gone to Heaven. The gifted cook had prepared a feast of the most delicious selections from the day's catch. I was never very hungry because my stomach was always upset, but that didn't stop me from eating my fill of fresh seafood.

On calm days, I enjoyed spending time with the cook and the fishermen. They all had stories to tell and were more than willing to educate me about the sea and its creatures. My understanding of Chinese improved with each story they told. Though I didn't understand everything they were saying, I listened with interest and let my imagination run wild.

Despite the education and excellent food I was receiving, I was anxious to get to solid ground. "When will we return to land?" I asked the vice captain.

"When we've filled the hold with fish," he answered.

One week turned into two, and two turned into three. With the hold only half full, another three weeks at sea was likely. We women began to tire of the monotony and took matters into our own hands by changing the focus of our prayers. We started to ask God to fill the hold with fish or rip the net. A damaged net would be irreparable at sea and would force the captain to return to port early for repairs.

In a matter of days, the fishnet broke. The captain called everyone together and announced that we would be heading home to Taiwan. We women exchanged guilty glances and cheered silently. We knew that our prayers had been answered and that God was responsible for the torn net.

With fishing suspended, our Chinese lessons intensified. One morning while we were in class, the vice captain pointed to a piece of land on the port side of the ship and said, "That is your old country. Say goodbye because you will never see it again."

His words pierced my heart. Until that moment, I had not given much thought to the possibility that I might never set foot in my homeland again. It's hard to explain why I felt such deep sadness considering the life I had lived in Vietnam. I had no strong attachment to any particular person, nor did I leave behind a house that felt like a home. Truly, there was no one or no thing that I would miss, just a way of life. Vietnam was all I knew—its language, culture, and customs. It fit me like a well-worn shoe. I felt as unsettled as the Israelites whom Moses led out of Egypt through the parting of the Red Sea. After just a few weeks in the desert, they were ready to return to Pharaoh and their lives as slaves. Like them, my life had been far from perfect, but it was familiar. I knew how to survive in Vietnam. The unknown future was frightening.

I pushed my anxious feelings down and told myself to concentrate on the lesson at hand. Taiwan might become my new home, and Chinese might be my new language. I had escaped Vietnam. I had escaped my family. This is what I had strived for and had achieved—I had won. But I didn't feel victorious. I felt cheated.

CHAPTER 17

The foreigner residing among you must be
treated as your native-born.
Love them as yourself, for you were foreigners in Egypt.
I am the Lord your God.
Leviticus 19:34 (NIV)

Early July 1975

A camera crew from a local newspaper marked our arrival in Taiwan by snapping shots of us as we disembarked the fishing vessel. I never saw the published picture, but I imagine we looked as haggard as we were elated. We may have appeared a little crazy as well, for we could barely contain our emotions. As our feet hit solid ground, we laughed and cried and danced for joy. My Christian friends and I lifted our hands into the air and praised God for our rescue. The Buddhists fell to their knees and kissed the ground. Praise and gratefulness was on everyone's lips.

The number of citizens who had come down to the port to welcome us into Taiwan surprised me. For a moment I felt like royalty. We were ushered onto trucks that transported us to a refugee camp on a marine base not far from the Port of Kaohsiung. When we arrived, the camp was empty. However, within weeks the tented enclosure was bustling with hundreds—and eventually thousands—of refugees from Vietnam, Cambodia, and Laos. The vast number of people spoke to the epic plight of citizens from across East Asia. With thousands of people seeking asylum in Thailand, the original stipulation that refugees had to learn Chinese was abandoned. Instead, the Red Cross and other government agencies focused all their energies on our care and eventual relocation to places within China as well as other countries around the globe.[18]

Provisions in the camp were simple but sufficient. Each person's personal space consisted of a cot and all that could fit under it. I didn't have anything other than the clothes I was wearing and the gifts Jun had given me. The camp, however, provided everyone with the necessary essentials for daily living—a toothbrush and toothpaste, a towel, soap and shampoo, a hairbrush, a blanket and pillow, and an extra set of clothes.

Meals were prepared regularly and consisted of a variety of fish, vegetables, and fresh fruit. With their tiny seeds and thick white flesh, lychees and longans became two of my favorite fruits. The lychees in particular were extremely juicy with a sour sweetness that dripped slowly down our chins whenever we bit into one. The longans were a bit drier, but just as sweet. Both were beyond delicious!

The summer weather in Taiwan was warm, and the cool breeze off the ocean offered perfect sleeping conditions. Families slept together in clusters. Whenever I awoke from a bad dream, which was often, I was comforted by Thanh's presence beside me. He was my protector.

It was easy to make friends in the camp. We had nowhere to go, and our tragic journeys provided a common experience on which to build relationships. Surrounded by refugees of all ages with their uniquely harrowing stories of escape, we bonded as one family and entered into a time of healing.

Thanh and I quickly adapted to life in the refugee camp, and it warmed my heart to watch him playing cards and laughing with his newfound friends. He was no longer the boy who had boarded the bus with me out of Saigon. Thanh had grown up and was, by all accounts, a responsible and mature young man.

There was a regular rhythm to our days that provided a sense of normalcy. Every time a new group of refugees arrived at the camp, we surrounded them like long-lost relatives and lovingly drew them into the fold. Backgrounds did not matter; here we were all equals. Under the tents, sorrow and hope were woven together to transform our ugly memories into a beautiful tapestry. I smile whenever I think of my time in the refugee camp. I believe I could have been happy living out the rest of my years there.

In addition to the essentials, refugees were provided with paper and pens with which to write to our loved ones. The purpose was twofold. First, to let the people we left behind know we were safe; second, to establish correspondence with relatives outside our homeland who could take us in.

I wrote three letters from the camp: one to my great Uncle Cuong in France, one to my pen pal Hubert in Switzerland, and one to my mother in Vietnam. Knowing my letter to my mother might be confiscated and read, I wrote to her in the third person.

> *Dear Mrs. Nguyen, how are you? I wanted to tell you that your daughter and her family are doing fine.*

Careful not to endanger any family members, I signed my letter using my baptismal name of Bernadette.

Cries of joy could be heard all over the camp when refugees received a return letter in the mail. Receiving a letter seemed to establish one's existence in the world. A person who had once been lost was now found.

The first letter I received came from Hubert. He wrote me a lengthy note and enclosed money for future postage. Hubert told me that he was relieved to hear that I was safe and hoped to see me soon. I read his thoughtful letter over and over again, crying each time. His concern for my wellbeing was so genuine, and his fear for my safety was touching. Hubert demonstrated a type of respect toward me that I had never experienced before.

The second letter I received came from Nicolas, my great Uncle Cuong's son. I was surprised to learn that I had a cousin in France. No one had ever mentioned him, and I had never considered the possibility that my uncle might have children. Nicolas informed me that he was completing the necessary paperwork for his father to act as sponsor and guardian for Thanh and me. He made it clear that we would have a new home in France.

Several weeks later, I finally received a letter from my mother. As expected, her letter to me was as cryptic as the letter I had written to her. It didn't contain any advice or encouragement. It simply indicated that she had received my letter and was aware that Thanh and I were safe in Taiwan. Her note was confirmation that she and Nhu had not made it out of Vietnam. I prayed for the safety of my family members, knowing full well that the communist regime would wipe them out if it discovered their past allegiance to the South Vietnamese government.

The first people to leave the camp were the Chinese refugees who had relatives on the mainland. It was incredibly difficult to say goodbye to those who had been passengers with us on Mr. Khoa's boat. After all we had been through together, their departure was simply gut wrenching. Because of their intervention with the fishing boat captain, we were now safe in Taiwan. We owed our lives to these people who we would never see again.

Visitors were commonplace at the camp—mostly reporters and government officials. Occasionally, our rescuers from the Taiwanese fishing boat would stop by, and our reunions were always joyful. Their visits, however, became less frequent once the Chinese refugees left the camp. Except for Jun's visits.

The vice captain's brother continued to drop by whenever possible to see me. Had I been raised with proper parental supervision, I might have discouraged these visits. Instead, I welcomed Jun respectfully. During one visit, he brought me two special gifts: money and a dress. I didn't really like the dress, but I tried to accept it graciously so as not to appear unthankful. I probably went a bit overboard in my expression of gratitude for the money, however, because Jun seemed quite pleased with my response.

Little did I realize, by continuing to accept Jun's gifts, I was leading him to believe that I viewed him as a love interest. As time went on, Jun started bringing family members to the refugee camp. He took great pleasure in telling how our small boat was first spotted in the open seas and how he came to meet me. He would become animated as he relayed the story of my rescue. I took it all

in stride, summing it up as a man's need to be the center of attention. I would nod and laugh as Jun told the story, careful not to
respond verbally because my Chinese was poor.

One day a representative from the American Embassy arrived.
Speaking through a translator to the entire camp, his message was
loud and clear: all were welcome to immigrate to America. It didn't
matter whether you had family to serve as a sponsor or not. It didn't
matter if you understood English or not. It didn't matter if you possessed a passport or not. The opportunity was available to everyone.

Interested hands shot up, but my arm remained pinned to my
side. I would be going to France. Though I had a strong desire
to follow my new friends to America, I had not been given permission to choose my fate. My mother had instructed me to go to
France, and my cousin Nicolas was completing the paperwork for
my immigration. Besides, I spoke French, not English. My destiny was set.

Administrative officials took my name and my uncle's address
in France telling me that they would alert the French Embassy in
Taiwan of my decision.

Camp life changed drastically the day the refugees left for
America. I was awakened that day by the sound of military vehi-
cles descending like thunder. Names were called, and people began
piling into the jeeps that would take them to ships heading to Guam.
Because no one knew where they would eventually end up, it
wasn't possible to exchange addresses. Therefore, each goodbye
was painfully final.

I watched in sadness as the last jeep pulled away. My heart
was broken. Thanh stood beside me, stoically silent. For all intents
and purposes, the camp was empty. Only four of us were left: two
women whose husbands were in France, Thanh, and me.

I remember asking myself, *How could America do this to me?* I
blamed the United States of America for my feelings of desolation.
In my mind, America was responsible for the war in my country,
responsible for breaking my family apart, and responsible for my
abandonment in a Taiwanese refugee camp. My newfound friends

were gone. Thanh and I were alone again. I felt as empty on the inside as the camp appeared around me.

A few days later, Thanh and I were relocated to a hotel in Taipei, about 200 miles north of the refugee camp. Though we felt rather isolated, there was much to explore in our hotel room that gave us a glimpse of Western culture. For example, we had never experienced a bed so big or so soft. We found it to be good for both sleeping in and bouncing on. Nor had we ever experienced sheets before. We were used to sleeping on mats with a simple blanket covering. Running water and flushing toilets were also quite intriguing, and we took pleasure in simply watching toilet paper swirl and disappear with each flush. We were delighted to discover that we could choose between a shower or a bath and between cold or hot water. Finally, the television in our room provided hours of entertainment, late into the night. These were all strange and alluring luxuries.

Every evening, a silver-haired representative from the French Consulate would stop by. Some of his visits were very short, about ten minutes, while others lasted for hours. He asked us a lot of questions and filled out many forms. Before he left each night, he would give us money with which to purchase the next day's food. Twice this gentleman took Thanh and me out for dinner, but most of our time was spent hanging out in the hotel room or wandering the streets of the city on our own.

I have three vivid memories of our time in the Taiwanese hotel. First, I remember watching *The Exorcist* on television, after which I was unable to sleep soundly for weeks. Even though I couldn't understand a single word of this American movie, the pictures scared me half to death. From what I could tell, an evil spirit had inhabited a little girl who had to be tied to her bed in order to protect her family. Two priests are called in to banish the evil spirit. That's when the real scary parts kicked in. The little girl spoke in a deep and creepy voice, her eyes rolled back in her head while she spit out bile and smoke, and at one point her head did a complete 360-degree turn on her neck. To put this in context, the Vietnamese culture not only believes in ghosts, it worships the dead.

This movie, therefore, felt more biographical to me than fictional and further enhanced my belief in evil spirits.

The second memory I have is of shopping for the perfect dress for my upcoming trip. I used the money Jun had given me in the refugee camp to purchase a navy blue frock with white piping. My mother had impressed upon me the importance of making a good impression. Therefore, I planned to wear this dress to France so I could impress my uncle and cousin. I wanted to look like a refined woman, not a poor refugee.

The third memory has to do with a proposal. One day there was a knock on our hotel room door. I opened it to find Jun standing there, crying. Through tears he asked, "Why did you leave?"

To him, my abrupt move to Taipei appeared as abandonment. I apologized profusely and asked for his forgiveness in broken Chinese, which he graciously gave. Then Jun presented me with a ring and asked me to marry him. His proposal hit me like a ton of bricks. It was only then that I realized his true intentions and the error of my ways.

"I can't marry you," I responded.

He looked shocked. I chose my Chinese words carefully to explain why I had to move to France. It was my responsibility to take care of my brother. My mother had instructed me to go to France. Thanh wanted to go to France. We had family in France. I could speak French. My cousin was expecting Thanh and me in France.

Oh, how he cried and cried! I felt so bad for Jun and embarrassed for myself. I promised him that I would stay in touch, but that was all I promised. He left a defeated man.

I felt terrible for breaking Jun's heart. I also felt relieved to have it out and over. Afterwards, I asked Thanh (who had been quietly staring at the floor during Jun's visit) if he wanted to stay in Taiwan. Without much emotion, Thanh replied, "Taiwan and China are always fighting. It's democracy versus communism. Everyday they fight, just like South Vietnam and North Vietnam. I don't want to live in a country that is fighting its own people."

Thanh was wiser than his years. I appreciated his answer and agreed wholeheartedly. I didn't want to live in Taiwan either, and

I didn't want to live in France without him. We would make the move together.

Our paperwork was finally completed. The next time the man from the French Consulate visited, he gave Thanh and me three items: permits to enter France, airline tickets, and satchels. Thanh and I were not given passports, but we were assured that the permits would suffice to get us into the country.

The man explained that we would be expected to reimburse the French government for the cost of the plane tickets once we were properly settled and working in France. The small satchels were ours to keep. Everything Thanh and I owned fit into them, along with the small shampoos and soaps we took from the hotel.

This man, with whom we had become familiar, then gave me his personal home address in France. "If you ever need help," he said, "call me."

I never did. Not because I didn't need help, but because I didn't know how to ask. I had been conditioned to follow directions, stay the course, and rely on my instincts to get through another day. Though I knew how to care for others, I did not know how to care for myself. I was unaware of what made me happy or what made me angry. I did not have a favorite pastime or a best friend. I lived in the present moment and accepted the future as it came. I knew how to survive, but not how to live.

PART II
FRANCE

1975–1977

CHAPTER 18

Though I scatter them among the peoples,
yet in distant lands they will remember me.
They and their children will survive, and they will return.
Zechariah 10:9 (NIV)

August 1975

Vietnam was behind me. Thanh and I were heading to France—a safe country, far from the Vietcong and communist rule. Family was waiting for us there, and the future appeared hopeful.

I was both scared and excited about the plane ride to Paris. I should have asked the French Consulate about air travel during one of his frequent visits, but it hadn't occurred to me to do so. Now, questions were spinning in my brain. Would I experience airsickness in the same manner that I had experienced seasickness? Would the plane smell like diesel fuel? Would we be packed in like sardines? Would the seats be similar to benches on a bus?

One thing I knew for sure was that the flight would be long, covering more than 6,000 miles. Fearing that I would not be able to hold my bladder for the duration of the 13-hour flight, I refrained from drinking any liquids during the preceding 24 hours. I donned my new, navy blue dress with the white trim and my brand new stockings for the journey. Plane travel was for the rich, and I wanted to look my best in order to blend in.

As Thanh and I walked through the airport, I noticed people staring at me. I wasn't sure if it was because I was Asian or because I looked so good in my new dress. Occasionally, someone would ask if I was serving in the Navy. I couldn't tell if they were being sincere or sarcastic, so I responded by turning away. The question perplexed me because I had no knowledge at the time of the uniform worn by American sailors.

Thanh and I—two Vietnamese orphans—were treated with special care at the airport. Every attendant we encountered was kind and smiled a lot. With no luggage to check, we were simply ushered to the gate where we sat quietly with our satchels on our laps awaiting further instructions. After some time, a woman in an Air France uniform approached us, took our tickets, and guided us onto the airplane.

It was astonishing, and nothing like I had imagined. The plane offered row upon row of individual seats that were clean and cushioned with backrests. We would be traveling in unbelievable comfort. I was excited beyond understanding. If this was any indication of what life would be like in France, I was ready for it to start!

A stewardess took our satchels and placed them in the compartment above our seats. At first, I didn't want to release our bags, but she assured us that they would be accessible during the flight. Then she showed Thanh and me how to use the seatbelt buckle and recline our seats after takeoff. It was all so fascinating and extravagant.

My excitement rose to new heights as I anticipated takeoff. *How on earth would this large vehicle get off the ground and soar through the air?* I wondered. As the engines grew louder, I braced myself by instinctively digging my nails into the armrest. Then the plane began to move, slow at first, then rumbling down the runway with increasing speed. I was terrified as I felt the large plane shaking around me. Surely, I thought, this wasn't normal. We were headed for disaster.

I closed my eyes and prayed. And then the shaking stopped. I jerked my head to look at the people in the seats around me for an explanation; they were calmly staring out the windows or reading as if nothing was wrong. That's when it hit me—nothing was wrong! The wheels had left the ground, and we were airborne.

Thanh and I peered out the window and watched as the land sank beneath us, turning buildings into unrecognizable dots on a green landscape. Then the water came into view—the beautiful South China Sea. The color was practically the same from this height, bluer than blue, yet it looked different somehow. Peaceful. Tame even. It was hard to believe that I had been lost and frightened on that placid, blue canvas. But the sea is a masterful impersonator—a wolf in sheep's clothing waiting to pounce. Sea travel was dangerous, and I hoped never to set foot on a boat ever again. Flying was different. Up here in the sky, miles above the earth, I felt safe.

An hour or so into the flight, the stewardess offered Thanh and me a beverage; we politely refused. A little while later, the stewardess offered us a beverage again. When we refused again, she asked me if something was wrong. In my best French, I explained that I was worried about not being able to hold my bladder all the way to Paris if I were to drink something. She smiled gently and offered me her hand. I then received an A-class tutorial on how to locate and use the plane's bathroom. The next time Thanh and I were offered a beverage, we graciously accepted freshly squeezed orange juice and promptly took advantage of the bathroom facilities.

Thanks to my ability to understand and speak French, the bathroom problem had been solved. However, looking at Thanh I realized that without me, he would be quite lost in France. I would have to be his ears and voice. Like never before, I would be responsible for his welfare. I contemplated this daunting task, but then I remembered that we were going to live with my grandfather's brother. He spoke Vietnamese. And since he had agreed to take Thanh and me in, he was probably willing to share the responsibility for acclimating us to our new home and surroundings. This gave me hope.

My excitement continued to rise with each passing hour as I pondered above the clouds what my new life might look like. I knew nothing about my uncle—only that he existed. The French nuns had taught me that Paris was the most refined city on the planet. I had to assume that if my uncle lived there, he must be refined too.

I imagined my Uncle Cuong to be well off, wealthy even, with a house that was bigger than the one I had been born in. It was probably a modern home with a fancy oven and flushing toilets, like the ones in the hotel in Taipei. I imagined there would be running water, both hot and cold, in the kitchen and the bathrooms. I wondered if Thanh and I would each have our own bedroom, perhaps with windows looking out over the city. I hoped my uncle had servants who would do the cooking so I wouldn't have to. If my uncle was very rich, he might even have his own fruit trees in his big backyard.

By the time we landed at Charles de Gaulle Airport, I had fabricated the most amazing uncle imaginable! I couldn't wait to meet him and begin my new life. Thanh and I grabbed our satchels and followed the exit signs toward the baggage claim. I had never been in a building as shiny and bright as Charles de Gaulle Airport. The long hallways lined with stores that offered everything from magazines to wine fascinated me. Thanh and I couldn't help but stare at the people around us; they represented every nationality and color. We blended right in.

Once we got through security, which was a relatively simple process in those days, we searched the crowd for an older man who likely resembled our grandfather. Instead, our eyes landed on a middle-aged couple holding up a sign with our names written in Vietnamese. I approached the man and woman skeptically, wondering if this was perhaps my cousin Nicolas and his wife.

"*Es-tu Minh Phuong?*" (Are you Minh Phuong?) the man asked.

"*Oui,*" I replied, adding, "*Thanh, c'est mon frère.*" (This is my brother, Thanh.)

The man's eyes lit up. He grabbed my arms and planted a kiss on both cheeks. Then he did the same to Thanh. The gesture threw us off guard and rendered us stiff as boards. Our reaction caused the man to burst out laughing. I didn't see anything funny about being kissed in public by a total stranger. While this greeting might be the norm in France, physical affection in a public setting is extremely rare in Vietnam. Thanh and I weren't comfortable with it. The last time I had been kissed was many years earlier by my father, and that was on the top of my head.

"I'm your cousin Nicolas," the man said cheerfully in French, "and this is my wife, Margaux."

My cousin looked nothing like my grandfather or any of my uncles. Nicolas had long hair and light colored eyes that masked his Asian ethnicity. He wore bell-bottom jeans with sandals and an untucked, button down shirt. Had I known any better, I would have called him an American hippy. The clothes looked odd, but I was more surprised by Nicolas's incessant smile; such a cheerful demeanor was abnormal among the members of my mother's family. Despite his strange attire and positive attitude, I liked him. Nicolas conveyed an air of confidence that I found quite beguiling.

Thanh and I were soon wrapped up in Nicolas's enthusiasm as he began to tell us stories about family members we had never met. I played the role of interpreter, relaying each story to Thanh in Vietnamese.

We learned that Nicolas's father, my Uncle Cuong, was married to a French woman, hence the reason for Nicolas's light eyes. Though Nicolas and Margaux had no children of their own, they had nieces and nephews by his two sisters and their husbands. This meant that I had two more cousins.

When Nicolas asked about my siblings, I told him their names and ages. Nothing more. In truth, there wasn't much to tell except that they existed. Thankfully, Nicolas didn't push for more information.

At one point in the conversation, Nicolas told me that he and Margaux were very impressed with my French fluency. Their compliment gave me confidence that I would be able to make my way in France.

Nicolas loaded us into his small car and headed out onto the motorway, the likes of which I had never experienced or imagined. He drove fast, zipping from one lane to another, passing cars on the left and the right. Thanh and I stared out the windows in fear and amazement. I could see the benefit of the paved highways with multiple lanes, but I found the pace of the traffic to be paralyzing.

All I could do was pray that God had not brought me to France to die in a car accident.

Our first stop was Nicolas and Margaux's home—a small yet charming apartment in the heart of Paris. It would have been a tight fit for the four of us to live there, but that was not an option. We had stopped simply to drop Margaux off, as she had no intention of going with us to her father-in-law's house. Why, I did not know and was too polite to ask. Sensing my concern, Nicolas confessed that Margaux felt uncomfortable at his parents' home for a variety of reasons. He didn't say what those reasons were, and his evasiveness put me on guard. Now I began to worry. Perhaps my uncle was mean and prone to pinching women. *After all,* I reminded myself, *Uncle Cuong is my grandfather's brother.*

As we drove to my uncle's home, the scenery changed drastically from quaint chic to working industrial to dirt poor. I got a sinking feeling in the pit of my stomach when Nicolas suddenly parked his car in a poverty-stricken section of Paris. The brick buildings appeared sad with their cracked concrete steps and mold-covered trim. Even the weeds poking through the cracks of the sidewalk looked discontented. This was not at all what I had envisioned.

Thanh and I clutched our satchels close to our bodies and followed Nicolas down a dark alleyway to a ramshackle, single-level home. There were four steps leading up to the weathered door. When Nicolas opened it, waves of cigarette smoke and the smell of decay smacked me in the face. This was to be my new home—not a place of light and hope, but a place of despair.

Despite the wretched conditions before us, Uncle Cuong seemed quite excited by our arrival. His warm welcome, however, could not drive out the darkness. What little light there was came from a small window that looked out onto the back alleyway. The window in my former jail cell had provided more light.

As my eyes adjusted to the dimly lit room, they landed on a tough looking woman sitting at a small wooden table in the center. This was Nicolas's mother, my Aunt Danielle. There she sat smoking with a look of disdain on her face, her light blue eyes throwing daggers at us. She did not stand up to greet Thanh and me, but Nicolas approached her and kissed her on both cheeks. It was obvious that she did not want any of us there.

I averted my eyes and examined the rest of the room while Nicolas and his father discussed our arrival at the airport. In the corner I could see a sink and a small combination stove and oven. Various items were scattered around the edges of the walls, such things as canned foods, old pots, and miscellaneous papers. Three doors ran down the left hand wall. Uncle Cuong opened the first to reveal a room about the size of a large closet. A single light bulb hanging from the middle of the ceiling illuminated the dirty mattress on the floor below. This was to be Thanh's and my room. I had never seen anything so depressing. If Thanh hadn't been with me, I think I would have run away in tears.

The last door led to Uncle Cuong and Aunt Danielle's bedroom. It wasn't much larger than our room. It, too, contained a single mattress on the floor along with a couple boxes of clothing. The door between the two bedrooms opened onto a stained toilet. No sink. No shower. Uncle Cuong informed us that physical hygiene could be addressed at the public showers several blocks away.

Our uncle spoke to us in rapid Vietnamese, asking about our trip, telling us about the letters he had received from my mother, and inquiring about the condition of Saigon. I got the feeling that he was enjoying the conversation, not only because we kindled his memories of home, but also because Aunt Danielle couldn't understand a word he was saying.

It didn't take long for me to realize that Nicolas's parents fostered a love-hate relationship that both drew them together and alienated everyone else. It was no wonder Margaux did not want to visit.

Uncle Cuong's home was, by far, the worst place I would ever live. It was small, smelly, dark, hot, and full of bitter tension. To make matters worse, I discovered that Uncle Cuong had a wicked streak like his brother. Fortunately, he did not aim it at Thanh or me. He aimed it at his wife. Aunt Danielle, however, was no wallflower. She stood up to his bullying, flinging back insults with ease. In no time, she was insulting Thanh and me as well, and Uncle Cuong became our protector. Once when Aunt Danielle said something very hurtful to me, my uncle responded by saying, "Don't listen to this crazy woman. Don't take her seriously. She has been crazy for years!"

Thanh and I were, without a doubt, both a burden and an embarrassment to Aunt Danielle. She was neither sufficiently able nor willing to provide for us. Our presence forced her to share what little she had with two distant relatives whom she did not want.

Meals were a distinct reflection of my uncle's impoverished state, for they were nothing more than canned foods heated in a pot on the small stove. With barely enough to go around, Thanh and I conscientiously refrained from eating as often as our stomachs would allow. It was ironic to realize that the food we ate in a refugee camp in Taiwan was better than that the meals we consumed in a home in the outskirts of Paris.

A common question Aunt Danielle often asked Uncle Cuong in front of us was, "How long are they going to stay here?" Though I could speak and understand French, she never spoke directly *to* me. Instead, she would talk to my uncle in front of me *about* me. I tried to keep my distance as much as possible; this wasn't always easy in such close quarters.

Thanh and I had stepped into a challenging environment on so many levels. Trying to make the best of it was a daily struggle. I often found myself wishing that I had either accepted the invitation to move to America or stayed in Taiwan. Either place would have been better than this.

Sleep did not come easy in Uncle Cuong's house with the rats scurrying behind the walls. I prayed they would not break through and crawl into bed with me. Thankfully, they never did, but the scraping sound of their claws haunted my dreams. The cockroaches were also disturbing. Whenever I turned the overhead light on in our room, I watched them run for cover. I had to shake my clothes out each morning in order to rid them of the roaches that had crawled inside.

Going to the public showers brought little relief. They were mildew-ridden, dirty, and just plain creepy. The first time we used them, I stationed Thanh outside the door to ensure no one entered or took a peek. Periodically I would call out, "Are you still there, Thanh? Are you keeping your eyes open?" No matter how many precautions I took, I still felt as if I was being watched.

Coins were needed to access the stalls, and since we had no money of our own, we relied on the kindness of Uncle Cuong to get clean. Every couple of days he would give Thanh and me a coin and caution us, "Don't tell your Aunt Danielle." I couldn't help but wonder if she really would have preferred that we not shower at all.

I watched in horror over the course of a few weeks as my skin changed in color and texture. I had developed a rash of red spots and pimples on my arms and legs that made me feel dirty and contagious. It might have been a reaction to the old mattress I slept on each night, the cheap soap I used to wash my clothes and body, the canned foods that made up the bulk of my diet, or a result of the stress I experienced daily. Whatever the cause, I felt the life draining out of me. I knew if I stayed long in this place, I was going to go crazy like Aunt Danielle.

Each morning Thanh and I would dress, then wait quietly in our room until we heard Uncle Cuong and Aunt Danielle leave. Since neither of them worked anymore, they spent many hours outdoors walking and smoking. Hanging with the bugs in our small room was preferable to hanging with Aunt Danielle. Once they were gone, Thanh and I would head outside as well. We spent most of our time in the more respectable areas of Paris looking for Help Wanted signs. I had one goal: to move as far away as possible from Uncle Cuong's neighborhood and Aunt Danielle. My dream was to one day rent an apartment on the finer side of the city, one with lots of windows, a bathtub, and no cockroaches. The first step toward achieving this goal was to find jobs.

Luckily, a relative provided an opening. Nicolas's sister's husband, Philippe, managed a small company, and he needed someone to fill in while an employee was on a four-week vacation. Nicolas showed up at the house one morning with details about the opportunity and directions to the office. I found it odd that Nicolas would offer me this position instead of Philippe himself, but I soon learned that Nicolas was the only one willing to venture into his parents' neighborhood.

Without hesitation, I accepted the job offer even though it required me to travel on the metro each day, which was an unfamiliar form of transportation. Nicolas explained the process and provided me with a metro pass. It sounded easy enough, but it wasn't! I was not equipped to navigate the complexity of the Paris metro system. Unlike bus stops with one entry point, train stations were huge underground structures with a number of exits. I got so confused and arrived 45 minutes late for my first day of work.

My only task was to file papers, but this proved to be difficult because I was not proficient with the order of the French alphabet even though I could understand and speak French rather well. Consequently, I was never able to complete the work assigned to me each day, and the work I did do was riddled with mistakes.

Recognizing my shortcomings, Philippe moved me to the front desk and moved the receptionist to the filing room. I did well at the front desk where I greeted visitors politely and managed the phones. I was never chastised or ridiculed for poor performance, and Philippe kindly took me out to lunch each day.

The time I spent working at Philippe's company was just long enough to whet my appetite for full-time employment. Thanh did not appear to have the same desire. After a day's work, I would return to my uncle's house to find him and Uncle Cuong playing cards or reminiscing about the good old days in Vietnam as if it was the Garden of Eden.

I refused to allow Thanh to settle in the past. I would pull him away from Uncle Cuong and force him to take walks with me through the better parts of Paris in the hopes of inspiring him to do something more with his life. I feared that if left to his own devices, Thanh might turn into Uncle Cuong or worse, our grandfather. I felt it was my duty to save Thanh from himself, to save him from accepting a life in the slums.

What I didn't realize then was that Thanh didn't need saving. I did.

CHAPTER 19

However many years anyone may live, let them enjoy them all.
But let them remember the days of darkness,
for there will be many.
Everything to come is meaningless.
Ecclesiastes 11:8 (NIV)

Fall 1975

I t was early autumn, less than three months since our arrival in France, when a morning visitor rocked my world. Thanh and I were still in bed when we heard the unexpected knock on the front door. My uncle and aunt were already out, so Thanh hurried to answer it.

"*Minh Phuong est-elle ici?*" (Is Minh Phuong here?) I heard a male voice ask.

I quickly jumped out of bed to dress and brush my hair. Since there was no phone in the house, I assumed the man might be a friend of Philippe's or Nicolas's coming to offer me a job. I heard the front door close and Thanh appeared before me with a strange look on his face.

"There is a man here asking for you," he whispered. "He's from Switzerland."

Could it be? No. Surely my pen pal from Switzerland hadn't tracked me to this godforsaken place! My heart started to beat with excitement. Just in case it was Hubert, I wanted to look my best. Thanh opened the front door a crack and, using hand gestures, told the man to wait. I quickly donned the navy blue dress with white piping, brushed my teeth in the small sink in the main room, and combed my long, dark hair till it shined. Then taking a deep breath, I opened the door and stepped outside.

There he was, a glimmer of sunshine in the dark alley. He was fairer than I imagined and shorter. His blonde hair was badly in need of a cut. He glowed confidence. I loved him immediately. "Hubert?" I asked cautiously. His blue eyes met mine.

"*Oui*," he answered with assurance. "I am your friend from Switzerland!"

How far had he come to find me? I pondered the question having no grasp of European geography. I must have appeared pathetic in my navy blue dress in contrast to his crisp button down shirt and khaki pants. Etiquette told me to invite him into my home, but that would have been an embarrassment for us both. I considered approaching him and kissing him on both cheeks, but I couldn't bring myself to do it. Unsure of the next move, I stood still and stared at the ground.

"Are you working today?" he asked. I shook my head no.

"Would you like to go for a cup of coffee or hot chocolate?"

Yes! Of course I would! I had never been asked out before. The full impact of the invitation did not escape me—I needed a chaperone. That is the way things work in Vietnam. I asked Hubert to wait a moment while I ran inside to get my brother.

Hubert, Thanh, and I spent the entire morning in a coffee shop drinking espresso and chatting in French. Well, only Hubert and I chatted in French. Thanh sat quietly sipping his hot chocolate, happy and content to be watching strangers come and go. At first, I translated for Thanh, but after an hour it got to be too much. I eventually turned all my attention to Hubert and completely ignored my brother.

The conversation between Hubert and I flowed freely. We had so much to talk about, and the espresso only served to heighten the vigor of our conversation. I had never felt such happiness, and I remember giggling like a young child. Hubert had memorized practically every little thing I had told him in my letters, and I soon realized that he knew me better than anyone else in the world. I had written things to him that I had never verbalized to anyone in my 18 years of life, and he had tenderly held my secrets close to his heart.

There were, however, other things he did not know about me, things I had no intention of ever sharing—the painful things, the shameful things. These were buried deep in my soul in a futile effort to obliterate them forever.

When we had had our fill of espresso, Hubert and I began a long walk through Montmartre with Thanh tagging along behind us like a puppy on an invisible leash. Montmartre is a colorful and heavily populated area in the north end of Paris. It is dominated by the white-domed Basilica of the Sacré-Coeur, a Roman Catholic Church that appeared before me as a symbol of hope. Hubert took this moment to inform me that he had worried himself sick when he hadn't heard from me for several months.

"The day I received your letter from Taiwan was one of the happiest days of my life," he said. "It was better than Christmas."

I smiled at his enthusiasm, but I couldn't understand it. For me, Christmas meant attending mass. There was nothing exciting about it. At the time, I knew nothing about Christmas trees, Christmas presents, or Christmas joy.

Hubert did most of the talking that day, and I was happy to listen. He explained in great detail the process for filing immigration papers, which he was prepared to do again so I could live in Switzerland with him. He spoke about his amazing family, how much they wanted to meet me, and what he liked to do for fun. He spoke highly of his love for his parents and his sister who was his only sibling. He told me that he was looking forward to taking me for a ride on his sailboat across the lake near his home. The thought of this made me seasick, though I didn't let on. I just listened attentively and savored his every word.

Several hours into our date, Hubert announced that he had made plans to meet his friends for dinner. Apparently, he had convinced three of his classmates to drive more than seven hours across Switzerland and France so he could meet me—his Vietnamese pen pal—in person. I was deeply touched by Hubert's determination to find me in France and his desire to spend more time with me. While I couldn't fully grasp the distance he had traveled or understand his fascination with meeting me face-to-face, I cherished our time together and felt blessed by his presence.

When Hubert invited Thanh and me to join him and his class-mates for dinner, I cheerfully agreed. I did not know if spending an entire day together was proper behavior for a first date, but I did not care.

Thanh, Hubert, and I were already seated in a casual restau-rant when Hubert's friends showed up with French girls hanging on their arms, one more beautiful than the next. They were a loud bunch—confident and cocky. Even though they greeted me politely, I was out of my league. With my foreign looks and shabby dress, I did not fit in. Hubert didn't seem to notice or care, and he seemed genuinely embarrassed by his friends' behavior. He apologized pro-fusely for them, saying, "I am so sorry about this. They are wild."

I was not able to eat much that night. My stomach was in French knots. Sitting in a restaurant with four men from Switzerland and three giddy French girls was far outside my comfort zone. Thanh's quiet but indisputable presence did not help. I didn't know how to act, where to look, or what to do with my hands. Hubert must have sensed my unease because he ushered us out of the restaurant before the meal was over. He told his friends he would meet up with them later at the hotel where they were staying.

Hubert walked Thanh and me home slowly, thus prolonging the inevitable end to the fairytale evening. Then, in the dark alleyway outside my uncle's home, Hubert asked if he could call on me in the morning. My heart leapt in my chest. Our time together was not ending; it was just beginning.

When the knock came the next morning, I was ready. This time I dressed in a simple apricot frock dotted with small white flowers. It had short sleeves and a Peter Pan collar. I also wore stockings in an attempt to make myself look more mature and to draw attention away from the rash on my legs.

Hubert came bearing gifts—two bags of clothing: one for Thanh (Hubert's own hand-me-downs) and one for me (his sister's hand-me-downs). I found this gesture to be extremely thoughtful. The clothes were neutral in color, neatly folded, and smelled of sunshine. It couldn't have been easy for him to squeeze these bags of clothing into a car with four men and their luggage. Yet, he had done it just for me.

Despite Thanh's gratitude for the gift, he refused to act as my chaperone for another day. Apparently, he had heard enough French for the week. Quite frankly, I was thrilled at the prospect of being with Hubert in public without a chaperone.

We ventured out and caught the metro to the Champs-Elysées. There we walked the tree-lined boulevard toward the famous Arc de Triomphe, which Hubert said was commissioned by Napoleon to commemorate his victories. Throughout the day, Hubert provided me with French history lessons while pointing out important landmarks along our route. He was so smart; he knew so much more than I would ever know.

Hubert also taught me how to use a payphone, which I considered amazing. I couldn't help but wonder why this invention had not yet been introduced in Vietnam or, if it had, why I hadn't seen it.

Hubert asked if he could hold my hand as we walked. I told him no, explaining that Vietnamese girls did not hold hands with men, only with their girlfriends or husbands. He accepted my refusal and compensated by walking a little closer to me instead. This slight adjustment made me tingle all over, and I suddenly understood the purpose of a chaperone.

For lunch, Hubert purchased food for us from a street vendor, and we ate our meal at the Jardin des Tuileries, the most beautiful public garden imaginable. As we sat down on a park bench, Hubert asked, "What's wrong with your skin?"

"Nothing," I answered a little too quickly. In truth, I didn't know how to answer him. I didn't know what I had, nor did I have the means to do anything about it. His question made me feel like a leper. Untouchable. Unlovable. Yet Hubert tenderly ran his fingers across the rash on my arm and said, "We need to get you something for it."

I can't quite explain the feeling that washed over me. I can only compare it to falling into a soft bed of pillows after a hard day's work. It's that feeling you get when the struggle has ended and you find yourself at peace, enveloped in a soft cocoon. Hubert was my cocoon. With him, I could be myself. My skin should have repulsed him, but it didn't. He didn't run away when he saw where I lived, and the clothes I wore didn't appear to offend him. He saw me differently than I saw myself. He saw beyond my imperfections. He saw my heart.

Hubert and I shared an absolutely lovely day, and I found myself dreading our goodbye as he walked me to my uncle's home later that night. The air had turned cool, so Hubert took off his jacket and laid it across my shoulders. It was just another small gesture that not only demonstrated his understanding of decorum but also his concern for me.

Hubert promised to call on me very early the next morning so we could spend as much time together as possible before he had to drive back to Switzerland. Returning his jacket, I bid him goodnight and slipped out of my sublime dream and back into my harsh reality.

Uncle Cuong and Aunt Danielle were sitting at the table, filling the house with their cigarette smoke. I went into my bug-infested room and joined Thanh on the well-worn mattress. The scent of Hubert lingered on my dress, so I used it as a pillow to cradle me to sleep.

Hubert knocked on the door bright and early the next morning. I was ready and waiting, wearing one of his sister's dresses that I found in the bag he had given me the day before. When I opened the door, Hubert said, "Ah, you are the same size as my sister. It looks good on you!" I felt beautiful. Simply beautiful.

One would think that Hubert and I would have run out of things to talk about, but we didn't. There was still the future to discuss. He told me that he would be returning to college in Switzerland to continue his studies as an engineer. He had just one more year to go. Hubert asked me if I had thought much about the future, and I had to admit that I had not. "However," I told him, "I have considered becoming a nurse in order to do something good for mankind."

Hubert seemed very pleased with my response. In fact, Hubert seemed pleased with me. Nursing, he said, was a noble profession. He gave me the blessing I needed. In that moment, I knew that I would someday pursue nursing as a career.

Continuing to talk about the future, Hubert asked, "Have you ever thought about getting married?"

Images of Nhu, Mr. Khoa, Jun, and the North Vietnamese captain who took my virginity flashed through my head. I pushed them back and responded, "No." My odd brushes with marriage prospects seemed so strange in light of the strong feelings I had for Hubert.

Then Hubert asked, "Would you *like* to get married one day?"

I wasn't sure if this was a hypothetical question or if he was actually asking me to marry him. I chose my words carefully. "I suppose I would like to be married someday," I said, "but right now I have to take care of Thanh."

Hubert said he understood. He didn't pursue this line of questioning any further, and for that I was grateful.

Try as I might, I could not imagine what life might look like if I were Hubert's wife. The house, the clothes, even the sailboat were not what rattled me. It was his gentleness, loving-kindness, generosity, and compassion—day in and day out—which I simply could not envision. How does one live in such a perfect environment? Life without agony was unknown to me.

To end our time together, Hubert took me to a traditional Swiss restaurant with white tablecloths and waiters wearing bowties. A number of forks, spoons, and knives fanned out from both sides of the plate in front of me. I felt quite uncomfortable, but Hubert was thoroughly at ease. He ordered for both of us—spiced pork cooked in red wine for him and veal covered with a mushroom and onion cream sauce for me. I had never seen anything like it, which is why I can still clearly picture these dishes today.

Hubert ate with enthusiasm while I watched. He finished everything on his plate before he noticed that I had not taken one bite of my food. "What's wrong?" he asked.

"I'm not hungry," I lied. The truth was, having never eaten in a fancy restaurant, I was not sure how to do it. Eating a sandwich in a park or a croissant in a coffee shop is not the same as eating at a table set with several utensils of varying sizes.

Hubert knew I was not telling the truth. After much prodding, I finally confessed my fears. Then Hubert did the sweetest thing to alleviate my discomfort. He called the waiter over and asked for a newspaper, which he opened up so he could not see me and I could not see him. Then he told me to eat, using the utensils furthest from the plate first.

Hidden from view, I was able to pick up the fork and knife and begin eating. Lessons on table manners that I had been taught in boarding school came flooding back into memory, and I slowly began to eat with the fork in my left hand and the knife in my right.

"Is the food good?" he asked through the paper.

"It is very nice!" I told him.

"Take your time," he said. So I did.

The newspaper eventually came down, and we shared a caramelized nut-filled pastry for desert. I liked his Swiss food very much. I felt full—physically and emotionally. Too full perhaps.

When Hubert looked at me, I had a hard time maintaining eye contact. My feelings for him were overwhelming and all consuming. I had no way to explain them or control them. If this was love, I was lost.

As he walked me home, Hubert handed me some money saying he expected both Thanh and me to spend Christmas in Switzerland with him and his family. I did not want to make promises I could not keep, so I told him that I would probably have a job by then that would keep me from leaving France. I tried to give him his money back, to sever the hold he had on me, but he would not take it.

Getting a job was just an excuse, of course. I couldn't fathom spending Christmas with Hubert and his family. Hubert was sophisticated and smart. I was not. Hubert had parents and a sister who spoke fluent French. Though I was competent with the French language, my brother acted mute. Hubert wore expensive clothes. My nicest clothes were his sister's hand-me-downs. Hubert had beautiful, smooth skin. I looked like a leper. He was Prince Charming, but I was not Cinderella. No, I would not be going to Switzerland in December. I was not worthy of Hubert or his affections.

Hubert asked if it would be all right if he hugged me before he left. Since the French hug all the time, I saw no problem with honoring his request. He put his arms around my back and gave me a strong, warm hug. The physical contact completely shattered my defenses, and I began to sob.

"Don't cry," he said gently. "We'll see each other again." I knew we wouldn't. I had fallen head over heels in love with Hubert, and it hurt too much to be with him.

I will forever be grateful for the light Hubert brought into my dark world—an illumination by which all other men would be evaluated. On that fateful night, I blew the flame out. That decision left a hole in my heart that rivaled the one left by my father's death. If Hubert was God's gift to me, I was not a gracious recipient. I pushed him away because I didn't know how to handle the feelings I had for him. Love was such a foreign emotion. I was still a child in so many ways, only capable of consuming baby food. Being offered the entire cake was too much for me.

Clouded by tears, I walked down the dark alley to my uncle's home. It was late, and Aunt Danielle had locked me out. Frustration, anger, and rejection surged through my veins; these emotions were familiar and served to remind me that I did not belong in Hubert's world. I slumped to the ground and cried my heart out.

CHAPTER 20

Out of the depths I cry to you, LORD; Lord, hear my voice.
Let your ears be attentive to my cry for mercy.
Psalm 130:1-2 (NIV)

Fall 1975–1976

T hanh and I possessed no marketable skills to speak of. Still, I refused to settle for the slums. I had spunk. I was resourceful. And I had inspiration. Hubert had shown me a better world in which to live, one I wanted to claim as my own. Thanks to him and my one-month working stint at Philippe's office, I was now familiar with Paris's metro and bus routes as well as its various neighborhoods. My desire to find a job in a prestigious part of town where employers were sure to pay a decent wage led me to strike up conversations with anyone and everyone along those routes. I would initiate communication at the bus stops, at the coffee stands, and while riding the trains.

One day I overheard a woman asking another woman if she knew of anyone who could clean house while she was on vacation. I interrupted their conversation, volunteered my services, and got the job. Another time a woman on a train directed me to a weeklong position as a nanny. And then there was the young lady at a bus stop who put me in touch with a couple from Greece who needed an aide for their disabled daughter. This six-day-a-week job lasted a little more than a year and taught me a lot about myself.

Monsieur and Madame Paquet and their adult daughter, Helena, lived in a beautiful penthouse in the lovely neighborhood of Pont de Neuilly. All three family members were highly educated; their conversations ranged from politics and research to music and history. Most of their discussions were way over my head, but I enjoyed listening and learning what I could.

My main responsibility was assisting Helena with her daily activities, such as bathing and dressing. Helena was confined to a wheelchair due to an accident suffered years earlier that left her paralyzed from the waist down. I never asked about the accident, as I did not think it was polite to do so, and the information was never offered.

When I wasn't assisting Helena, I was cleaning the house. I distinctly remember polishing a lot of silver because it always turned my hands a dingy color of gray. Madame Paquet often worked alongside me, like a mentor. At first, her presence was to ensure that I met her standards. After awhile, I believe she stayed because she appreciated my company. I enjoyed her company, too.

Madame Paquet instructed me on how to properly transfer Helena from her bed to her wheelchair, how to differentiate between a table setting for lunch and a table setting for dinner, how to dust an antique properly, and how to store silver correctly. I was immersed in western culture and etiquette, which would serve me well in later years.

"I am going to call you Turtle," Madame Paquet announced. I assumed she chose that nickname because I was working too slowly, so I focused on increasing the speed at which I tackled each chore. Madame Paquet noticed my efforts and told me to slow down. Then she shared the story of *The Hare and the Tortoise*, one of Aesop's fables. She explained that while the tortoise was much slower than the hare, the tortoise was able to achieve more because he didn't race through life. Looking into my eyes, Madame Paquet told me that I was like the turtle. Though I was a slow learner, once I had mastered the information, my work would prove exemplary.

"Someday," she said, "you will achieve your dreams. Just stay the course." Her words were encouraging and gave me hope that one day I would pursue the path to nursing.

Because I was learning so much, I viewed Madame Paquet like a wise teacher. She viewed me as the hired help. We never ate a meal together or even shared a cup of tea. The dining room table was off limits to me unless I was serving the family and their guests a meal. I always ate in the kitchen by myself. Class divisions were clearly defined, and I never tested a boundary.

Working for the Paquets provided me with both an education in life as well as a decent wage. My salary was not only enough to reimburse the French government for the plane tickets they had purchased for Thanh and me, it was also enough to cover our daily living expenses. This meant we no longer had to rely on Uncle Cuong and Aunt Danielle for food, soap, and other essentials.

I much preferred my time at work to my time at home. So whenever Madame Paquet asked me to work late, I always said yes, even though it made the commute challenging. The Paquet home was not on a metro stop, so I had to take both a train and a bus to get to work and home again. On a good day, the commute was 45 minutes each way. On a bad day, the commute was closer to two hours. On those rare occasions when I missed the last train, I would have to take a taxi; this was something I could not afford.

One evening, after finishing a little later than usual, I found myself waiting at the bus stop alone. If the bus didn't come soon, I would miss the last train. I kept peering nervously down the street, pacing the sidewalk, and wringing my hands. In retrospect, I now see that I exhibited all the signs of a perfect target.

"Excusez-moi, mademoiselle," the man said, as he rolled down the window of his expensive, sporty convertible. I gave him my full attention, noting that he was middle-aged, French, and professionally dressed. He told me that he was lost and asked for directions to an office building. I was not able to help him.

"Where are you going?" he asked inquisitively.

I told him I was waiting for the bus to take me to the train station.

"Do you know the way to the station?"

I told him I did. He was sure the place he was looking for was near the station. He wondered if I would be willing to take a ride with him and direct the way. This was just what I needed, or so I thought. Grateful for the offer, I jumped into his car.

Several blocks later the man claimed he had acquired his bearings. "Ah," he said, "I know where we are now! Thank you for your help."

I, in turn, thanked him for his help, even though we still had a several more blocks to go to get to the train station.

"Oh, wait a minute," he said suddenly. "My office is right around the corner. Do you mind if I stop and pick something up?"

I did mind! I couldn't afford to miss my train, but I didn't want to appear ungrateful. "Where is your office?" I asked.

"It's on the way," he said. "Don't worry, it will only take five minutes."

I did not feel I had any right to tell him no, so I nodded my consent. It's strange to look back on this scene and remember myself as a young woman who did not feel she had any right to speak up for herself. I had been raised to respect and obey my elders, not to complain, and certainly not to question authority. So when this well-dressed man pulled into an underground parking lot and told me, "It's not safe for you to stay down here alone," I reluctantly followed him into the elevator, more worried about missing my train than about my own safety. I did not recognize the blatant signs of a predator. I had never been taught what to look for.

For just a moment I thought, *this is not right!* The feeling quickly faded when he took out a key and unlocked the door to an office. I hoped he would move quickly and get what he needed so I could connect with my train. I positioned myself by the door hoping my stance would encourage him to move fast. It did not. He took his time.

His office was quite messy, and his search for the alleged item had him systematically lifting stacks of papers and opening drawers over and over again. This was taking too long, and I started to get nervous. "We have to go," I told him.

He wasn't listening. He offered me a drink instead. I declined.

"Come here." He motioned for me from behind his desk. "I want to show you something."

Hesitantly, I moved toward him. The man pointed to a framed picture of himself with his family. He had a wife and two kids. They were all smiling. As I looked at the photo, the man suddenly put his arm around my waist and pulled me to him. "You are a very nice, pretty woman," he said.

"Thank you," I replied politely, as I had been taught to do when complimented. The man did not let go of my waist. I felt strangely sick, yet I didn't move. As calmly as possible, I said, "We need to go."

"I'm really attracted to you," he said tauntingly, squeezing my waist. Now I was scared. This was all wrong.

I tried to make a run for it, but he grabbed me. The harder I fought, the more excited he got. Fighting him was no good; he was at least twice my size. With one quick move, he picked me up and threw me down on top of his messy desk. As his wife watched from the family photo, he hoisted up my skirt, pulled down my panties, and entered me.

I froze. I wanted to cry out, but I could not. I closed my eyes so I wouldn't have to watch what was happening, but I felt it all. Fearing for my life, I prayed silently to God that He would keep me alive. This was not how or where I wanted to die.

It didn't last long. When he was done, he asked, "Do you still want to go to the metro?"

Without looking at him, I pulled up my panties and answered, "Yes, please." For some reason, it seemed appropriate to say "please."

"Come on," he said, somewhat annoyed. "Let's go."

We went down the elevator, got in his car, and drove off. I was numb to the core yet grateful to be alive. He needed no help navigating to the train station. He knew exactly where it was. He had known all along.

As I ran to catch the train, I heard him yell, "Can we meet again?" I thought I was going to puke.

I caught the last train and cried the whole way home. I felt dirty, like my skin was crawling with lice. I felt stupid for trusting a man who drove an expensive car. I felt ridiculous for being so polite to him. And I felt weak for not trying harder to escape. Then anger began welling up inside me like a pot of boiling water—the anger was directed at myself. I blamed myself for the rape. A voice in my head kept repeating, "You stupid, stupid girl."

Before I knew it, I was at the door of my uncle's home. I was a wreck, but it would do no good for Thanh to see me in such a state. This was my burden to bear, not his. I needed to appear strong; it was the only way to survive. I walked up and down the alleyway until I was drained of emotion. Then I entered the house as if nothing was wrong.

The next day I told Madame Paquet that I couldn't work late for her anymore. "All right," she said. She didn't ask for an explanation, and I didn't offer one.

Hubert continued to write, pleading with me to visit him in Switzerland. His letters had become more intimate since we had spent time together. My heart fluttered every time I read one of them. I tried to respond virtuously, but after the rape, the right words would not come. I did not spend Christmas with Hubert that year. I excused myself by telling him that my work commitments hindered me from taking any kind of trip.

Will you come to visit later? Hubert wrote. *My family is asking.*

I wanted to run to him, but I couldn't. My shame ran too deep, creating a chasm between us that was too wide to cross. Hubert deserved someone better than me, someone who was worthy of his love—someone who was pure. I was damaged, broken beyond repair. For his protection and mine, I simply avoided his requests and basked in the knowledge that I was desired.

About a year after his visit to France, I received a final letter from Hubert. In it he informed me that he had become involved with another girl and, therefore, had to break off our relationship. Though I had anticipated such an end, his letter pierced me like a knife.

I wrote to Hubert one last time. I told him that I understood his decision and wished him much happiness. My heart broke that day, and the pain of true love remains lodged in the fracture.

One morning Madame Paquet informed me that her family would soon be returning to Greece. She wanted me to come with them, to live with them permanently. It would have been so easy to say yes, but I could not bear the thought of starting over again in another country and leaving Thanh behind. I told Madame Paquet that my brother was dependent on me.

In truth, I was dependent on Thanh. He brought a vague sense of stability to my life. He was the anchor that kept me grounded and the buoy that kept me afloat. He was also my crutch and my excuse for not moving forward.

CHAPTER 21

All our days pass away under your wrath;
we finish our years with a moan.
Our days may come to seventy years, or eighty,
if our strength endures;
yet the best of them are but trouble and sorrow,
for they quickly pass, and we fly away.
Psalm 90:9-10 (NIV)

1976–April 1977

I was certain that God had either abandoned me or was punishing me. He had taken away my protector—the father I loved. He had allowed me to be molested and raped. He stuck me in the slums of Paris and had not provided a clear way out. And he had moved my employer back to Greece, thus eliminating my job and my income.

I couldn't see then what I see now: I was not able to feel comfort from God because I had not made room for Him in my heart. Instead, I blamed Him for every miserable aspect of my life.

My Uncle Cuong and Aunt Danielle were not believers, so I used them as my excuse for not going to church. I had been in Paris for over a year and had never explored the possibility of attending mass. My prayer life, which had proved so fruitful on the Taiwanese fishing boat, was a distant memory.

Relying on my own strength and determination, I made a plan. If I wanted to escape life in the slums, I needed to find jobs for both Thanh and me because it would take two incomes to afford a decent apartment in Paris.

I found what I was looking for in a respectable section of the city where an Asian restaurant had a Help Wanted sign posted in its window. Upon inquiry, the owner of the restaurant told me she was looking for a cook who could prepare Chinese, Vietnamese, and Thai dishes. Given my background, I had no desire to work in the kitchen, so I made a pitch. I offered to wait tables if she would hire my brother as the cook.

The owner was a Vietnamese woman named Madame Binh. She was mean and shrewd and knew how to negotiate. In the end, she agreed to hire both Thanh and me for a flat rate in return for six days work. Though the pay was not great, it included two meals a day for each of us. According to my calculations, if we skimped and saved, Thanh and I would be able to afford our own apartment within the year. This was a goal worth straining for.

The restaurant could seat about 80 guests, and Thanh and I were its only employees. It was our sole responsibility to set the dining room and prep the food. Sunday was our only day off. This created a window of opportunity for us to go to church, but we didn't even entertain the idea. Instead, we used the day to rest.

Each workday began with a trip to the market to purchase fresh produce that was not included in the daily food deliveries. Then we would prepare the dining room by covering the tables with white tablecloths, placing full sets of silverware before each chair, and folding a cloth napkin into each water glass. Back in the kitchen, we peeled and chopped 100 pounds of onions as tears streamed down our faces. Next we chopped bok choy, diced chicken and beef, and deveined shrimp. Then soups and sauces were mixed and left on the stove to simmer. Finally, we prepared the fritter batter for the fried bananas and pineapple desserts. Our lack of experience in the restaurant business resulted in plenty of mistakes at first. However, in due time we mastered our tasks, and eventually we were able to run the restaurant without Madame Binh's direction.

The restaurant was closed after each lunch shift. This gave Thanh and me a chance to clean and prepare for dinner. If we finished our chores in record time, we would push some of the chairs together to create a bed and take a nap. Once the dinner shift ended, we repeated the cleaning process and vacuumed the floor. It was truly a full day's work! Though Thanh and I were perpetually exhausted, our jobs provided us with a reason to get up every morning.

Thanh became a superb cook, and I wondered why I hadn't assigned him cooking duties years before when we lived with Nhu and his mother. Meanwhile, I discovered that I was quite skilled at waitressing. I could take orders, serve drinks, bus tables, and seat the next party without missing a beat. The years of serving in my grandfather's house were paying off.

While I worked the floor, Madame Binh worked the cash register and hobnobbed with the customers. To encourage them to spend more, she would tell them they could buy me a drink if they liked my service. She would then add the price of an alcoholic beverage to their bill, though I never actually received the drink. In this way, Madame Binh was able to pocket extra money without wasting liquor.

All transactions had to be cycled through Madame Binh, which meant all tips went into a tip jar that went right into the cash register instead of my pocket. It didn't bother me too much because the French are notoriously poor tippers. At the end of each week, Madame Binh would pay Thanh and me our salary in cash. We stashed as much of it away as was humanly possible.

It took only a few months — not a year — for Thanh and me to scrape together enough money to rent our own apartment, complete with its own bathroom that boasted a toilet, a sink, *and* a tub. There were two drawbacks, however. The first was the apartment's location; it was situated on the other side of the city and several blocks away from a train station. In order to make it to work on time, Thanh and I had to get up before 5:00 a.m. to begin our commute, and we were lucky to get home by midnight. The second drawback was that Thanh and I needed a reference to vouch for our ability to cover the apartment's rent. Madame Binh agreed to do this if we would work on Sundays. I couldn't imagine working seven days a week, so we settled on a compromise: Thanh and I would work longer hours on weekends in exchange for Mondays off.

Now that I had the apartment I had dreamed of, I had no time to enjoy it. The stress of working long hours on little sleep began to take its toll. Within the year, I was wrestling with panic attacks, bouts of depression, and night sweats. My coloring appeared gray to me in the mirror, and my bones protruded through my thin skin.

In an effort to maintain some semblance of control, I poured all my energy into becoming the perfect employee. Instead of resting, I worked harder, bouncing from one activity to the next. I smoothed every tablecloth and chopped onions into uniform pieces. I rewashed dishes and dried them till they shined. I also created a system for seating people that improved overall service—the best-dressed customers got the best seats; the loud customers were seated at corner tables where they were less likely to disturb others; and foreigners (who were likely to tip well) were seated where I could give them attentive service. My mind was forever churning as I looked for new ways to improve workflow. I was no longer Minh the refugee and victim; I was Minh, captain of restaurant efficiency.

Thanh and I would pool our pay and purchase only those items that were necessary to get us through the next month, like soap and toilet paper. We sent the rest of the money back to Vietnam. First, as obedient children we sent money to our mother, knowing that whatever she received would go a long way in a communist environment. Second, we worked on fulfilling my commitment to Captain Quan. I was under no legal obligation to send him money, but it would have been dishonorable not to carry through on our agreement, and I did not want to be remembered as a dishonest person. I would put the French bills in an envelope and mail it to the address he had given me with a simple message: *This is good luck money for brother Quan.* Several weeks later I would receive a return letter that simply stated: *Money received. Thank you from brother Quan.*

Despite the respectable apartment and decent wage, Thanh and I lived as paupers on the fringes of poverty. We were politically free in France, but we were not any happier or healthier for it. In fact, I felt like a prisoner—captive to Madame Binh, captive to my mother, and captive to Captain Quan. I was living for everyone else but myself. Like a gerbil on a wheel approaching warp speed, I was going nowhere fast. The cost of freedom was proving to be higher than I had anticipated and perhaps higher than I could physically or emotionally afford.

One day I broke down and told Thanh that I couldn't go on living like this. It all seemed so meaningless. Thanh agreed but had no solution to offer. I believe his exact words were, *"C'est la vie."* (This is life.)

If this was life, I thought, it was no way to live. Working to stay alive is not the same as working to live, and I wanted to live.

The day came when I was simply unable to will myself to go to work. Thanh went without me and told Madame Binh that I was ill. I stayed in bed for several days, sleeping and crying. It was during this time that the dream to become a nurse resurfaced, and I strengthened my resolve to pursue this goal. By the grace of God I realized this was something I could not do on my own. I needed help.

I made my way to a public telephone and called cousin Nicolas. It had been months since our last conversation, and his upbeat voice heartened my weary soul. He brought me hope when he said that he would gladly look into the process of becoming a nurse.

After dutiful research, Nicolas met me at a coffee shop to share his findings. They were not promising. I would need to become a naturalized French citizen before I would be allowed to attend nursing school, and citizenship would take a minimum of four years. I felt the rug being pulled out from under me. I couldn't wait that long. There had to be another option.

Determined to become a nurse by another route, I wrote to my Auntie Khanh in Australia. I explained the situation and asked for her help. *Would it be possible for a refugee to become a nurse through the Australian education system?* I sent the letter and crossed my fingers.

It had been years since my last correspondence with Auntie Khanh, and I wondered if she would even bother to send me a return letter. If she didn't, I would just add it to the growing list of injuries she had inadvertently inflicted upon me.

While I waited, I picked up housecleaning jobs to make ends meet. Returning to the restaurant to work alongside Thanh was no longer a consideration. Though Madame Binh would have taken me back, I was unwilling to go. The long hours on my feet had been too much, and I realized, unapologetically, that restaurant work would kill me if I stayed on that path.

I decided I needed a back-up plan in case nursing was nothing more than a pipe dream. The community college offered a paid internship program for refugees willing to learn how to solder wires in computer circuit boards. This skill would allow me to earn a decent wage on a factory assembly line. I applied and was accepted into the program.

The months dragged on with no letter from Auntie Khanh. I assumed she had forgotten about me, but that was not the case. She was ardently working on my behalf. Australia had recently relaxed its strict immigration policy and was evaluating potential immigrants for citizenship based on one of two criteria: family reunion and professional expertise in areas where there were gaps in the Australian workforce.[19] Not only was Auntie Khanh my closest family member outside of Vietnam, Australia was experiencing a shortage of medical personnel. These conditions made my move to Australia a possibility.

Through the Catholic Church she attended, Auntie Khanh was able to secure a couple to serve as my sponsors. Harry and Rosie were both doctors and wanted to support a Vietnamese refugee who aspired to work in the medical field. It was the perfect match.

I was over-the-moon excited when I received Auntie Khanh's letter! A door had opened, and all I had to do was walk through it. Though my sponsors were Catholic, this did not inspire me to attend mass. Nor did I consider getting on my knees and thanking God for His blessing. Instead, I dropped out of the soldering program and enrolled in an English language class at the Australian Embassy. After all, I needed to understand the English language to participate in nursing classes. Between work, classes, and study, there was simply no time for God.

My Australian teacher spoke with a dialect that sounded nothing like the American English I had heard in Vietnam. He not only opened my ears to this new language, he also opened my mind to a totally new and unique culture. The pictures of red rocks and the vast outback of red sand ushered me into another world. I marveled at the descriptions of strange wildlife—kangaroos carrying their babies in pouches and vegetarian koala bears nibbling on leaves. What shocked me most of all was learning that seasons below the equator were experienced backwards. I had no idea! Summer was in December, and winter was in July. No wonder Australia was called the Land Down Under. I don't know why, but I had hoped to learn that I would get to experience snow in Australia, so I was a little disappointed when my teacher informed me that flip-flops were the predominant shoe of choice year round. In the end, it didn't matter. The more I learned about Australia, the more excited I was to move there.

When the paperwork and plane ticket—subsidized by the Australian government—arrived several months later, I was ready to go. I told Thanh our separation was temporary, and I sincerely believed it was. Had I considered the move to be permanent, I'm sure I would not have gone to Australia at all. My plan was to quickly acquire a nursing license and return to France to work with the Red Cross in the hopes of traveling around the world to care for other refugees and displaced persons.

Thanh supported my dream by acknowledging that it was a noble endeavor. I believe he was happy for me though it wasn't in his nature to display much emotion. Instead, he demonstrated his support by buying me a new suitcase and a bottle of French wine. "This is the last bottle of French wine you can have," he teased.

The night before I left, we lay on our apartment floor and drank the whole bottle while we reminisced and relived our painful past.

"Life is good," he said in reference to how far we had come in the world.

"Yes," I agreed, "but it is not good enough."

That night, Thanh and I took a bittersweet journey down memory lane, one I will always treasure. We could finish each other's sentences or each other's thoughts when no words would suffice. As the wine dwindled low in the bottle, I suddenly feared I might drift off course without Thanh's constant presence in my life. He calmed my fears by telling me that he thought I was making the right decision. With his support, I knew I could make the move to Australia without him. After all, it was only temporary.

We sat in silence for a few moments, unsure of how to proceed. The reality of having to say goodbye hung over us like a dark cloud. Then Thanh emptied his glass and called it a night.

When I arose the next morning to catch my plane, my brother had already left for work. On the counter was a simple note: *Bon Voyage.*

Minh Phuong, age 1 (1958)

Minh and Thanh (1959)

Left to right: Thanh, Duc, Mom, and Minh (1961)

Back Row: Minh and her father
Front Row: Chau, Dan, Duc, and Thanh (1965)

Minh's mother and Nhu on their wedding day (1970)

Minh with her mother (circa 1973)

Thanh and Minh (circa 1974)

Minh in front of the Sydney Opera House (1977)

Earl and Minh when they met in New Zealand (1981)

Minh on her wedding day with Harry walking her down the aisle (1981)

Minh as a registered nurse and Rosie (1983)

Minh holding Eddie (1988)

Eddie and Emily heading to school (1995)

Minh with Martha (circa 1996)

Jason and Emily's wedding (2001) with Earl, Minh, Emily, and Eddie

Giang, Minh, Thanh, and Duc in France (2002)

Emily and Minh on a mission trip to Vietnam (2009)

Emily and Eddie with Minh on her graduation day,
Pittsburgh Theological Seminary (June 2013)

Michelle Layer Rahal, Paul Towner, and Minh
the day she became a U.S. citizen (Mt. Vernon, Virginia—July 4, 2014)

Minh and Pastor Pete James during her ordination
at Vienna Presbyterian Church (November 18, 2017)

PART III
AUSTRALIA

1977–2006

CHAPTER 22

Friend deceives friend, and no one speaks the truth.
They have taught their tongues to lie;
they weary themselves with sinning.
You live in the midst of deception; in their deceit they refuse to
acknowledge me, declares the Lord.
Jeremiah 9:5-6 (NIV)

April–October 1977

Neither of my aunts was at the Sydney Kingsford Smith Airport to greet me when I arrived in Australia. Instead, a mini-bus driver picked me up and drove me straight to my new living quarters, the Villawood Migrant Hostel located in the industrial section of Sydney.

Villawood was a series of grouped apartment buildings that housed migrants and refugees from all over the world. Residents and their dependents were allowed to stay in the hostel for free for up to a year while they participated in resettlement training and looked for employment. The hostel was conveniently located within walking distance of a number of factories in order to encourage residents to seek jobs that would allow them to contribute to their room and board.

Many residents did indeed obtain employment, but with little oversight they pocketed their earnings rather than turn them over to the government. On the whole, refugees do not spend their earnings on frivolous items. They scrimp and save so they can send money back to family members in their home country who need support to survive.

Unlike France, Australia's resettlement program was quite generous. In addition to having my plane ticket purchased by the government, I was also given food, lodging, and a small stipend. By providing for our basic needs, the resettlement program ensured that participants were able to fully attend to daily lessons in language, etiquette, and culture. In the ten years following the fall of Saigon, Australia would welcome more than 90,000 refugees from Vietnam, Laos, and Cambodia, permanently changing the landscape of Australia's white population.[20]

Not all refugees at Villawood were from Asia. Many came from Western and Eastern Europe, Africa, and South America. It was an eye-opening experience for me to learn that the Vietnamese people were not the only ones in the world suffering hardships and persecution. Though different in backgrounds, we all shared a common bond: a desire for a better life.

I was assigned to an apartment with three young women—one from Russia, one from Cambodia, and one from Laos. With each of us speaking a different language, it made for a rather odd living arrangement. The mismatch was intentional, however; living together forced us to use English to communicate.

We all had our own bedroom, but we shared one bathroom and a communal living space. Unfortunately, there was no kitchen because we were all expected to eat in the large dining hall known as the canteen. The food there was not particularly appealing to me. Lamb, a staple of the Australian diet, was served often and tasted strange to my Vietnamese palate. My Asian companions and I would bring our own spices to the canteen in an effort to mask the taste, but we were only mildly successful. On days when the distinct aroma of lamb wafted across the courtyard, I would do an about-face back to my apartment and make myself three-minute noodles in a Styrofoam cup.

Due to the varied cooking practices of its residents, Villawood would routinely conduct random apartment inspections in search of banned kitchen appliances that were deemed a potential fire hazard—things like electric burners, toasters, and coffee pots. But with lamb being served so often, I was practically forced to purchase a rice cooker so I wouldn't starve to death. My Cambodian roommate and I managed to keep the rice cooker hidden from the authorities during our entire stay at Villawood, and I'm sure we saved the Australian government a chunk of money by regularly skipping dinner at the canteen. Why that place continued to serve lamb when half the residents didn't eat it is beyond me!

Life at Villawood was similar to life on a small college campus. The main focus was education, and everything else we might need or want could be found within the compound. There was a post office, convenience store, recreation hall, sports field, TV hut, and movie theater.

I attended English language classes every morning, afternoon, and evening, though such a rigorous schedule was not required. I spent most nights watching American movies and TV shows like *Bewitched, I Love Lucy, Bonanza,* and *Little House on the Prairie.* I didn't watch because I liked these shows, I watched to learn the language, paying particular attention to the cadence of the actors' delivery. I carried my French-English dictionary everywhere with me. I never left home without it. I would have carried a Vietnamese-English dictionary with me as well, but I could not find one.

Determined to master the English Language, I spoke in English all the time, everywhere and to everyone. Sadly, it was always difficult for the person on the receiving end to understand what I was saying because certain sounds were impossible for me to reproduce—sounds like the hard "r" and soft "s." The muscles in my tongue had simply not been trained to form these sounds that do not exist in Vietnamese speech.

Oftentimes my teacher would ask me to repeat a word after her, again and again. To my Asian ear, I was mimicking her perfectly, like a parrot. However, her repetitive ritual alerted me to the fact that I was not hearing the same articulation she heard. I have come to believe that this is the problem most students encounter when learning a new language: hearing the subtle differences in pronunciation, not learning the words themselves.

In my new environment, I also took to praying in English, though my prayer life was sporadic at best. When I did pray, my prayers were pleas for mastery of the English language. I figured God didn't care how poorly I pronounced the words, and He would understand what I was saying anyway. I wish I had considered attending Catholic mass during this time because that would have provided me with an educational opportunity to hear the rote prayers and responses in English, but worshipping God couldn't have been further from my mind. I was on my own mission that included classes — not church.

My favorite class, by far, was the Australian etiquette class. Though I had been exposed to some Western manners during my years at boarding school, the lessons there had been beaten into me rather than explained. They did not stick. Under the gentle guidance of my etiquette teacher, valuable social skills and proper manners were ingrained in my brain, and these have sustained me well over the years.

For example, I learned that it was never acceptable to barge into a conversation without saying "excuse me" first. This, however, was not the phrase to use when answering a phone. In that case, we were to give a greeting, then state our own name so the caller would know whom he had reached. It is a greeting I still employ today. "Hello. This is Minh Phuong."

One surprising lesson I learned was that it was totally fitting to ask for clarification when confronted with information that did not make sense. We were encouraged to use sentences like "Could you repeat that?" and "I'm not understanding what you mean." Asians don't typically ask for help. That would be rude. Instead, we nod our heads and say, "Yes, yes," as if we perfectly understand the information being relayed, even when we don't.

I also learned that the proper way to end a conversation was by showing appreciation. In other words, we were instructed to say "thank you." I remember one German student asking, "What if the conversation ends badly? Are you still supposed to thank the other person?"

The teacher smiled and kindly informed him that no dialogue should end ever badly and that he should still show gratitude, no matter what course the conversation took. The German student boldly announced that he would do no such thing, and I couldn't help but think that his response was indicative of *his* nation's values.

Another class I enjoyed greatly focused on Australia's cultural norms. The teacher dressed just like my cousin Nicolas—in bell-bottoms, sandals, and tie-dyed shirts. He was several years older than me, yet he insisted that we call him by his first name, Michael. I viewed this as disrespectful; still, I did as I was told.

Michael liked to incorporate American music into our lessons though it had nothing to do with Australian culture. His favorites were Simon and Garfunkel tunes like *Scarborough Faire* and *Cecilia*. He would play 45s on the record player while explaining the words to us. *"You're breaking my heart. You're shaking my confidence daily. Oh Cecilia, I'm down on my knees. I'm begging you please to come home."*

Come to find out, Michael's wife had left him for another man, so he had firsthand experience with such things and was apparently using our class to work through his pain. Nevertheless, I enjoyed the music greatly and found his teaching style quite entertaining.

Michael also offered his students weekend field trips to familiarize us with such places as the Sydney Opera House and the Royal Botanic Gardens. These daylong excursions would involve train travel, which was an education in itself. I remember once watching the landscape pass by as I stared out the window on a particularly long ride; I saw miles of nature unlike any I had ever seen before. There were mountains towering in the distance, houses splattered on barren red soil, and the occasional wallaby. It all looked so peaceful.

Coming upon the city of Sydney for the first time, I was taken aback by the beautiful buildings, clean sidewalks, and well-dressed people who didn't seem to be in any type of a hurry. To me, Australia seemed perfect—a slice of Heaven on Earth.

To round out my educational experience at Villawood, lessons were offered in personal hygiene, a subject as foreign to me as the English language. Here I learned to wash my hands before and after every meal and to wipe them on a towel instead of my clothing. I also learned to blow my nose into a tissue rather than into toilet paper, and that spitting on the street was simply not acceptable under any circumstances. At the time, I couldn't understand why the Australians were so paranoid about germs. After all, I had never gotten sick from communal living, eating scraps from trash bins, or crawling through sewage lines. Later, however, I did come to fully understand the value of all these hygienic habits.

My personal opinions aside, I respected all my teachers and committed every lesson to memory. I always left my classes feeling smarter than when I arrived.

After several weeks at Villawood, Auntie Khanh and Auntie Linh finally came to visit me. I was like a little girl waiting with anticipation at Villawood's gate. As their car pulled up, I began jumping up and down with excitement. They returned the enthusiasm by rolling down the car windows and waving profusely.

Auntie Khanh had aged quite a bit, but Auntie Linh had grown into a lovely young lady, polished and confident. She was only 14 years old when she left Vietnam prior to the fall of Saigon; and from the looks of things, she carried no unpleasant memories to haunt her. Now she was a senior in high school, and though I was several years older, I felt like a child in her presence.

My aunts didn't speak French, and I hadn't mastered English, so we spoke in Vietnamese. I gave Auntie Khanh and Auntie Linh a tour around the campus, showed them my room, and introduced them to every classmate I passed.

Auntie Linh made it a regular practice to visit me on weekends. She would strike up conversations with the most popular girls and the most handsome boys. I was in awe of the way she could ingratiate herself to total strangers. As a result of her visits, I ended up gaining the attention of an outspoken group of boys from Germany that was fluent in French. When they asked me to join them out on the town one night, I accepted and eagerly jumped on the back of one of their motorbikes.

Our destination was an Oktoberfest celebration on the streets of a nearby town. I had never been to a street festival before and was delighted by the live music, high-energy crowd, and overflowing beer. Caught up in the fun of it all, I was soon dancing, conversing, and drinking with abandon. The German boys made sure I always had a full beer in my hand, which I continued to sip throughout the night to show them my gratitude.

I was having a great time, and I loved the attention, but I went too far. The next thing I remember is waking up in my bed, though I had no idea how I got there. I was partially dressed, and my pants were on backwards. When I tried to sit up, a dull pain between my legs alerted me to the horror of what had obviously taken place. I had been raped. Again. I struggled to recall any details that would identify my rapist; none came to mind. The reality was it could have been any one of the German boys—or all of them.

I sat on the edge of my bed; my breath coming in short spurts. The guilt and shame I felt were harder to bear than the physical pain. *What had I done to encourage this?* I had no answer; the evening's events were missing from my memory. I had trusted these boys; they were my peers. *How could they do this to me?* My shame soon turned to anger. I wanted revenge, but I did not know where to begin.

Then another thought rushed through my head. Perhaps it wasn't one of the German boys at all. Perhaps a stranger had brought me home and took advantage of me. *Did I wander away from the group? Did I ask someone else to drive me home?* I just didn't know.

Only one thing was certain: I had no right drinking—I didn't know how. Like the rape I had experienced in France, I accepted the blame. It was my own stupidity that had led me into both predicaments.

In an effort to settle my nerves, I filled the bathtub and slipped beneath the warm water. I seriously contemplated suicide, but I didn't have the courage or the pills to carry it out. I tried to put things into perspective by reasoning that this was a minor offense in comparison to other events in my life. *You've been through worse,* I told myself. *You can get through this. You will survive.* All I needed to do was bury this rape like I buried the last one. Forget it ever happened. With that, I got dressed and headed to class.

Several of the German boys sat up and took quiet notice when I entered the room. Though they said nothing, their cagey glances told me that the rapist was one of them—or all of them. Strangely, I felt detached from the situation, like an observer, not the victim. I averted my eyes and took my seat. My head was spinning and I could not concentrate. I needed to know. I turned to the boy nearest to me and flatly asked, "What happened last night?"

"You got pretty drunk, so we had to take you home," he answered.

They all laughed. This was funny to them. Taking advantage of me was funny to them. My heart began to pound in my ears, and I felt the anger boiling up in my throat like bile. Keeping my voice low, I sternly asked, "Who took me home?"

They looked around and started pointing to each other. Him. No him. The laughter rose again. It was a game. It was all a game, and I was the lone loser.

My voice rising, I demanded, "Who put me to bed?"

Looking to each other for support, they all started talking at once. First they said they all took me to my room, they all put me to bed, and they all left together. I couldn't tell if they were protecting someone or if they were all guilty. I felt sick to my stomach looking at them, so I turned away and faced the front of the classroom. I would not allow them to intimidate me any further. They would not control me. I—and I alone—was in charge of my feelings, not them. I knew how to block out pain. I had had plenty of practice.

The teacher walked in and started class. I focused all my attention on her, intently listening to every word she uttered. I pushed the rape to a far corner of my brain, sealing it with an iron door. Everything would be fine—as long as the iron door to my painful memories held.

When class ended, I picked up my notebook and, without so much as a backward glance, walked out.

CHAPTER 23

...we also boast in our sufferings,
knowing that suffering produces endurance,
and endurance produces character, and character produces hope,
and hope does not disappoint us,
because God's love has been poured into our hearts
through the Holy Spirit that has been given us.
Romans 5:3-5 (NRSV)

1978–1979

They say time heals all wounds. I don't agree. I think time merely alters wounds and changes the person who is housing them. Our only hope for actual healing lies in our willingness to release our pains to the one who died for our sins. Unfortunately, at this time in my life, such a concept was beyond my reach.

No one knew the baggage I carried, and I was hell-bent on keeping it that way. No one knew that I had escaped an abusive uncle, an unloving mother, a Vietnamese jail cell, and poverty in France. I hid the scars of a molested child, a tortured teenager, and a victim of multiple rapes. No one asked, and I never told that I had attempted suicide before the age of ten, slept with a North Vietnamese captain for comfort, and drank my own urine to survive.

I went to great pains to reinvent myself, pretending to be someone I was not. From all outward appearances, I was an upbeat, hardworking Vietnamese refugee from an upper-middle class family who sadly lost everything in the war. The real me, however, was held captive by defeat and regret. In the presence of others, I stuck to pleasant conversations that did not touch on the personal, and I looked for distractions that would occupy my mind so past memories could not creep in. One of these distractions was tennis.

I had never played the game before, but there were several courts at Villawood and plenty of tennis players who were willing to teach the rules of the game. Not one to do anything half-heartedly, I spent many hours on the courts perfecting my swing. It felt good to hit the balls, and within a matter of weeks, I was beating the more experienced players—the more experienced *male* players. Winning gave me a sense of confidence and sparked the beginning of my first real friendships in my new country.

Debbie and Claudia were fellow tennis players. Debbie hailed from South Africa and Claudia from Switzerland. Like me, they had come to Australia in search of a better life. Debbie was loud and smoked like a chimney. Claudia was quiet and levelheaded. By choice, I was somewhere in between.

The three of us became inseparable and pushed the limits of our independence by strutting around campus like we owned the place. Such behavior was empowering. We were three young chicks testing the boundaries and learning how to spread our wings. When we got together, we would laugh until our bellies ached. Never before had I experienced that sensation, and it was the perfect cure for shame-induced nausea. For the first time ever, I felt like I was completely accepted and had nothing to prove.

Just as I was beginning to enjoy life again at Villawood, it was time for me to move on. According to government regulations, refugees could live in Australian hostels for only one year with few exceptions. My biggest fear was being kicked out of my home without a way to support myself. I needed a job.

A government agent named Joyce was assigned to help me with my transition. "What would you like to do?" she asked.

"Anything," I said, "as long as they pay me!"

I did not divulge my desire to become a nurse. Such boldness would have been considered rude by Vietnamese standards. Plus, without any credentials, I simply assumed that I needed to find a job first that would help me pay for nursing school.

"Can you type?" Joyce asked.

I couldn't, but I told her I was familiar with the process and willing to learn. With her connections as a former secretary, Joyce enrolled me in secretarial classes at a community college. She also secured me a part-time job as a secretarial assistant in a legal firm. The best part of this arrangement was that I could remain at Villawood as long as I was enrolled in college classes. The worst part was that I was expected to type in English, which was incredibly difficult because I hadn't yet mastered speaking this language. I still thought in Vietnamese and spoke in French. As a result, I was not capable of producing an error-free paper. It was only a matter of time before I was let go—three months to be exact.

"What *can* you do?" Joyce asked compassionately at our next meeting.

"I know how to take care of people," I told her.

"Sick people?" she asked.

"Yes!" I assured her. *Now,* I thought, *we are closing in on my goal of becoming a nurse.*

Though Joyce had no connections to healthcare or medicine, she had the wherewithal to contact my sponsors who did. Rosie was an anesthesiologist, and her husband, Harry, was a family doctor.

The first time I met Rosie was several days later when she drove into Villawood in her canary yellow BMW to pick me up for an interview with Matron Wheen, the Director of Nursing at the New South Wales Masonic Hospital. I knew I was in trouble the moment Rosie introduced herself because I couldn't understand a word she said. With her thick Australian accent, and my thick Vietnamese accent, no trace of the English language sounded familiar to either of us. Unable to communicate effectively, the hospital interview seemed doomed. But Rosie was very encouraging and spoke to Matron Wheen on my behalf.

I had never been interviewed for a professional job before. Luckily, I knew enough to say "excuse me" before speaking, to blow my nose into a tissue if necessary, and to thank Matron Wheen for her time. When all was said and done, I was offered a job—not as a nurse, but as a nurse's aide. I was thrilled!

At that time, courses to become a licensed practical nurse, or LPN, were taught in hospitals rather than colleges or universities. This meant that I would be working at a hospital that also functioned as a teaching college. With approximately 150 beds, the hospital boasted an Accident and Emergency Unit, an Intensive Care Unit, and a Maternity Unit. It was large enough to present nursing students with a wide range of experiences, but small enough to feel like home.

In addition to classes, the hospital provided its students with lodging and meals. I wasted no time packing my bags and moving into the small, private dorm room in the employee building on the hospital grounds. The hardest part was saying goodbye to Debbie and Claudia. I promised them that I would stay in touch so we could get together for rounds of tennis whenever our schedules aligned.

A typical workday for me at Masonic Hospital ran from 6:00 a.m. to 3:30 p.m. My duties included brewing tea and perking coffee each morning and afternoon, delivering it to all the patients and hospital employees, serving the noon meals, and collecting the dirty trays for kitchen staff to wash. The final chore of the day was the worst, but I performed it with zeal—picking up all the bedpans, emptying them out, sterilizing them, and scrubbing them till they shined.

There were other nurse's aides, but I was the only one in charge of tea, coffee, and bedpans. In reality, I was nothing more than a glorified waitress and janitor. Nonetheless, I felt incredibly privileged to perform the tasks I was given. At the end of each day, Matron Wheen would personally check my work and give me permission to leave. I beamed like a child whenever she complimented my efforts.

Occasionally I would see Rosie as I made my rounds. She always made it a point to ask me how I was doing. My relationship with her, the Chair of the Anesthesiology Medical Board, may have had something to do with why staff always treated me with respect.

At the time, I didn't know about the clout she carried and prefer to think that staff was kind to me because I performed my duties well.

Though I didn't actually tend to the medical needs of the patients, I knew the work I was doing was important and valued. My job as a nurse's aide was my pride and joy, and I wore my uniform like a badge of honor. I felt like I was living a dream come true. I also remember feeling filthy rich when I received my first paycheck, flabbergasted that I would be paid so much for doing so little. Since I was not required to pay for rent or food, I sent most of my earnings to Thanh who would then reroute them to Vietnam. Most of it went to our mother, and the rest went to Captain Quan to pay off my lingering debt.

I managed to save some money for myself with which to purchase a small guitar and a beginner's music book. I had my heart set on learning how to play Simon and Garfunkel tunes. I also purchased a few flowers from a local nursery and planted them outside my dorm window. I thought the guitar and flowers would bring me much joy, but they only brought limited happiness.

I was lonely. I missed Thanh. Though I interacted with staff and patients on a daily basis, I could not call any of them my friend. This was of great concern to Matron Wheen who often encouraged me to make friends with some of the other employees. This was easier said than done. I had nothing in common with anyone, and my broken English kept most people at arm's length. They did not invite me into their social circles. To them, I was an outsider.

I would often call Debbie or Claudia to play tennis, but our get-togethers were infrequent due to our differing work schedules and our dependence on public transportation. I had no choice except to push through my loneliness. In retrospect, I see that this wasn't healthy. I have since come to realize that friends are a necessary ingredient for good mental health. Matron Wheen obviously knew this. When she saw how isolated I had become and how difficult it was for me to make friends, she insisted that I complete my English language certification. "After all," she said, "you cannot enroll as a nursing student at the hospital until you can speak English satisfactorily."

That was all I needed to hear. I immediately enrolled in an English course at the local community college. Though I didn't make any friends there either, I did enjoy the classes, which the Australian government paid for due to my status as a refugee.

English language classes at the community college were nothing like the English language classes back at Villawood. These were more stringent and goal oriented. In other words, they weren't very fun. There were no Simon and Garfunkel tunes to discuss or field trips to the beach. Instead, there were criteria and deadlines to contend with. Certain things had to be learned by a certain date in order to take a certain test. I sincerely enjoyed studying, but I did not like being assessed.

My college language teacher focused on speaking and listening skills with a specific bend toward pronunciation. To ensure our success, she quizzed her students weekly on grammar and spelling. She was driven to make us English literate within two semesters, and I was determined to make her proud. I studied hard and practiced my pronunciation daily, mostly on unwilling patients at the hospital. My efforts paid off. In less than a year, I completed my English language course and passed the English language exam.

Certificate in hand, I approached Matron Wheen and asked, "Now can I start my nursing studies?"

I was enrolled in the LPN program at Masonic Hospital along with six other students who were all several years younger than me. Despite the five to six year age differences, I expected to bond with these young women through our shared goal. That was not to be. Our life experiences were too disparate for us to find common ground. They were silly; I was serious. They looked for ways to shortcut their studies; I used every spare moment to review my notes. They had lives outside of the hospital; I did not. My life was the hospital. They had no compassion for the refugee or under-standing of what it meant to be one. Likewise, I could not identify with their simple, carefree lives.

There was only one nursing teacher assigned to our cohort, and she was tough. Nurse Williams's mission was to drill as much information as she could into our heads in the shortest amount of time possible. She had little tolerance for slow learners—she talked fast and was visibly annoyed by my questions. In truth, I seemed to be the only one asking any. The other girls would whisper behind my back, and that only served to further alienate me from the group.

In time, Nurse Williams came to blatantly favor the younger, Australian students. She would assist them while ignoring my raised hand for help. I tried to demonstrate my commitment to the program by desperately scribbling notes onto my pad of paper, but more often than not they were just that: scribbles. My mind could not comprehend the information Nurse Williams was conveying at the speed with which she was conveying it.

I spent many late nights pouring over my notes, my textbook, and a dictionary attempting to decipher my lecture notes. I was no quitter. I had the most to gain and the most to lose. Madame Paquet had been right—when it came to learning, I was a turtle—slow and steady. Her faith in me was the image that I clung to during those late nights. I knew I would eventually finish the race, though it would be long and difficult.

At the end of two years, I nervously sat for the national LPN exam. The multiple-choice questions were relatively simple, but I struggled to write the essays. Before the test time was up, I knew I had failed.

Several days later, Matron Wheen called me into her office and asked me to sit down. She must have given considerable thought to how she would break the news to me. She began by sharing stories of famous men who had failed in the earlier part of their lives—Einstein, Lincoln, and Monet. I was touched by her attempt to make the information palatable, but I wished she would just drop the bomb and get it over with.

I believe my failure hurt Matron Wheen more than it hurt me. I apologized for falling short of the goal, and I admitted that a nursing career was possibly just my castle in the sky. Matron Wheen would hear none of it. She told me to start studying and get ready for the makeup test that would be administered in six months.

Six months was a short amount of time, especially in light of a greater decision that loomed in front of me: my French residency visa was about to expire. Either I could remain in Australia and continue to pursue a nursing degree, or I could return to France and to Thanh, whom I missed terribly. There was no guarantee that I would pass the next test. If I didn't, I would lose my rights as a French resident and be forced to remain in Australia indefinitely. The pressure was too much to bear on my own. I called Thanh.

"Sister," he said, "if you can become a nurse you will have greater potential in the world. You must stay in Australia and try."

It couldn't have been easy for Thanh to speak those words. He was still working as a cook in Madame Binh's restaurant and had no ambition to pursue anything else. His French was poor, and he made ends meet by sharing an apartment with two other Vietnamese boarders who did not have his best interests at heart. My greatest fear was that Thanh might end up like our Uncle Cuong—cloistered in a cheap apartment, smoking cigarettes, friendless and reminiscing of happier times in Vietnam.

"You can always visit," he said. I could hear it in his voice. He was unhappy and lonely, too.

Having to say goodbye to Thanh just about broke my heart. Staying in Australia was the right decision, but it felt awful. I cried like a baby when we hung up. Our relationship would never be the same. He was there; I was here. The separation in miles and opportunity was vast, and it was permanent, not temporary.

I needed to pass the nursing test, not only for my future but also for Thanh's. He had no dream but mine.

CHAPTER 24

"For I know the plans I have for you," declares the Lord,
"plans to prosper you and not to harm you,
plans to give you hope and a future.
Then you will call on me and come and pray to me,
and I will listen to you.
You will seek me and find me
when you seek me with all your heart."
Jeremiah 29:11-13 (NIV)

1979–1980

Six months after failing the LPN exam, I sat for the test again. I failed. Again. By now it was too late to return to France because my residency visa had expired. I had no choice except to study some more and sit for the exam a third time.

I was angrier than ever with God. The omnipotent creator of the universe surely knew I would fail the test again. Yet He chose not to spare me the grief of failure, nor did He alleviate my loneliness by allowing me to return to my brother in France. Instead, He had the audacity to use Thanh's words to keep me in Australia. *What did He want of me?*

During the day, I continued to work as a nurse's aide making coffee, delivering meals, and cleaning bedpans. Sadly, I no longer found the work rewarding and cringed whenever I thought about doing this the rest of my life. Rosie and Matron Wheen refused to let me fail and offered much needed advice. Rosie suggested that I start paying closer attention to how things operated at the hospital beyond my assigned duties. Matron Wheen blessed her suggestion by ordering me to spend extra time on the hospital floor shadowing the nurses and asking questions of them as they worked.

I came in early and stayed late, observed and asked questions, read and reread my notes—and my efforts paid off. Somewhere and somehow, the information I had learned during lectures started to make sense. I was no longer relying on memory to retrieve answers; I was actually comprehending medical facts. Lo and behold, on the third try I passed the LPN exam and became a licensed practical nurse.

When Matron Wheen shared the assessment results with me, she was as excited as a kid in a candy store. So was I. So was Rosie. I couldn't have done it without either of them. And then it hit me. God apparently had my back after all! He had blessed me by putting these two women in my life—women who believed in me and had been praying for my success.

Rosie was a committed Catholic who went to church every Sunday, and Matron Wheen had once served as a missionary in India. I hadn't been to church in years, and I hadn't asked for God's help with my studies, but Rosie and Matron Wheen had. They had stepped into the gap, thus bridging the link between God and me by interceding on my behalf.

To show my gratitude, I thanked them over and over again, like a broken record. If I had the chance to relive this moment, I would tell them both that I loved them. I loved them for being there for me, for believing in me, and for praying for me. And I loved them for being more than my mentors, for being my surrogate mothers. At the time, words of love were not in my vocabulary, so I gave them my respect instead. They deserved so much more.

My first paycheck as an LPN brought with it a feeling of personal pride and giddy exhilaration. Unfortunately, there were no job openings at Masonic to match my new status. So even though my pay increased, I had to continue working as a nurse's aide. With no indication that a nursing position would come available at Masonic in the near future, Rosie and Matron Wheen advised me to look for employment elsewhere.

In a matter of weeks, I landed a job as an LPN in an adult nursing home. The change in employer meant I could no longer reside in Masonic's dormitory. Before I had a chance to search for suitable housing, Rosie offered me a room in her home.

Back then I considered myself lucky to have Rosie and Harry as my sponsors. Now I know I was blessed. Rosie and Harry not only provided me with free housing, they embraced me as a member of their family. Having no children of their own, they loved me like a daughter—challenging me, nurturing me, and teaching me how to navigate the bumps along the road of life.

It's hard to find the words that accurately describe the sensations I felt living under Rosie and Harry's roof. Bliss. Tranquility. Joy. Unity. In Rosie and Harry's home there was no arguing, no back-stabbing, and no inappropriate behaviors. Only mutual admiration, respect, and love. Their differences were celebrated as assets rather than identified as traits that needed to be changed. Where Rosie was complex, Harry was simple. She examined and investigated every nuance of every situation while he sat back and simply let life run its course. They complemented each other perfectly, and because they loved each other—and God—deeply, they provided me with a glimpse of what a healthy marriage should look like. Until this time, I had been unaware that such loving relationships existed in the world.

Whenever I appeared distressed, Harry would say, "It does you no good to be unhappy. You might as well make the most of your circumstances." He had the uncanny ability to cheer me up when I was down and give me hope that better things were yet to come. Never satisfied with how much knowledge he or anyone else possessed, Harry would routinely quiz me on the names of the bones in the body. This always set me laughing. Then he would call me his "happy little Vegemite," which incited me to deeper laughter. He was unflappable, confident, and kind.

It was Harry who encouraged me to apply for employment at Concord Hospital. His reasoning was sound: if I could get hired as an LPN, I would have the opportunity to enroll in the registered nursing program there. Concord Hospital had a long and respectable history dating back to World War II. In 1963 it became a teaching hospital within the University of Sydney and provided a hands-on nursing experience that could not be rivaled. With more than 700 beds, it was significantly larger than Masonic. A bigger facility meant better pay and greater chance for advancement.

The possibility of becoming an RN felt too big to me, and I told Harry as much. He brushed my concerns aside like unwanted lint. I promised him I would think about it.

Without any exams to study for, Debbie, Claudia, and I were able to start playing tennis again. Occasionally I would complete a foursome for a game of squash with Claudia, her boyfriend, Mario, and his best friend, Angelo—both immigrants from Italy. I didn't particularly like squash, but I liked Angelo.

Angelo was tall, thin, dark, and handsome. He drove a motor-cycle and wore a leather jacket. He was confrontational and insensitive, argumentative and a bit narcissistic. Despite his negative qualities, I found myself attracted to him like a moth to flame. And though I knew he was no good for me, I set my sights on making him my husband. Why I set my sights so low, I do not know. Perhaps I did not think I deserved any better, or perhaps I was simply tired of being single. Now in my early 20s, I was considered an old maid by Vietnamese standards.

Angelo and I were an unlikely pair. Our common bond was that we were both outcasts, immigrants from different countries with thick, foreign accents. English was not our first language, yet that was the language we used to communicate—poorly, I might add.

In the beginning, to demonstrate that I was available, I would show up every time Angelo got together with Claudia and Mario, whether I was invited or not. Over the course of time, Angelo started to include me on weekend outings with a larger group of immigrants that traveled as a pack. Inclusion into this group gave me a sense of belonging, and soon everyone started treating us like a couple. So when Angelo made a move to get me into bed, I went willingly. And once we started sleeping together, I assumed marriage was inevitable even though we did not see eye to eye when it came to relationships.

Angelo told me in no uncertain terms that it was a woman's responsibility to care for her man, and a woman's place was in the home raising babies. He clearly wanted someone who would cook and clean for him and bear his children. I didn't mind cleaning, but I hated cooking, and I wasn't keen on becoming a mother. In spite of the red flags, I was unwilling to walk away from the relationship. Expecting him to change, I demanded that Angelo support me in my desire to further my career.

"You want everything!" Angelo would chide. "Why can't you be happy with what you've got?"

This was a question I could not answer.

The one good thing Angelo did for me was encourage me to drive. Unwilling to teach me himself, I enrolled in driving school. My instructor, Heinz, spoke in a thick German accent that often morphed into German profanities when I took the wheel. In true Minh fashion, I failed the driving test twice. Heinz, exasperated with my performance, told me that I made his record look bad. When I finally passed the test on the third try, he cheerfully stated, "Finally, I get rid of you!" Believe me, I was just as happy to be rid of him.

Angelo, who worked as a mechanic, found me my first car—a light green Leyland Mini with beige vinyl interior. It also boasted a cassette player, and I wore it out playing songs by my favorite band: Air Supply. Now that I had my own wheels, there was no reason for me to remain in Rosie and Harry's home. I was ready to move in with Angelo. He hadn't asked me to move in with him, but he hadn't discouraged the idea either.

When I shared the news with Rosie, she hit the roof. Not only did she look down on premarital living arrangements, she did not approve of Angelo. Though she never said why, I believe she did not consider him a suitable match, mainly because he did not support my pursuit of higher education.

"Why do you need to move in with him?" she asked.

"I thought I could save some money," I lied.

"If you need money, I'll give you money," Rosie declared maternally. "Get your own apartment. I'll help you pay the rent."

Against Rosie's sound judgment, I moved in with Angelo.

I can't honestly say that I was in love with Angelo. He was more like an obsession. I craved him like a diabetic craves sugar. Willing to do whatever it took to make him mine, I pretended to be what he wanted me to be. The stresses of this manipulation thrust me into a vicious cycle: I would binge eat; then I'd starve myself to lose the extra pounds. To numb the pain, I would drink heavily at night. Then Angelo and I would fight, and I'd run to Rosie and Harry's house to escape for a few days.

Rosie would always let me in, but she would give me the cold shoulder and leave the room to avoid speaking to me. Her rejection cut like a knife. Harry, however, always welcomed me with open arms. He filled the role of a father figure in my life by being there for me and listening with love.

After one particularly bad fight with Angelo, I decided to take Harry's encouragement to heart and submit my application to Concord. This would be the first step toward enrolling in the registered nursing program there. Knowing Angelo would never support my efforts to advance my career, I completed the paperwork behind his back. Within weeks, I received a call for an interview and was hired as an LPN floater. My new job would start in a little less than two months.

By now Angelo and I had made up, yet I couldn't bring myself to tell him about my new job. I feared the news might destroy my plans for marriage, and I desperately wanted to marry him! What I needed, I thought, was the support of *his* family. If they accepted me, Angelo would too. So I quit my job at the nursing home and arranged for a month-long trip to Europe. I told Angelo that I was going to visit my brother and would like to take a side trip to Italy to meet his mother, father, and sister. Angelo didn't object and willingly gave me their addresses.

There was no ring on my finger, nor had there been a proposal. Still, in my mind, Angelo and I were as good as engaged.

It has taken me years to come to terms with the manipulative, selfish ambitions I had during this time of my life. I knew from the start that my relationship with Angelo was unhealthy, but I was unwilling to accept this as fact. I justified my actions by telling myself that things would change once we got married. So, I pushed forward, acting as if I held all the cards as well as the acumen to play them.

CHAPTER 25

May my prayer come before you; turn your ear to my cry.
I am overwhelmed with troubles and my life draws near to death.
I am counted among those who go down to the pit;
I am like one without strength.
Psalm 88:2-4 (NIV)

Early 1980

It had been three years since Thanh and I had seen each other. He was still the little brother I so dearly loved though he had not aged well. His clothes hung on his haggard body, and his eyes betrayed a lack of joy as well as a lack of sleep.

No longer a cook, Thanh was now employed as a house painter. The hours were not as grueling, but the work was just as physical. He lived in a small apartment, a poor rendition of the one we once shared together. All he owned was the mattress he slept on and a few sets of clothing. I wanted more for him, so I begged him to return to Australia with me. I even offered him a bed in the apartment Angelo and I shared.

Thanh had no interest in moving. Now that he had learned how to speak in French, he considered France his home. "Besides," he said, "my birthday is July 14—French Independence Day. The whole country celebrates my birthday! What else could I ask for?"

I told him it was painful for me to accept his response. "Minh Phuong," he said, "lighten up!"

I couldn't say with certainty that Australia was my home, but I knew beyond a shadow of a doubt that France never would be. I had built a respectable life for myself in the Land Down Under. I had hopes and aspirations while Thanh had none. My visit with him was sad and sobering.

I spent the second half of my vacation in Italy with Angelo's sister in her college dorm room followed by several days with Angelo's parents at their home. They were all very kind to me and quite happy to learn that Angelo was planning to settle down. However, they expressed surprise over the fact that he hadn't mentioned anything about marriage to any of them. When asked whether we had set a wedding date, I said we were considering the early spring. When his mother beamed with happiness, I interpreted this as the stamp of approval I was looking for.

I had not spoken to Angelo even once during my vacation; this was not considered strange in the years before cell phones. Like the saying goes, "absence makes the heart grow fonder," and I hoped that Angelo had missed me as much as I had missed him. I couldn't wait to jump into his arms and discuss our wedding plans when I returned to Sydney.

I exited the airport to find Claudia and Mario waiting for me. "Where's Angelo?" I asked.

"He had to work," Mario answered.

They took me back to their apartment and insisted that I spend the night with them. The next morning when Angelo had still not put in an appearance, it became clear to me that something was terribly wrong. Carefully choosing his words, Mario explained that Angelo did not want me back in the apartment because he thought it best to terminate our relationship.

I was in shock. This was not supposed to happen. A breakup was not in the plan. We were to get married in the spring!

I slept on Claudia's couch for three days with my apartment key burning a hole in my pocket. I kept expecting Angelo to show up once he had to come to his senses. When it became obvious that he was not about to change his mind, I headed to the apartment to pack up my belongings. Claudia insisted that she go with me to help. Secretly, I think she wanted to make sure I didn't damage the place in a fit of revenge.

The first thing that hit me when I unlocked the door was the perfume of another woman. Then I saw her clothes everywhere. They were clothes I had seen before on someone I knew. I was finding it hard to breathe. Humiliated, I turned to Claudia and asked, "Is Angelo sleeping with someone else?"

Claudia broke down in tears. "Angelo and Debbie are together. I should have told you before you left for France. I'm so sorry!"

Claudia kept talking, but I had tuned her out. She and Mario had known about the relationship. They could have protected me from making a fool of myself in front of my brother and Angelo's parents, except they didn't. They were as much to blame as Angelo and Debbie. My life was a sham.

Claudia told me I could stay at her place as long as I needed. I didn't want to stay with her; she had betrayed me. Harry and Rosie would have taken me in, but I was too embarrassed to ask, and there was no one else. Reluctantly, I returned to Claudia's apartment and slept on her couch for several weeks until a room opened up in the dormitories at Concord Hospital.

Work was a welcomed reprieve from the realities of my life. The staff at Concord warmly welcomed me as a new member of their professional team, and I was not ostracized for my strange accent. Having now entered the professional world, I was no longer considered a peon of low social standing.

As an LPN floater, I was assigned to different areas of patient care each day. I was never bored, and the change in scenery helped to improve my spirits. Best of all, Rosie was back on speaking terms with me now that I had separated from Angelo and was living at Concord. We would pass each other in the hallways and Rosie would always acknowledge me warmly, which was a great boost to my fragile ego.

Regrettably, I could not stop thinking about Angelo. I foolishly hoped that he would call to tell me that he had made a mistake and wanted me back in his life. To keep my mind off him, I threw all my energy into work.

My performance gained the attention of the hospital manager, and within months I was promoted to a permanent LPN position in the operating arena. My main duty was to monitor the phones in the office outside the operating rooms and obtain instruments for the surgeons as needed. This allowed the doctors to complete a surgery with little interruption while maintaining contact with their personal office staff offsite. The position, however, posed serious obstacles for me because it relied heavily on clear communication, and my English abilities were still quite limited.

One day the phone rang, and the voice on the other end said, "Dr. Smith." I told the gentleman to hold on.

Getting out of my chair, I proceeded to enter each operating room in search of a Dr. Smith. With the surgeons changing on a daily basis, I rarely knew who was behind each surgical mask, and I didn't like to ask. Several minutes later I came to the conclusion that the caller had the wrong number.

I picked up the phone and informed the man that there was no one in any of the operating rooms by the name of Dr. Smith. The voice screamed back at me, "I AM DOCTOR SMITH!"

I thought for sure I was going to lose my job, but I didn't.

Another time during a vascular surgery, a doctor gave me this order: "Get me a pack of peanuts."

I had never had a doctor order food before, and I was unsure of how to accommodate him. Frantically, I left the operating room and found an orderly. "Get me a pack of peanuts!" I yelled. "In fact, get me two."

While the orderly made the run to the nearest vending machine, I began to worry about how to sterilize the peanuts for the operating room. I did the best I could. I wiped down both packets with disinfectant. Then I stood at the door waiting for the doctor to notice me. When he looked up, I held up the peanuts, unsure whether it was safe to get any closer to the patient with food products. The surgeon looked at me confused, brow furrowed above his surgical mask. Then he gave me a very clear directive.

"Get those out of here! Call Nurse Shipton and ask her for a packet of peanuts!"

Nurse Shipton was in charge of sterilized supplies. It never dawned on me that she might already possess sterile peanuts. As I left the operating room, I heard the doctor ask, "Who is that idiot nurse?" He was right. It was stupid of me to purchase peanuts on my own to take into surgery. Such an error could have been fatal!

I called Nurse Shipton and requested two packets of peanuts. Moments later the materials arrived via the lift. Imagine my shock when I discovered that peanuts are small cotton swabs used to soak up blood and fluids during some vascular surgeries. This was not something I had been taught at Masonic.

Once again, I thought I would lose my job, but I didn't. The experience did, however, teach me a valuable lesson in communication. It was one I had been taught during culture classes at Villawood, though I apparently hadn't taken it to heart. *Always ask for clarification when confronted with information that does not make sense.*

Truly, it's a miracle I survived in the operating theater.

Rosie used to encourage me to read the newspaper daily as a means of improving my English. Whenever I would visit, she would hand me an edition. One day I found an ad that read, "Want to meet pen pals from all over the world?" I did, but only if they spoke French. It had been years since I had corresponded with a pen pal, and I hoped the distraction would take my mind off Angelo. I filled out the form, paid the initiation fee, and waited. A few weeks later I started receiving letters. I chose to respond to just one man: Simon. He was Swiss, spoke French, and worked as an engineer for an oil company on a rig in the middle of the Pacific Ocean.

In a strange sort of way, Simon became my rock, the listening ear I so greatly needed. I told him about my job and the struggles I had with the English language. I told him what I missed about Vietnam and what I knew of France. I told him all about Australia and how difficult it was to assimilate into the culture. My six-page letters elicited two-page responses. Still, I appreciated the fact that he was diligent in corresponding.

A couple of months after arriving at Concord, I was called in for an interview for admission into the RN program. An intimidating group of professionals confronted me: the Director of the Hospital Board, a staff psychologist, the Director of Nursing, and the Director of the Nursing School. I tried to remain calm and answer their questions thoroughly and succinctly, but I was a nervous wreck.

Several days later I was informed that I was not qualified to be an RN. I was sure the decision was based either on my misunderstanding of surgical peanuts or my poor English pronunciations. It wasn't. It was based on my status as a wartime refugee. The news shed light on the reasoning behind certain questions I had been asked during my interview, such as "Do you still have nightmares about the war?" I had responded, "I have restless nights, but not nightmares." Come to find out, that answer alone deemed me unfit to work as a registered nurse.

It wasn't fair, and I approached the Director of Nursing to tell her how I felt. She listened and took my concerns back to the committee. I was proud of myself for speaking up and hoped the committee members would change their minds. Several days later I was given an ultimatum: if I could pass all the entrance exams within the first three months, I would be admitted into the RN program. If I did not pass, I would not be allowed to reapply ever again and would remain in employment at Concord as an LPN.

I accepted the challenge. I had no other choice.

There were five tests in all. I spent each day asking the RNs on the floor every relevant question imaginable, and I spent my evenings buried in my textbooks. The only time God entered my consciousness was when I would occasionally squeeze in a prayer for success.

One by one I passed each test, thus proving that I was a fit candidate for the RN program. The ordeal, which exhausted me physically and mentally, also empowered me. I was no longer the victim of circumstance—I was the architect of my destiny.

Strengthened by my accomplishment, I called Angelo to share the news. *If only he could see how well I am doing,* I thought, *he would want me back.*

Angelo agreed to visit me in my dorm room. I had decorated the place nicely and had put on one of my better dresses. My stomach was in knots as I waited for his arrival. When he knocked, I immediately jumped up to welcome him in.

Angelo did not look happy to see me. Without even stepping into the room, he said, "Debbie and I are going to get married."

I couldn't believe what I was hearing. "Are you sure?" I asked. Then I added, "She smokes."

"I know," he said. Then he turned around and left. That was it. He just walked away.

I was devastated. Angelo was choosing an uneducated, loud-mouthed smoker over me. I couldn't fathom his rationale. He had come all the way over to my dorm to stab me in the heart. I slowly stepped back into my room and crumpled to the floor in tears.

Behind the closed door I felt more alone than ever. I may have been accepted into the RN program, but I felt like a failure. I was unlovable.

With each passing day, I slipped deeper and deeper into despair finding it harder and harder to focus at work after a fitful night of sleep. Perhaps I was not cut out to be an RN after all. Perhaps I was not worthy of such a vocation. What was the point anyway if I would never be loved?

I began to collect pills. Any pills would do. Allergy pills. Sleeping pills. Pain pills. I needed enough to make a potent sedative that would put me to sleep forever. By the end of the week, I had an extensive collection. My plan was to consume all of them on Friday night to ensure my death by Saturday morning.

Friday finally arrived. As soon as my shift ended, I hurried to the dorm and washed all my clothes and tidied up my room, as I did not think it right to leave a mess for someone else to clean up. Then I sat on the edge of my bed and began swallowing the pills. I was perfectly calm with what I was doing and entirely sure of its success.

I started consuming several pills at a time until I started to choke when memories of my childhood attempt at suicide invaded my thoughts. Determined to complete the task, I switched to swallowing just one pill at a time. It took me a while to finish the whole batch. Once I did, I took a shower and dressed nicely so I would look presentable when I was found dead.

Before I lied down to die, I wrote a note to Thanh.

Dear Thanh,
I am glad you decided to stay in France rather than come to Australia. Often in search of our dreams, we land in the wrong place. I am in the wrong place. Don't worry about me though. I will watch over you now and be closer to you than ever. Please forgive me. I am sorry I left you to pursue my own happiness. With love, your sister,
Minh Phuong

Around 2:00 a.m. I woke up and went to the bathroom. I was somewhat shocked that I was able to urinate with complete clarity. I did notice that my urine was dark and smelled like ammonia, which was a byproduct of the medications. Otherwise, I felt fine. I told myself the pills had obviously not kicked in yet and that I just had to give them more time.

I ended up sleeping all day on Saturday, and then awoke on Sunday with excruciating stomach pain. That's when I realized that I was not going to die after all. It would have been risky to take myself over to the emergency room to have my stomach pumped, so I spent the next several hours hunched over my toilet instead, sticking my fingers down my throat till I gagged and threw up. I did this again and again. I was so disappointed in myself. I couldn't even commit suicide correctly!

Later that day, I decided to get some fresh air to help clear the feeling of nausea. While walking around the parking lot, I bumped into a nursing colleague who was returning from church. "You look hideous!" Neville exclaimed.

I told him I was sick and depressed, suffering from a broken heart. And then I promptly broke into tears.

Neville sat me down on a nearby set of stairs. He listened as I sobbed on about my pathetic life. He didn't ask any questions, nor did he offer any words of advice. He just listened. When I was all talked out, Neville told me he was going to pray for me.

At first I found his response to be disappointing. I wanted to be held, physically comforted; but as he prayed, a peace washed over me that was calming and strange. It was as if I had been lifted out of my aching body. I was vaguely aware that something had changed inside me because I no longer felt like I wanted to die, and I no longer wanted Angelo back. I could see clearly that he was not the right man for me. Of course, he had told me as much—Angelo had said that he wanted a woman who would cook and clean and bear his children. He did not want an independent woman like me, one who put her career above him.

I had not heard him then, but I heard him now.

The tears stopped as suddenly as they had started. Neville gave me his phone number and told me I could call him anytime if I needed to talk. I never did.

CHAPTER 26

Get rid of all bitterness, rage and anger,
brawling and slander, along with every form of malice.
Be kind and compassionate to one another,
forgiving each other, just as in Christ God forgave you.
Ephesians 4:31-32 (NIV)

March 1980–January 1981

Thirty students entered into the grueling pace of the RN program at Concord. Leftover military influences from its glory days as an army hospital were evident in the program's strict rules and rigid expectations. Everything had to be perfect, down to the 90-degree angles on the corners of the bed sheets. The program was lovingly referred to as "slavery" because of the way students were required to respond to orders without question.

My fellow classmates and I were split into groups that worked and studied in cycles. Several weeks of classes were followed by several weeks of hands-on practice. At the end of each day, all the student groups would meet up to discuss our experiences, share our struggles, and eat a meal together.

I loved the camaraderie of the program. We functioned like a herd of cattle, moving in the same direction and refusing to accommodate stragglers. We were all responsible for one another's progress. This was especially helpful in the days leading up to an exam when we gathered to quiz and strengthen each other. On testing day, students would pass around encouraging notes that read "Good luck" and "You can do it!" If one of us failed, we all failed. The success of the group was more important than the success of the individual. As a member of this elite and loyal team, I felt like I belonged to something quite extraordinary.

My closest friend was an older woman who had already had a full career. Zuzana, a single mother with two young children, had worked for years as a registered nurse in her home country of Czechoslovakia, but her qualifications did not meet Australian standards. Though Zuzana's understanding of medical processes and procedures greatly overshadowed mine, we connected through our struggles as immigrants. English was not our first language, and we had to work twice as hard as everyone else to stay in the game. Zuzana pushed me hard to memorize what was needed for each exam, even if I didn't entirely understand the reasoning. When I wanted an explanation, I would bombard Zuzana with questions that could push her to the point of exasperation.

"Who cares?" she would yell in her thick Eastern European accent. "Just memorize the right answer so you can pass the exam!"

Zuzana did not tolerate fools well, and when I got too caught up in the details, she would remind me that I was my own worst enemy. "Why do you have to complicate your life?" she would ask. "If there is a shortcut, just go for the shortcut!"

I lived vicariously through Zuzana. She was just the type of friend I needed and everything I wanted to be — self-confident, strong, and smart. Whereas I looked at life like a puzzle to be solved, she looked at life like a party to be experienced. She had a wicked sense of humor that she liberally laced with cusswords. Sometimes she used profanities just to make me squirm. Then she would laugh like a hyena.

One thing that cracked us both up was the titles we used to address our teachers. "Mister" preceded the names of the male instructors, while "Sister" preceded the names of the female instructors. At first, I thought all the female instructors were nuns until I saw one of them kissing a man. Zuzana would say, "Only in Australia!"

During our first year of RN classes, we studied microbiology and germs, the cardiovascular system, the respiratory system, and anatomy. Physiology, which addressed how the body's organs and systems worked together, was my most memorable class. I distinctly remember the lesson where I finally learned the truth about the birds and the bees. My teacher, Sister Robertson, used an overhead projector to show us pictures of a woman's uterus and a man's scrotum. It was both fascinating and embarrassing to watch as she animated the lesson for us by drawing on her transparencies as she explained sexual intercourse.

"This is what happens," she said. "The sperm is all revved up, running around in the scrotum. The man is having a great time. Then the sperm shoots out through the penis into the woman's vaginal canal."

Sister Robertson enthusiastically drew the ejaculation process to the squeals of the students. Then she illustrated how the sperm attached itself to an egg. By this time, everyone in the class was laughing. Everyone except me. I had never given much thought to how babies were made, and now I knew more than I cared to know. Images of my parents having sex flashed through my head uncontrollably. This kind of information, I surmised, should only be told behind closed doors in gender-specific settings.

The whole lesson was rather shocking, and I questioned whether it was entirely true. I had heard that Sister Robertson was previously employed as a lawyer, so there was a slight possibility that she had fabricated the reproduction process for our enjoyment. Nonetheless, I took furious notes in case we were tested on the material later.

I loved classes with Sister Robertson because she was full of energy and brought vivid life to each lecture. I can still see in my mind's eye the lesson she taught on tracheotomies where she intensely described how she had once performed an emergency surgery at a bus stop in the Caribbean Islands using the barrel of a ballpoint pen. Her rendition of the incident had her grabbing a pen from her purse, pulling out the ink chamber, and jabbing the clear outside cylinder into the man's throat to create a passage through which the air could flow.

I later heard that this story had circulated as a tall tale across the globe and that Sister Robertson had merely adopted it as her own. Whatever the case, it created the desired effect. If you had been able to look around the room during that lesson, you would have seen mouths agape and eyes wide open in awe and reverence. I was sure that my teacher on Infection Control would not have been pleased with the instruction we received that day even though Sister Robertson did tell us that such a procedure should only be attempted in emergency situations.

The rhythm of the educational process, the captivating lessons, and the support of my classmates and friends strengthened my resolve. There was simply no way I would not achieve RN status. Failure was not an option. I remember thinking that this was the happiest time of my life. Restless nights were at an all-time low, and thoughts of suicide did not seep into my mind. Then I received a letter from my mother that rocked my world and reminded me that no matter how far I went in life, I could not escape my past.

The letter read: *My husband left me. I do hope that Bernadette will help him if he contacts her.* Translation: Nhu had possibly made it out of Vietnam and could be on his way to Australia.

As I read the note, I felt my chest constrict and I gasped for air. My visceral response caught me off guard. Being in the medical profession, I wondered why this information triggered a physical reaction in me. I considered asking Zuzana but decided against it. There were some things that were best left hidden.

Try as I might, I could not shake the weight of the letter from my mind. It crept into my consciousness at the most inopportune times and began to affect my ability to concentrate in class. Questions ran unceasingly through my brain. *Had Nhu actually escaped? If so, how? Why wasn't my mother with him?*

At first, sleep was my only protection from haunting flashbacks. Eventually, I was robbed of that when I began to have unsettling dreams of being lost at sea or locked in prison. Memories I had buried were surfacing against my will.

I cursed my mother for writing me the note. She had two sisters living in Australia; she could have reached out to one of them. She knew how I felt about Nhu. I did not want him in Australia.

Zuzana knew something was wrong, but she didn't probe. I think she suspected it was a new love relationship because I remember her telling me, "Minh, do not let men control you!" Though she was always able to make me laugh, the dark memories of my earlier life continued to wreak havoc on my psyche. I desperately wanted to be a compassionate nurse who would never wish ill on anyone, but I found myself hoping that Nhu would just disappear in the South China Sea.

The letter I hoped never to receive showed up in my mailbox several weeks later. Nhu had sent it from a refugee camp in Malaysia. In it he described the harsh living conditions and oppressive lifestyle he and my mother were forced to endure under communist rule. Until that moment, I had no idea how difficult life had been for those who were left behind. Nhu also informed me that the government had confiscated much of the money I had sent to my mother over the years. It was deeply disappointing to realize that all the sacrifices I had made to financially support my family had been for naught.

Nhu's letter then shifted to a plea for forgiveness. He reminded me that we had both led terrible lives in Vietnam. As Christians — and family — we needed to forgive and forget in order to move forward. I heard the sincerity in his words, but forgiveness was not his to offer. I took my time in responding. When I finally did, my letter was short and to the point.

> *We cannot change the past, and I will always remember what you did. However, you need not worry that I won't sponsor you. I will help you because you are my mother's husband, and it is my responsibility as my mother's child to respect her wishes.*

I dropped the letter in the mail. Then I called the immigration office in Sydney and explained the situation. They sent me some forms, which I filled out and submitted with a small application fee. One of the questions on the form asked whether the refugee would be sheltered in the sponsor's home or in a hostel. I checked hostel. I also had the option of selecting the location of the hostel. I chose the one in Wollongong City because it was over an hour's drive from where I lived and worked.

The situation with Nhu distracted me from my studies and continued to affect my sleep. As the first-year exams approached, I worried whether I would be able to pass them. I had to remind myself that my priority was passing the exams, not tending to Nhu's needs.

Several weeks later, I received a letter from the Australian government informing me of Nhu's arrival date. I was relieved to learn that I was under no obligation to see him once he arrived. I did not even have to pick him up from the airport. This information brought me incredible relief. The nightmares subsided, and I was able to apply my full attention to preparing for the upcoming exams.

Late one night, after consuming several glasses of wine with Zuzana while we quizzed each other on medical terminology, she made an announcement. "I want to have a holiday," she said. "Are you interested?"

My whole life had been all work and no play. A holiday sounded extravagant, mainly because we weren't even halfway through the RN program. "Do you think we should?" I asked.

"Hell, yes!" Zuzana responded. "We deserve it."

I had to agree. I *did* deserve a holiday.

Zuzana found us the perfect trip: a bus tour across New Zealand that was designed for singles. I would use the money I had been saving to send to my mother to pay for my first real vacation. I nervously pulled the cash out of the bank and went with Zuzana to a travel agent to book our trip.

The excursion was billed as a fourteen-day adventure for single men and women to experience the country while looking for the partner of their dreams. That sounded good to me. I was ready to be married. I was tired of caring for myself. I wanted a man I could lean on for protection and support, someone I could trust. At age 25, I was already old by Vietnamese standards.

Zuzana, on the other hand, was spoken for. Though not married, she was in a committed relationship with her boyfriend with whom she had been living for several years. "Does Robert know you are planning to take a trip for singles?" I asked her.

"Hell, yes!" she said. "Robert would rather I party with single men than married men. Ha! Besides, this trip is all about you. We need to find you a man!"

I appreciated her intentions, but I worried that the man of my dreams might not sign up for this particular trip. If the goal was to find me a husband, I thought it best to stock the bus with men I was interested in. There were only two.

The first was Jasper, a friend of Mario and Claudia's that I had met years earlier. Jasper was a tall, skinny, Swiss fellow with a great sense of humor. "Look me up if you ever come to New Zealand," he had once told me. I had not been attracted to him at the time; anything was possible now. I sent Jasper my itinerary and asked him to catch up with the bus somewhere along the route if he was able.

The second person I reached out to was Simon. In his latest letter, Simon stated that he would soon be on leave from the research station. He wanted me to come to Switzerland to meet his family. I wrote back and told him that I already had vacation plans. Then I invited him to join me on the trip across New Zealand, and I included my itinerary as an incentive.

Zuzana hit the roof when I told her that I had extended invitations to Jasper and Simon. "Men are idiots," she said. "We can't let any bloody men come between us on this trip!" I assured her that that wouldn't happen. However, her response confused me. I was under the impression that this trip was all about finding me a husband, not partying with Zuzana.

Exam week finally arrived. In spite of myself, I passed every test. So did Zuzana. There was much celebrating to be done. Zuzana and I packed our bags and headed to the airport to begin our much-deserved holiday.

CHAPTER 27

Be careful, or your hearts will be weighed down with carousing,
drunkenness and the anxieties of life,
and that day will close on you suddenly like a trap.
For it will come on all those who live on the face
of the whole earth.
Luke 21:34-35 (NIV)

January 1981

Zuzana and I were as giddy as schoolgirls from the minute we left Sydney to our arrival in Christchurch, New Zealand. The laughing stopped when we went to board the tour bus. There, standing in line for the trip, was Simon. He had flown all the way from Switzerland to accompany me on this trip. Even though I had invited him, I didn't really expect him to show up. Perhaps I should have been flattered by his appearance, but I was disappointed.

It took me only minutes to figure out that Simon was not my type. Narcissistic and aloof, his somber demeanor darkened my bright attitude. He was not there for fun; he was there for conquest. He was not interested in wooing me; he was planning to seize me as his wife. Simon wanted nothing to do with the other passengers, and he practically shunned Zuzana when I introduced him to her. He couldn't be bothered with anyone else. He wanted me.

"You can entertain him if you want," Zuzana said, "but I'm having a good time."

Throughout the trip, Simon snapped pictures on his 8mm camera and took copious notes about everything he saw. At first I thought it was for posterity's sake. Later, I realized the practice protected him from having to interact with people. No one wanted to interact with Simon anyway. In his self-assigned seat on the bus, he would spread a small cloth napkin out on his lap and nibble on chunks of stinky cheese that he had brought with him from Europe. The smell had an adverse affect on the passengers. I overheard one person ask with an air of disdain, "Does he have to eat that smelly stuff on the bus?"

Since I had invited Simon, I felt it was my responsibility to tell him what others thought. "Simon," I said, "the cheese you are eating has a terrible smell and is offending the other passengers on the bus."

He didn't care. "It is my right to eat cheese," he replied.

Simon was more than a rigid engineer; he was an eccentric. Completely lacking in social skills, he did not belong in the company of others. The best place for him was on an oilrig in the middle of the ocean, by himself. I felt obligated to pay him some attention; however, the more attention I gave him, the more possessive he became and the less I wanted to be around him. I found myself looking forward to the end of each day when Zuzana and I could just lock ourselves in our hotel room far away from Simon.

It had been a huge mistake to send Simon an itinerary. I feared the other passengers might ostracize me if they discovered my role in his presence. That would truly ruin the trip; but everything changed when Jasper drove up on his motorcycle on day three.

I had just stepped off the bus at one of our scheduled stops when I felt someone grab me and spin me around. Jasper's playful attitude was a welcomed change from Simon's austere temperament.

Jasper did not join the tour; he offered me a new one. Each morning he'd show up after breakfast at the hotel du jour. Instead of getting on the bus with the other passengers, I would jump onto the back of his motorcycle. Jasper took me to places a bus would not dare go, and we ate at obscure little rest stops along the way.

Each evening he would drop me off at the next hotel where the bus had parked for the night. Then I would find Zuzana, and together we would share our stories of the day over a glass of wine before falling asleep.

One place I fondly remember visiting with Jasper was the Hole in the Rock at Piercy Island off the north coast of New Zealand. Standing on the mainland, we had a clear view of the uninhabited island, which is nothing more than a sheer cliff with an opening at sea level—just large enough for jet skis to pass through. The hole in the rock was created by centuries of wind and waves. It was truly breathtaking.

Looking out over the vast waters made me feel small and insignificant. I remember Jasper putting his arm around me and pulling me close as we gazed out across the ocean. I instinctually leaned against him and felt content. Caught up in the moment, I imagined myself married to Jasper. I asked, "What do you see in your future?"

He told me he wanted to be married and have a ton of kids. Though motherhood did not really appeal to me, I found myself strangely attracted to Jasper and wondered what it would be like to raise a family with him. Jasper wasn't incredibly handsome, but he was naturally charming, easy to talk to, and kind.

That night, I confessed to Zuzana that I thought I was falling for Jasper. She told me I was crazy. "He's too nice," she promptly assessed. "Something is wrong with him."

The next day I discovered what was wrong. Jasper was a practicing Mormon. Unfamiliar with Mormonism, I asked him to explain his religion to me. He was happy to do so. Jasper talked for a long time, but the only thing I remember learning was that Mormon men could have several wives. This information made me want to run away. I wanted only one husband, and I was sure I wanted a husband who wanted only one wife. Jasper's attempts to assure me that he wasn't really interested in having multiple wives did not take root. I had already checked out, and I asked him to take me back to the bus.

Simon was thrilled to see me back. "Now that he's gone," he said referring to Jasper, "let's leave the tour. We can drive around and see the sites on our own."

His offer was less than enticing. I told Simon, as kindly as I could, that I was not interested in spending time alone with him, that he was not my type, and that I was sorry I had misled him. Simon didn't take my apology well. He got angry. He said some choice words, called me a few disrespectful names, accused me of leading him on, and then promptly left the tour. I felt terrible until I realized that all the passengers on the bus were grateful for his departure.

Simon and I never wrote to each other again. In fact, the experience left such a bad taste in my mouth that I vowed never to respond to pen pal correspondence ads in the future. I just didn't need the headache.

During my days away from the tour group, additional passengers had joined the excursion. The women greatly outnumbered the men with odds at six to one. They were a competitive group and uninterested in forming friendships. Like me, they only wanted one thing—to find a husband.

We must have been a desperate lot. To this day I can still remember the names of all the men. First there was the bus driver, Jim. He was a quiet man who seemed uninterested in any of the ladies, so I could only assume that he was already spoken for, like Zuzana. Then there was Jack, a psychologist from Australia who was a non-stop talker. I couldn't help but wonder if he ever allowed his clients a chance to speak. I avoided Jack and prayed I would never have the misfortune of running into him when I returned to Sydney. Rene was a local New Zealander, commonly referred to as a kiwi, which is a flightless bird native to the island. Rene wore the same baseball cap every day, which was covered in stupid little pins. It looked awful, and I imagined the inside stained with perspiration.

Another man who also wore a baseball cap was Earl; his, however, wasn't covered with silly paraphernalia. He was tall and fair—the most decent-looking guy of them all, even though he was in desperate need of a tan. Earl had a hug and a cheerful "good morning" for every woman on the bus. This acquired him the name of Cuddle King. Earl was acutely aware that he was the most popular man in the group, and that bothered me. Whenever I saw him coming, I'd turn the other way.

Though I was not attracted to any of the men on the bus, they seemed to be interested in me. Maybe it was because I was the only Asian, or maybe it was because I was the most outspoken. Whatever the reason, I was grateful for Zuzana's presence because the other women would have devoured me without her. I had a tendency to read into every situation and worried about what others thought of me. Zuzana couldn't have cared less. She was entirely comfortable in her own skin—derogatory comments and piercing glances never bothered her.

The trip ended with two days and nights on the beach. After the first day of sun and surf, we spent the night around a large campfire drinking gin and tonics. The more we drank, the chummier we all got. Now that the trip was coming to a close, even the other women became friendly. Time flew, and we dragged ourselves to our cabins, drunk and happy, just as the sun was coming up.

I remember thanking Zuzana for planning our holiday and for teaching me how to play. Free from the demands of work and school, I felt refreshed and energized.

The last night of our trip was simply a repeat of the night before. When the gin ran out, one of the men suggested we play spin-the-bottle. Normally, the object of the game is to force participants to kiss each other. The thought of kissing some of these men was repugnant to several of us, so one of the women suggested a variation on the game: whoever was at the end of the bottle when it stopped spinning would have to take off a piece of clothing. We were all drunk enough to think this was a good idea—all except Zuzana. She wisely excused herself saying she did not want to be hung-over for the trip home. I considered accompanying her back to our cabin, but decided against it. I was having too much fun, and I wasn't worried about losing. In total, I was wearing about seven pieces of clothing, not counting my socks.

Earl sat next to me during the game. I hadn't paid much attention to him during the entire trip. However, the more I drank, the better he looked. The bottle twirled. Someone removed a sandal. The bottle twirled again. A T-shirt came off. The spinning went on and on. I thanked God each time I was spared. The game progressed quickly. It wasn't long before some of the women were as naked as jaybirds. I, on the other hand, was still safely wearing my shorts and two T-shirts.

Then someone noted the time. Hot water got turned off at midnight, so if anyone wanted a warm shower, it was time to go. The showers were not free, but they were cheap. The game came to an abrupt end as everyone picked up their clothing and ran to their cabins for cash, soap, and shampoo.

Several people boarded the bus the next morning either hung over or suffering from guilt and regret. They slipped quietly into bus seats and hid behind their sunglasses. When Zuzana took advantage of a bathroom break, Earl slid into the seat next to me. Our conversation flowed more easily than I expected as I learned his story.

Earl had dual citizenship in both New Zealand and the United States. While visiting his uncle in New Zealand earlier in the year, Earl was informed that the company he worked for back in the U.S.A. had folded. This left him without a job to return to. Earl was not particularly crushed about his change in circumstance. Instead of boarding the next plane back to America, he signed up for the singles' bus tour.

I found myself intrigued with Earl's knowledge of the world and his untroubled attitude about losing his job. An incident like that would have pushed me over the edge, but Earl seemed to take it all in stride. He was not the showoff I had made him out to be. He was smart and easy going. Quite likeable.

Before we got to the airport, our bus driver pulled into a souvenir shop where we were encouraged to deplete our New Zealand currency. I roamed around the store looking at kiwi scarves, kiwifruit body lotion, and posters of kiwis when I spotted Earl looking at jewelry under a glass case. Suspecting he might have a girlfriend, I asked, "What are you looking for?"

"Something for my sister," he responded. Pointing at a pair of opal earrings, he asked, "What do you think of those?"

I peered into the case and evaluated the iridescent stones mounted in gold. They were lovely, and I told him so. Earl bought the earrings. The purchase was sweet and rather extravagant. I concluded that Earl loved his sister as much as I loved my brother.

While our group made their purchases, I headed back to the bus and dropped into the seat next to Zuzana. My time with Earl was over.

At the airport, everyone fondly bid each other goodbye. We hugged, exchanged addresses, and promised that we would stay in touch. Earl waited to hug me last. When he did, he asked for permission to contact me.

"Sure," I told him rather offhandedly to demonstrate that I would not be waiting with bated breath. Then Earl smiled, reached into his pocket, and pulled out the jewelry box containing the opal earrings.

"I bought these for you," he said.

I must have looked like a kangaroo in headlights. I had never been given such an extravagant gift, and receiving it made me a bit uncomfortable. "Thank you," I managed to blurt out before jamming the earrings into my bag and making a quick exit to the gate. I don't think I even said goodbye to Earl.

Once I was safely seated on the plane, I reached into my bag, pulled out the box, and lifted the top. There inside were the lovely, opal earrings. They shimmered as I tilted them in the light. They were perfect. *Did this mean Earl was interested in me? Could I expect to hear from him again?* My stomach felt queasy. *Was I actually attracted to the Cuddle King?*

I pondered my next move. Either I would sell the earrings or get my ears pierced.

CHAPTER 28

Love is patient, love is kind.
It does not envy, it does not boast, it is not proud.
It does not dishonor others, it is not self-seeking,
it is not easily angered, it keeps no record of wrongs.
Love does not delight in evil but rejoices with the truth.
It always protects, always trusts, always hopes,
always perseveres.
1 Corinthians 13:4-7 (NIV)

February–April 1981

A few weeks after our New Zealand trip, I met up with Zuzana at her house. I was eager to show her my newly pierced ears and the Valentine's card I had received from Earl. The outside was red with a heart and flowers; the message inside read: *I enjoyed the time we spent together.*

Zuzana looked at my card without emotion, gently turning it in her hands before handing it back. Then she got up, walked to her bedroom, and returned with her own Valentine card. Handing it to me, she said, "Minh, I got a card from Earl too. He probably sent one to every girl he knows."

Choking back my disbelief, I asked, "Why would you think that?"

"Because I heard him promise all the girls a Valentine card as we were saying goodbye," she answered. "Didn't you hear him? Where were you?"

I was probably lost inside my head, running to the plane after being surprised by the gift Earl had given me. Touching the earrings that now graced my pierced earlobes, I felt crushed. I shook it off and smiled, grateful to have a friend like Zuzana who would protect me from going down the wrong path. The pain of being jilted by Angelo years earlier still weighed heavily on my heart, and I doubted my ability to choose a man who would be a suitable partner. I reminded myself that while I hadn't been particularly attracted to Earl, I had found him interesting and charming. And, I must admit, I had enjoyed the chase because it made me feel desirable.

When I received a letter from Earl a few weeks later, I had to ask Zuzana whether she had received one too. She hadn't, and this rekindled my interest in him. I faithfully wrote Earl a letter every week. For every one I sent, Earl wrote three in return. I barely had time to eat let alone write that often. Though I didn't share his enthusiasm for writing, I did enjoy reading his letters. Unintentionally, Earl became my new pen pal.

Earl and I had very little in common—practically nothing, in fact. Born in New Zealand, Earl called America home, but he would have been just as comfortable living in a yurt in Mongolia. I, on the other hand, missed my homeland and yearned for stability. Earl was free spirited, always ready to jump on the next wave of life. I was cautious, forever planning my next move. I set goals and lived to work; Earl had adventures and lived to play. I was quite serious; Earl was always joking. I saw the glass as half empty; he saw it as half full. Having stepped into the role of caregiver at age 11, I approached life with a sense of responsibility, sadness, and struggle. Earl approached life with childlike wonderment. I didn't understand how his brain worked. His edges were soft; mine were hard. Earl was everything I was not, which is probably why I was attracted to him.

I began my second year in the RN program with a newfound sense of purpose. The focus of the lessons shifted from anatomy to a holistic approach to care, away from knowledge of body parts and how they functioned and towards the wellbeing of the entire patient. Learning how to evaluate an individual's emotional and psychological needs not only helped me appreciate the struggles others were dealing with, it gave me some insight into my own personal battles.

I began to consider how my past was possibly affecting my sleep, my decisions, and my relationships with others. Nightmares and panic attacks could be attributed to life's stresses, but I was sure I could overcome them through sheer willpower. I was, after all, a nurse. I was trained to care for others. Surely, I was capable of caring for myself.

Thanh had told me to lighten up, and that was exactly what I planned to do. I wanted to enjoy life, to live for today and not worry about tomorrow. I needed to take more vacations. I needed to laugh more. I needed to take myself less seriously. A dose of Earl, I thought, would do me good.

After several months of letter writing, Earl started to contact me by phone. I found myself looking forward to his calls, knowing that he would pull me out of whatever funk I had fallen into.

One night Earl called me from the Whitsundays Islands off the coast of Queensland. "What are you doing there?" I asked.

"I've taken a job as a groundskeeper for a resort," he answered matter-of-factly.

"Do you like it?"

His response was, "Sure," as if there was no other answer. For him, there probably wasn't.

I enjoyed our long-distance relationship. It fit perfectly into my safe and structured life, sandwiched between challenging RN classes and an intense work environment.

Life was good. I had friends, a cute dorm room on the grounds of Concord Hospital, I still drove my light green Leyland Mini, and there was money in the bank. My achievements would have made my father proud.

When I look back on this period of my life, I see an incredibly self-centered woman driven by personal gratification. Though I had experienced the peace of God and had accepted His existence, I was further from Him than I had ever been. My top priorities were work, finding a husband, and status—worldly symbols of success. Friends and family were a lower priority, and God didn't even make the list. And why should He? Things were going well enough in my life that I had no need of a savior. I had everything under control until the day I received another letter in the mail from the Australian government.

My brother Duc and his girlfriend, Trong, would soon be arriving in Australia. I had no idea their immigration was even in the works. The letter informed me that they would be living with Nhu, which meant he must have sponsored them. My heart leapt in my chest at the prospect of seeing my brother again. As soon as I had worked up enough courage, I called Nhu to tell him that I was planning to drive to his home the following weekend for a visit.

Duc was the third child born to my parents, in their third year of marriage. I had fond memories of him as a young boy as he fetched water with Thanh from the community well in Dalat while I cooked eggs over an open fire. Before my mother married Nhu, it had been just the three of us. We were poor, naïve, and content.

I had never met Duc's girlfriend, but I knew something about her through my mother's cryptic letters. Mom had made it clear that she did not approve of Duc's relationship with Trong because she came from a poorer family. I knew that if my mother didn't like her, I would love her.

The weekend arrived, and I jumped in my car to make the drive to the coastal town of Woolongong in New South Wales. I had packed an overnight bag in case I was invited to stay. The 90-minute drive seemed to drag on forever, and I questioned whether my decision to send Nhu to the furthest hostel had been the right one. Until now, it hadn't been an issue. Nhu had been in Australia for two years already, and I had fortunately never run into him. For that I was grateful.

My brother was waiting outside when I pulled into the driveway of the rental property. There were no words, only tears. It would have been inappropriate to hug, so we just stared at each other and cried. The sadness of the past mixed with the joy of our reunion spoke volumes in the space between us. Duc had been, and still was, a sensitive soul.

Trong bowed respectfully when I entered the apartment, and I immediately adored her. She had cooked us a nice Vietnamese meal to converse over. With all my attention focused on Duc and Trong, I was barely aware of Nhu's presence.

As new immigrants, Duc and Trong wanted to know about Australia, what I did for a living, and what the future might look like for them. I believe this is what immigrants everywhere want to know. We talked for hours. Our conversation flowed naturally, and

I was blessed to see traces of our childhood mannerisms emerge. There were so many stories to cover. Childhood stories. Prison stories. Communist stories. Boat stories. Love stories. We were both careful to keep the conversation light, to hold back our deepest pains and hardest struggles. As Duc's big sister, I wanted him to be happy and enjoy life in Australia. I did not want to burden him with the scars I carried and the insecurities they had created, although I did wonder whether he experienced nightmares too.

According to an old Vietnamese proverb, "Brothers and sisters are as close as hands and feet." I think this is especially true for siblings who have experienced trauma. We laughed, we cried, and sometimes we just sat in silence. It was a beautiful reunion.

I was graciously invited to spend the night, and though I had planned to go home the next morning, I ended up staying the next night as well. Sunday evening came too soon; I had work and school I needed to return to. Duc also had work the next morning; Nhu had secured him a position as a janitor at the steel factory in which he worked. I knew I would see Duc again, but we still cried when we parted. Leaving brought on a flood of painful "goodbye" memories and reminded me of just how much I had lost when I was forced to flee Vietnam. I drove away feeling drained yet strangely full.

Despite my disdain for Nhu, I made it a point to visit Duc and Trong once a month, and each time it became a little easier to leave. I was grateful for Trong's presence in Duc's life because it took the self-inflicted burden of responsibility for his happiness off my shoulders. They were a good couple, and I envied their relationship, which seemed to illuminate my singleness. I wanted what they had— someone to care for and comfort me.

One evening Earl called and complained about the lack of tourists at the island resort due to the bad weather forecasts. "Just to let you know," he said, "you might not hear from me for a while if the power gets knocked out."

I didn't think much about it until I caught the news reports the next day. A tropical hurricane was making its way toward the coastal islands, and everyone was being evacuated to the mainland. Now I started to worry. War had not only stripped me of my childhood, it had left me in a perpetual mode of rescue and survival. I felt it was my duty to protect Earl. I paced the floor that night, hoping that he would call again. He did.

"Where are you?" I asked frantically.

"At the resort," he answered calmly.

"There's a hurricane headed right towards you!" I screamed. "Everyone is being evacuated."

Unaffected, Earl responded, "I know."

"What are you going to do?" I demanded.

"Wait it out."

I was pretty sure Earl was insane. "What are you thinking?" I shrieked over the phone. "You need to evacuate like everyone else! Get off the island! Move to Sydney! If you weren't so picky, I'm sure you could find a job right here!"

Earl heard my plea as an invitation.

The next day while I was witnessing the hurricane's devastation on TV, Earl called to tell me he had landed safely in Sydney. I instinctively took responsibility for his welfare. He needed me. Earl had no job, no job prospects, no place to live, and no car. I couldn't bring him to my dorm room at Concord Hospital, so I called on Zuzana for help. Her response was, "Send him to my house."

Earl was calmly waiting for me at the airport curb. I should have felt a twinge of excitement when I saw him, but I didn't. My first reaction was anger. *How can he be so damn calm?* I thought. In contrast, when Earl spotted me, he jumped up like he had just won the lottery; a look of excitement brightened his face. He promptly gave me a big, friendly bear hug. Though there were no butterflies in my stomach, I liked the warm feeling of his embrace. He felt comfortable, like an old pair of woolen slippers.

Zuzana kindly welcomed Earl into her home and gave him one of her daughter's rooms to use. He didn't blink twice when confronted with pink walls and a frilly bedspread. And Zuzana didn't seem to mind housing another man in her home. That's because Zuzana and Earl were cut from the same cloth—two carefree spirits, gratefully accepting whatever life had to offer rather than attempting to steer it toward a defined goal. Neither of them bore any resemblance to me in terms of character or approach, yet these were the two individuals I chose to spend most of my time with.

Zuzana probably would have been fine with Earl living in the pink bedroom indefinitely. I was not. I insisted that Earl keep my car so he could search for a job and an apartment. At the end of my shifts he would be waiting to drive me to the places he had seen during the day to get my opinion. Because we were spending so much time together, I assumed we were dating, but I wasn't certain. Earl had never actually asked me out on a date; he didn't hold my hand when we were together, and he never tried to kiss me. The bulk of our affection was a strong hug each time he picked me up or dropped me off.

One evening Earl and I took a walk around the hospital's neighborhood. On a charming little side street we saw a sign that read "Room to Rent." It turned out to be a tiny in-law suite on the back of the owner's house. It offered a kitchenette built into the living space and a small bedroom. The shower and toilet were in a separate building outside. Completely furnished, it was lacking only in kitchenware—pots, utensils, glasses, and plates. Earl loved it. However, since Earl had no job, he couldn't afford the rent.

"How much is it?" I asked.

Instead of giving me a price, the owner asked a lot of questions. He wanted to know how Earl and I had met, who our parents were, and what had drawn us together. I kept thinking, *it's really none of your business,* but Earl graciously answered each and every question. It soon became clear that the owner had no intention of renting the apartment to an unmarried couple. I assured the man that I had my own place at the local hospital and would merely be covering Earl's expenses until he found a job. When the man learned that I was a nurse, he offered the apartment at a reasonable price in exchange for information on how to treat his gout. Cautiously, I signed the rental agreement.

Earl and I spent practically every hour together when I wasn't working. I'm sure the people around us thought we were madly in love; we weren't. When Earl did try to kiss me goodbye one night, I turned my head and offered him my cheek instead. I knew where kissing would lead, and I did not want to fall into a sexual relationship like the one I had had with Angelo.

Things started to change when I started spending nights at the apartment. Having grown up in a culture in which entire families slept in the same room on mats one right next to the other, I did not feel strange sleeping next to Earl night after night. Earl, on the other hand, was not used to such an arrangement and assumed my nightly presence meant I was ready for a relationship.

Earl's attempts to kiss me increased. Still, I avoided his advances because I was determined to keep our relationship platonic. Around the same time, I decided to give up my apartment at Concord and move in with Earl permanently. After all, I was paying the rent and my car was parked in the driveway. It was just more convenient. My behavior sent Earl mixed messages. While this arrangement made little sense to him, it worked well for me—until we got a phone installed.

Earl's parents, who lived in the United States, started calling right away. Following one of their conversations, I asked Earl if they knew that we were living together. Earl responded, "Probably."

His answer induced in me a feeling of shame, and I didn't like that. Even though we weren't having sex, Earl's parents' assumption that our cohabitation was sexual touched a nerve. The perception of our relationship held more weight than the truth. Had we been living in Vietnam, our living arrangement would have made me an outcast. I would have been considered a loose woman, not fit for proper society.

For the first time in a long time I found myself struggling with my identity. Who was I? What did I want out of life? I thought I had been acting like a liberated woman who could come and go as she pleased without any strings attached. I was wrong. My relationship was not only ruining my reputation, it was ruining Earl's.

With one foot in the past and one foot in the future, I felt the ground splitting open beneath me. Something had to change. That something was me.

CHAPTER 29

So I say to whose who aren't married and to widows—
it's better to stay unmarried, just as I am.
But if they can't control themselves,
they should go ahead and marry.
It's better to marry than to burn with lust.
1 Corinthians 7:8-9 (NLT)

April 1981–1983

The next time Earl tried to kiss me, I didn't turn away. However, kissing was as far as I wanted to go. I can't honestly say whether this was due to a lack of chemistry between us or because of the mental damage of past sexual experiences. Whatever the reason, I had no desire to have sex, but I wished I did. I decided to share my confusion with one of my coworkers.

"Why are you living together if you aren't romantically involved?" she asked.

"Because he needed a place to live," I explained. "He moved to Australia to be with me."

"If you don't like him," she said, "kick him out."

"I do like him," I explained, "I just don't love him."

"Why not?" she asked.

"I don't know," I answered. "I want to love him. He's a good man. He's a kind man. I just don't feel a spark." In retrospect,

I'm not sure I would have recognized a spark even if it started a small fire.

My coworker's eyebrows furrowed. "Why don't you try sleeping with him to see if your feelings change?"

I thought for a second before answering. "I'm afraid of getting pregnant."

"You know," she said, "you can take a pill for that."

I'm sure I had learned about the birth control pill in one of my pharmacology lectures, but somehow it hadn't registered in my brain as an option that was available to me. I took my colleague's advice and headed to an offsite clinic—far from the eyes of the hospital staff—to obtain the pill.

That very night, Earl and I had sex. I didn't enjoy it, but it did push our relationship to the next level. We became a real couple.

Around the same time, I recognized that Earl's limited skillset was making it difficult for him to find a job. Earl had a degree in forestry and had been trained to work with softwoods like pine. Australia is predominantly made up of hardwoods like eucalyptus. Positions that suited him were in short supply and nowhere near Sydney.

Now that Earl and I were a real couple, I expected him to pull his own weight. Therefore, I insisted that he take the next job that came along—whether it was in forestry or not. I hoped that my admiration for him would improve once he was earning his keep and not so dependent on my goodwill.

My Auntie Linh was able to secure a job for Earl as a shipping container transport administrator at the company where she was employed. It had nothing to do with forestry, nor did it put Earl in the great outdoors, but it provided him with a paycheck. With both of us working, we fell into a comfortable and predictable pattern.

Four influences that would alter the course of my single life converged almost simultaneously. I don't remember the exact order in which they fell, but they all pointed to the same outcome: marriage.

First there was Rosie. I would occasionally run into her at the hospital. She did not approve of cohabitation before marriage and took every opportunity to challenge my lifestyle. As a strong

Catholic, she considered premarital sex a sin. Though not particularly keen on Earl, Rosie preferred that I marry him rather than live with him. To move the process along, she would subtly offer to pay for our wedding. I would kindly thank her and promise to think about it. We were both strong-willed women and determined to have our way.

Next there was my mother who arrived in Sydney several months after Earl and I started living together. I was both nervous and excited about her arrival knowing our reunion could be either tense or joyful depending on my mother's attitude. As a result, I was on my guard when I joined Nhu and my brother, Duc, at the airport to meet her.

She arrived with three children in tow—my youngest brother, Giang, who was still in his teens, and my half sister and half brother by Nhu. Like a spectator, I watched from the sidelines as Nhu greeted them all with joy, and they returned the emotion. It was a moment unlike any I had personally witnessed as a child between my own parents.

When my mother finally noticed me, I respectfully said, "*Chào mẹ.*" (Hi Mom.) She responded in kind, patting me on the arm and holding my hand for a few seconds. Then she turned all her attention back to Nhu.

I could not deny the fact that there was a genuine connection between them. They had looked forward to this reunion and were undeniably happy to be together again. I wanted someone to want me the way my mother and Nhu appeared to want each other.

The third influence was Duc and Trong's wedding a few months later. Earl and I attended with around 150 of my mother's closest friends. I say that tongue-in-cheek because these people were merely acquaintances. In the Vietnamese culture, a wedding is for the parents, not the bride and groom. The parents on both sides of the aisle invite whomever they choose to the ceremony, often trying to outdo each other with the guest list. The newlyweds are left to foot the bill. In so doing, they honor their parents with respect and gratitude.

While it hurt to know that my mother had successfully depleted Duc's bank account with her guest list, I desperately wanted to join the ranks of the married. Everyone my age, and many of those who were younger, had a spouse. I felt like an outsider.

Finally, there were Earl's parents. Earl proposed marriage to me following one of their phone calls. His offer came with no great fanfare or romantic gesture. He simply offered, "Why don't we get married?"

My response was no less charming. "Why?"

Earl thought a moment before answering, "Because I want my parents to accept you as my wife and respect you."

Respect. Earl wanted me to be respected. I had to appreciate his concern for my reputation. Perhaps this was the first step towards love. Earl hadn't asked me to marry him because he loved me or couldn't imagine life without me. He didn't want me as his wife because I made him laugh or because I added value to his existence. He wanted to marry me because he was trying to make things right with his parents.

Earl had been married once before to a Malaysian woman who had used him to gain American citizenship. A year into their marriage, she left him for another man. Earl's parents were understandably leery of Asian women, but I found the whole matter rather odd. I did not have the same motives as Earl's first wife. I wanted a man who would take care of me, protect me, and love me. I wanted to be married to a man who would improve my rank in society.

Earl was not that type of man. Truth be told, I would not gain much by marrying him. Earl, on the other hand, had much to gain by marrying me—a steady income, a roof over his head, immediate health care, and someone to keep him focused.

"I'm quite happy to be your girlfriend," I told Earl. And though I meant it, I also felt that marrying Earl would be the right thing to do. Consequently, his proposal gnawed on my psyche.

A few days later, I told Earl I would marry him. He became ecstatic and started jumping around the apartment. I was taken aback by his response and actually quite moved by his joy. That was the confirmation I needed to make me believe I had made the right decision. Whatever my true feelings were, I was determined to make the marriage work.

Practically everyone we knew was thrilled with our announcement. However, I do remember one of my colleagues saying, "I bet your marriage won't last more than five years."

"Why would you say that?" I asked.

"Earl's a nice guy," she confirmed, "but he's not your type."

Her words haunted me. *Who was my type?* I didn't know.

I began in earnest to plan the wedding, which was to take place in Rosie and Harry's backyard. Meanwhile, my mother began assembling her guest list. She had been in the country for less than a year and had managed to ingratiate herself into the Vietnamese community by joining a local church. I knew that if she were left to her own devices, I could expect over 300 people to show up at my wedding. I didn't want Rosie and Harry to be overrun by my mother's guests, so I called her and informed her that my wedding was to be a private affair. The guest list would be limited to immediate family members and close friends of the bride and groom, and she would be allowed to invite only ten friends. Mom was irate, but I held my ground. Unable to choose just ten, she invited no one.

My wedding day was everything I hoped it would be. It was a beautiful spring day, and Rosie and Harry's backyard turned out to be the perfect venue. Less than 30 people attended the ceremony on November 12, 1981, with my family representing most of the guests. There were also friends from work and Earl's parents, whom I met for the first time the day before. My Uncle Vinh and his wife provided the music, and Harry—the closest man I had to a father—graciously gave me away. A licensed marriage celebrant performed the wedding service. I would have preferred a Catholic priest, but that was not an option because I was not a member of any church. Earl was dead set against a Catholic wedding anyhow.

I wore a traditional Vietnamese wedding suit known as an Áo dài that my mother specifically brought for me from Vietnam in the hopes that I might one day marry. My Áo dài was bright red with a golden dragon emblazoned down the front, an imperial symbol of prosperity. My mother beamed with pride when she saw me in it, and I felt beautiful.

All my life, family members had called me ugly names and had spoken in whispers behind my back that I would be lucky to find a man to marry me. For years they had tried to pawn me off to American servicemen. I had vowed never to marry an American, yet I had done just that! At least he wasn't in the military, didn't live in America, and I had picked him myself.

The high I felt on my wedding day dissipated as quickly as our guests. There was no honeymoon; Earl and I simply fell back into our normal routine.

I felt empty. Duped. I falsely expected marriage to inspire Earl to become a provider like my father had been, but he was nothing like my father. Earl did not have much ambition, and he was not motivated by money. He was content to simply be with me, piddle around the yard, go fishing, and read the newspaper.

Earl demonstrated his love by planning dates to jazz concerts or the movies. I found his efforts insulting. To me they were a waste of money and time. Special events, I thought, should be experienced sparingly—otherwise they weren't special.

I once made the mistake of complaining *about* Earl to his parents during one of their visits. "If Earl doesn't get his act together," I told his mother, "he's going to lose his job." She was so hurt by my accusation that she went into the back room and cried.

Earl's father approached me several minutes later and calmly stated that he and his wife did not appreciate my criticism of their son. "Look Minh," Earl's father began, "I am going to be straight-forward with you. We do not want to hear you say anything negative about your husband to us again."

I was dumbfounded. Wasn't it my prerogative to point out Earl's shortcomings to his parents so they could talk some sense into his head? Didn't they want a better life for him? Was it acceptable to let children go astray and say nothing? Why should I pretend that things were fine when they were not? "I don't mean to criticize Earl," I replied. "I was just sharing my concerns."

"We'd rather you didn't," Earl's father said. "We love our children, and we are proud of Earl. You should be too."

I honestly didn't know what Earl's father was talking about. What had Earl done to make them proud? They certainly couldn't be proud of his accomplishments; from my point of view, there were none. He wasn't hardworking or a stellar provider, and everything he had was mine.

I didn't see Earl the way his parents did. As a child, Earl had suffered from dyslexia and had struggled long and hard to obtain a college degree. He had the perseverance to overcome educational hurdles that I should have been able to identify with. They also saw Earl's heart, which was—without question—big and soft. He was kind and gentle. He had a positive attitude and a peaceful demeanor. Earl's parents were not proud of what he had earned but of who he was.

This kind of mindset was foreign to me. I viewed the value of a person from the Vietnamese perspective, which is based on achievement. I had been groomed to work hard in an effort to prove my worth. As a child, I studied diligently to increase my rank. As a teen, I worked obediently to avoid ridicule and pain. And as an adult, I had worked zealously to become a nurse and send money back to Vietnam to honor my mother. Still, no matter how far I went, no matter how much I did, no matter how much I earned, I never felt like I had accomplished enough. Where I had failed, Earl had succeeded.

My tense encounter with my husband's parents did not change Earl, but I learned a valuable lesson that day: A wife should never complain to her in-laws about their son. I would not make that mistake again. To criticize a child is to criticize a parent, and my relationship with Earl's parents was now tainted. Never again would they stay in our home during their rare visits to Australia. I had crossed a line that could not be erased.

My concerns about Earl's employment came to a head when he was fired from his job as a shipping container transport administrator. He simply lacked the organizational skills required to keep the orders moving efficiently. This made me the sole breadwinner for our family, and I resented Earl for it.

Luckily, I'd recently passed the RN exam, which was accompanied by a raise in pay. Still, I picked up extra shifts at a neighboring hospital to ensure we would always have money in the bank. My anger toward Earl would escalate when I would come home exhausted and bitter to find him ready to play. The last thing I wanted was to be touched or dragged out of the house for a movie. There was cooking and cleaning and laundry to be done. None of that mattered to Earl. He did not see the dishes piling up, the dirt on the floor, or the dust on the furniture. This irritated me to no end. Earl wanted romance, and I wanted help.

The extra income I earned allowed us to move into a one-bedroom apartment with a bathroom indoors. Though it was a respectable move up, it still wasn't enough for me. I wanted to purchase a home.

"Why do you want a house?" Earl asked.

Why wouldn't I want a house? I thought. Purchasing a house was the next logical step for married couples. Purchasing a house would prove that we were a success. Purchasing a house would be a good investment; it was better to own a house than rent one. But Earl didn't care about owning a house. Earl wanted children. I told him there would be no children until there was a house.

"If children come, they come," he'd say.

Earl obviously assumed I had stopped taking birth control pills after the wedding; he assumed incorrectly. There would be no children until I said there would be children. I was in control.

Eventually Earl found a job as a truck driver making local deliveries for a store. The work wasn't very fulfilling, but he did it without complaining. This, however, did not stop me from complaining. Even though I was safe in Australia and held a steady job, even though there was food on the table and roof over my head, I lived in constant fear that the world was about to cave in. I blamed my fears on Earl, and I lashed out at him every chance I got.

I was acutely aware that I was bitter and downright mean, but I wasn't able—or perhaps I wasn't willing—to change. Instead, I expected Earl to change. I was forever criticizing him and pointing out his faults in an attempt to push him to go beyond his God-given abilities. He seemed to take my verbal attacks in stride; he would stare at me like a deer in the headlights or simply walk away.

It's strange to look back on those times and realize that my relationship with Earl was much like my mother's relationship with my father. Earl's unwillingness to engage in a fight provoked me to higher and higher degrees of anger, much like my father's unwillingness to battle with my mother incited her to throw things at him. While Earl's passive behavior brought out the worst in me, my aggressive behavior crushed the spirit in him.

Had I married a stronger man, he probably would have left me for good. Had I married a conscientious man, he would have worked himself into an early grave. Had I married a wiser man, he may have noticed that I needed professional help. But I was married to Earl. He simply put up with me, which allowed my demons to flourish.

CHAPTER 30

For when they see their many children
and all the blessings I have given them,
they will recognize the holiness of the Holy One of Jacob.
They will stand in awe of the God of Israel.
Then the wayward will gain understanding,
and complainers will accept instruction.
Isaiah 29:23-24 (NLT)

1984–1987

M y first brush with pregnancy came in 1984, four years into our marriage. I had gone off birth control, not because I wanted to have children, but because the pill was making me gain weight. Earl and I were barely having sex, so I didn't think I would get pregnant. When I missed my period, I was incredibly upset. We were still living in an apartment, and Earl was only earning minimum wage. This was not the right time to bring a child into the world.

Cautiously, I waited another month to tell Earl the news, just in case it was a false alarm. After I missed my period again, I told Earl I was pregnant. He was thrilled. I did not share in his joy. I saw the pregnancy as a hindrance to the goals I had set for myself, as well as the goals I had set for him. I told Earl we had to move quickly and buy a house before the baby came.

We bought a cheap fixer-upper in a good neighborhood. Though it was unfit for the cover of any magazine, home ownership made me feel like I was moving up in the world. It had two small bedrooms, a tiny kitchen, and a living room. The toilet and shower were housed in a shed outdoors. The biggest eyesore was the outdated wallpaper that covered the walls of every room, the worst of which was in the dining area. Large, faded yellow sunflowers that stretched from the floor to the ceiling were impossible to ignore or conceal. They didn't look right in the house, but they blended in perfectly with the overgrown bushes and questionable debris in the backyard.

The place needed a lot of work. A lot. Thankfully, Earl was handy and willing to tackle some of the larger projects. He was especially excited about cleaning the backyard and designing a permaculture garden in which he could grow his own vegetables.

"Whatever you do," I told him, "don't plant any sunflowers!"

Having lived only in furnished apartments, Earl and I had no furniture of our own. Consequently, each weekend I would drag him to church bazaars and yard sales in search of secondhand pieces we could use. Earl would have preferred to sit back with a movie or concert; I had no time for that.

"Why can't you just relax and enjoy life?" Earl would ask, to which I would respond in reference to him, "Somebody else is enjoying life so much that I have to worry for the rest of the world."

Our first Christmas holiday together in the new old house was a disaster. It was excruciatingly hot that day—over 90 degrees Fahrenheit—and our home felt like an oven. Earl hauled his sweating body into the overheated attic to discover that that house had no insulation whatsoever. The roof with its black shingles was radiating heat through the ceiling, raising the temperature to an unbearable degree inside. We did not have enough money in our savings to hire someone to insulate, so we had to do it ourselves. Earl purchased the materials, and I supported his efforts by confiscating several surgical masks from the hospital to protect his lungs while he worked. When it was all finished, Earl decided he needed a vacation and went fishing. I returned to work.

One day, near the end of my first trimester and during my regular work rounds, I started bleeding. My first reaction was, *Thank God! I am not going to be a mother after all!* The nurse in charge sent me to the ER.

It was protocol in those days to be admitted into the hospital for bleeding and to notify the next of kin. Phone calls to Earl went unanswered because he had already left for a fishing expedition with some buddies. So I jumped in the car and drove home to leave him a note. Then I drove myself back to the hospital where I was admitted and kept overnight for observation.

By the next morning the bleeding had subsided. I was discharged to go home for bed rest. I told the doctors I felt perfectly fine and would like to stay and work, but they wouldn't hear of it. Bed rest was crucial because there was a slight chance the pregnancy was still viable. It would have been wise for me to ask a colleague to take me home, but I didn't. I defiantly drove myself.

Within a few hours, the bleeding worsened. I drove myself back to the hospital and was admitted again, this time for a D&C. A dilation and curettage is a short surgical procedure where doctors scrape the uterine lining following a miscarriage to prevent infection. I remember the doctor who performed the surgery being quite compassionate, saying on behalf of the entire staff, "We are SO sorry!" I accepted his condolences and tried to express grief. Little did they know, I was cheering on the inside.

Earl showed up at the hospital later that day to take me home. The look of disappointment on his face was condemning. We barely spoke on the drive, and I wondered whether Earl blamed me for the loss of his child. I admit I *did* feel somewhat guilty for the miscarriage. It was possible that I had caused it by working long hours and ignoring doctors' orders to take it easy and not drive. I gave Earl space to grieve and threw myself back into work. I had goals.

Several days later, I told Earl that if he wanted to try for another child, he had to get a better-paying job. This was motivation enough for the would-be father. He soon found a position as a butcher, cutting cows into pieces five days a week from 5:00 a.m. to 2:00 p.m. He didn't like the work, but he did it without complaining. Of course, Earl never complained. He had a way of looking for the silver lining in every situation. In the meat factory, the silver lining was his workmates. They were a good crew, and I could tell that Earl enjoyed the camaraderie. He always came home with stories to tell. Though I tried to show my support by listening with interest, I couldn't have cared less about the people Earl worked with.

What I, the ambitious nurse, did care about were the people *I* worked with. I loved tucking patients in, administering their meds, checking their vital signs, and completing the necessary paperwork. My hard work captured the attention of my superiors, and I was promoted to the step-down cardio intensive care unit. Most of the patients in this unit had pacemakers, but they were not considered as critical as those in the regular ICU who were hooked up to monitors around the clock. After my first week on the job, the manager told me, "If you keep up this pace, you will put the patients into cardiac arrest!"

I couldn't slow down. I had so much energy! I even requested additional shifts in the ICU, but I was turned down because of the stressful nature of the job. Driven by the unrealistic need for more money, I signed on with an independent health agency so I could serve as a private nurse on my days off. I slept little, worked often, and chastised Earl for his lack of motivation every time I saw him.

Earl ignored me and poured his extra energy into yard work. I could not deny that Earl had a knack for horticulture. He turned our backyard into a sanctuary of flowers and vegetables. One day, I happened to notice that sunflowers were blooming in the backyard. I'm sure Earl planted them to spite me, so I pretended not to see them.

During those months, when my anxieties took a backseat, I became pregnant again. It would be a lie to say that I was happy this time around. I was not. In truth, I was simply not as disturbed by the prospect of bringing a child into the world as I had been before.

This pregnancy was nothing like the previous one. I was terribly nauseous for the first three months. In fact, I threw up so often that I had to be hospitalized twice for dehydration and fed intravenously. I was sure this baby was going to kill me before it was born. Then, as quickly as the sickness had started, it ended. By the beginning of the second trimester, I felt fine, and soon my stomach was showing the first signs of a baby bump. That's when I knew motherhood was inevitable.

It was time to turn one of the bedrooms into a nursery. Hoping to paint the walls a pale color that would be calming to the baby, Earl began stripping off the antiquated wallpaper. Beneath the first layer he discovered another layer of paper. Then another. And another. Four layers of wallpaper in all! By the time he found the actual wall, Earl was drained of energy and enthusiasm. We decided to forgo the paint till we knew the sex of the child and instead focused on furnishing the room.

A garage sale yielded a tall standing dresser and a secondhand twin bed that we scrubbed fervently till they looked almost new. From the St. Vincent de Paul Society thrift store, Earl purchased a bassinette constructed of bamboo and white plastic with two sturdy handles for easy carrying. We set it on top of a secondhand table that could double as a changing station. Finally, the nursery was complete. It was far from beautiful, but it would do.

Earl and I signed up for prenatal classes where we were taught relaxation techniques and breathing exercises. Earl would carry his small, portable tape recorder into our sessions and pop in a cassette tape of John Denver singing *Take Me Home, Country Roads* to put me at ease. While Denver sang, I took breaths in sync with the music. I was sure delivery was going to be a breeze. What worried me was living day to day with another person in the house. I couldn't imagine what that would be like, and I had a hard time envisioning myself as a mother. That might have been because I did not have the best role model. I had to admit, Earl would definitely be the better parent.

I worked right up until the day I went into labor. My mother, thrilled at the prospect of becoming a grandmother, had told me that labor pains were not as bad as everyone made them out to be. I stupidly believed her thinking I was cut from the same cloth. I was nothing like my mother. Oh my God! What agony!

When my water broke, Earl drove me to the nearest hospital, which was not Concord. Every 20 minutes or so, I would buckle over in pain and scream profanities at Earl that would not be acceptable even in R-rated movies. Between the contractions, I silently prayed for God's forgiveness for all my bad deeds. It was my hope that he would have mercy on me and relieve my suffering. He did not.

I begged the nurses for pain medication; they gave me laughing gas instead. They had no idea who they were dealing with. "I'M NOT LAUGHING!" I yelled. "GIVE ME PETHIDINE!"

I knew what I wanted—I wanted the pain to be wiped out. But the pain of childbirth is required to keep the mother pushing. The maternity nurses knew this and ignored me. Earl did his best to divert my attention away from the nurses, whom I had deemed incompetent, by turning on the tape recorder. Suddenly, John Denver's sweet voice began singing *Take Me Home, Country Roads*.

"TURN IT OFF!" I screamed.

Earl did as instructed. Exasperated, he asked, "What do you want me to do?"

"GET ME SOME BLOODY DRUGS!"

The more I screamed the more the nurses avoided me. I could see the frustration on their faces every time they came into the room to check on my progress.

After 17 hours of excruciating agony, our child finally arrived. Earl cut the umbilical cord. "He's a beautiful boy," he announced.

In my exhausted state, I instructed Earl to check his eyes. "They're big and round," he said. I was relieved to hear that they weren't slanted. I did not want my son to be ostracized for being Asian.

The nurse took our baby away from Earl and laid him on my chest. Though he was only minutes old, I swear he looked up at me and smiled. His small, warm body was comforting against mine, and he felt like he belonged there. I thought to myself, *I can do this,* and I really wanted to.

We named him Edward after Earl's father, but we called him Eddie. He was perfect, and he was mine. Something truly good had come out of me.

By the time we left the hospital, I had fallen madly in love with my baby boy. Hence the reason I felt terrible bringing him home to our imperfect house and his secondhand nursery. None of it was good enough for my son. He deserved better. Earl didn't care about such things. He was content to have a healthy son and a roof over our heads.

Eight weeks of maternity leave flew by fast. Since Earl worked until 2:00 in the afternoons, I requested an evening shift at the hospital. My mother agreed to sit with Eddie every morning while Earl was at work, which allowed me time to clean, cook meals, and catch up on sleep.

Eddie became the apple of my mother's eye, which infuriated Nhu. As a traditional Vietnamese man, he expected my mother to put *his* needs first. He told her that if she was going to spend all her time at my house, she needed to be paid for her services.

To keep the peace and maintain in-house childcare, I started paying my mother. Giving money to her was nothing new. However, the stress it put on me threw me into a state of hyper-attentiveness. I snatched up extra work shifts where possible and begged my mother to spend the night when I didn't have the energy to care for Eddie. She didn't mind, but Nhu hated it. As their fights escalated into nasty exercises of verbal intimidation, Earl and I bizarrely found ourselves playing the roles of confidant and counselor for my mother.

Earl, with the patience of a saint, would give Mom his undivided attention as she ranted on in her broken English about how cruel Nhu could be. Earl would nod sympathetically, which served to validate her feelings and encouraged her to complain more. I, on the other hand, wanted to control my mother's situation. Though I had no right to give anyone marital advice, this did not stop me from suggesting divorce. I made my case by pointing out the glaring problems with my mother's marriage: she was a kept woman, totally dependent on Nhu because she had no job and did not drive, and he did not respect her. I even went as far as to take my mother to an attorney who wrote up the paperwork for a divorce. Mom threatened Nhu with the papers, but she never carried through. It was all a charade to get him to apologize for his behavior, which he did. Eventually.

Once the apology had been given and my mother no longer felt disrespected, she went home to her husband and left me hanging. "You'll have to find someone else to babysit Eddie," she said with a wave of her hand. My mother had abandoned me again. Hurt and angry, I promised Eddie I would never desert him, no matter how difficult life got. And life did get more difficult without my mother's help. Unable to afford daycare, Earl and I were forced to reevaluate our work schedules.

I wanted to keep working the overnight shift because it paid better than the day shift. That meant that Earl had to quit his job as a butcher so he could watch Eddie in the early morning hours before I got home from work. It also meant he would have to find a new job that meshed better with my nursing schedule. Earl was glad to quit his job, but not happy about finding a new one. It took him quite awhile to secure another position. In the end, he landed a front desk job with a rental car company that allowed him to head to work shortly after I got home.

I would feed Eddie, play with him, and then put us both down for a nap. After a few hours, I would get up, do some chores, and cook dinner. When Earl got home from work, he'd take over Eddie's care so I could catch some sleep before my 11:00 p.m. night shift started. This became our routine.

While I poured my energy into worrying about meals and money in between nursing and changing diapers, Earl poured his love and wonder into our son. I was so task-oriented that I totally missed out on enjoying those first few months with Eddie. In retrospect, it was a perfect balance. God gave Eddie a father who provided loving support and a mother who provided for his physical needs. Though the traditional roles were reversed, Eddie had everything he needed to thrive in his early years.

It was during the first year of Eddie's life that I remember seeing Earl with a Bible in his hands. Sometimes he would read me a passage and ask me what I thought it meant. I never bothered to answer. Interpretations were best left to the priests. Eventually, Earl stopped asking for my opinion.

Life was hard. Money was tight. Sleep was scarce. But Eddie was pure joy—such a sweet, contented child. The highlight of my days was watching his face brighten each and every time he saw me. I delighted in watching him grow. As he began to crawl, Eddie explored each room with innocent wonder completely fascinated by all the things he could now get his hands on.

One day as I watched him analyze something he had found on the floor, an incredible sense of panic set in. *What if I were to die tomorrow? Would Eddie remember me? Would he know how much I had loved him? What kind of legacy was I leaving for him? What can give him now that will make a difference in his future?* The answer came in a flash: GOD.

How strange. I hadn't been to church in years and didn't feel I had a right to set foot in one. My life was less than exemplary, and my marriage was far from perfect. I had too many sins to confess, and I honestly couldn't remember them all. Wasn't there something else I could leave Eddie?

The answer was clear: *No.* Only God could protect and care for my son. Only God could love him like I did. Only God knew what was best for him.

Besides, I had nothing else to give.

CHAPTER 31

Trust in the Lord with all your heart
and lean not on your own understanding;
in all your ways submit to him,
and he will make your path straight.
Proverbs 3:5-6 (NIV)

1988–1993

"We should go to church," I announced.

Earl jumped at the idea, and I had to wonder why *he* had never suggested it. He had invited me to plenty of concerts and movies, but never to attend worship. I had incorrectly assumed he was opposed to organized religion because he read his Bible in the solitude of our home and had not supported my desire to get married by a Catholic priest. Earl apparently had a problem with the Catholic faith, not Protestant denominations.

By Sunday, Earl had selected a church where we could worship together as a family. It was a Presbyterian church with a Scottish pastor, which was a good fit for Earl because he had been raised as a Presbyterian. It was not a good fit for me.

I dressed Eddie up in his cutest outfit, eager to show him off. In Catholic churches, children attend mass with their parents or sit with other children of their age; but in the church Earl had picked, children were relegated to the nursery or Sunday school classrooms. This meant Earl and I attended worship service without Eddie, and he was the whole reason why I wanted to go in the first place! I found it odd to be separated from my child even though the volunteers doted on him. Without children, the sanctuary was strangely quiet.

There were other differences in this church as well. The prayers were different. The music was different. There weren't any kneelers in the pews or holy water fonts to dip my fingers into. And to make matters worse, I couldn't understand a thing the pastor said with his Scottish accent. I was as lost as a child in a snowstorm. For Eddie's sake, I was committed to making the most of it. So each week I forced myself to sit quietly in the pew and pray silently for Eddie's future and for my marriage.

I would like to tell you that church was a life-changer, but it wasn't. As time went on, Earl became more involved in church life, which made me feel more and more like an outsider. The chasm between us grew even wider. Then, after Earl was fired from his job at the rental car company, the chasm became a canyon that was too large to bridge.

Instead of looking for another job, Earl volunteered to serve as a Sunday school teacher and to facilitate a Bible study one night each week. The pastor was thrilled, and the students and parents loved him. Everyone loved Earl. Everyone except me.

Without Earl's income, I was forced to pick up extra day shifts at the hospital following my night shifts. Knowing a degree would lead to higher pay, I also started taking classes toward a BA in nursing. The additional work made me exhausted and resentful. While I carried the weight of providing for our family, Earl socialized with students and spent quality time with our son.

What irritated me the most was that no one at the church had the faintest idea about what I was dealing with, and no one ventured to ask. Instead, they asked Earl, "Why does Minh work all the time?"

He would shrug and say, "That's how she is."

I was viewed as a workaholic while Earl got all the accolades. Church was not the place of respite and support I had hoped it would be. Feeling misunderstood and unwelcomed, I stopped going altogether.

I was sure God was punishing me when I discovered that I was pregnant again. I barely had time for Eddie, who had not yet turned two. I had no right bringing another child into this world. I cursed myself for not being on birth control, let alone allowing Earl to touch me at all. Unlike the last pregnancy, I was not angry with this one—just incredibly sad.

With money tighter than ever and another child on the way, I feared we might lose the house. I told Earl that he either had to find another job or we needed to consider moving to the United States. Earl's parents owned two homes in the Richmond, Virginia area, and they had offered to let us rent one.

Earl did not want to move back to America, so he started applying for jobs immediately. Meanwhile, I began looking into job prospects in hospitals in Virginia. What I learned was crushing: my nursing licenses would not be recognized in the United States, nor would my health insurance cover the cost of medical care for the birth of our baby outside of Australia. So even if Earl's parents did allow us to rent from them, we would have no immediate income with which to pay. Earl took this as a sign that we were to stay put.

I did empathize with Earl's frustration over the job prospects available to him. His degree in forestry was of no use in Sydney. Fortunately, he was willing to apply for *any* openings that offered work in the great outdoors. We both knew he did not do well in enclosed spaces that required administrative skills. And I did not do well every time Earl got fired. So I challenged him to really think about what he wanted to do with his life and pursue only those jobs that would make him happy.

"Minh," he said, "I want to go back to school for horticulture."

Earl did have a green thumb and an eye for landscape design. Our backyard was a testament to that. Though his degree selection was fitting, his timing stunk. This meant we would both be in school at the same time while trying to raise a family. Still, since I was already taking classes toward a BA degree, I felt I had no right to tell Earl that he couldn't go back to school too. With my approval, he enrolled in the horticulture program at the community college. My hope was that he could finish his degree and find a decent-paying job within the year.

Emily came kicking and screaming into the world on a cool July morning. Her birth was so much easier than her brother's. She looked just like Eddie, but Emily was nothing like him. She was loud and fearless, a demanding tyrant who barely slept. I had to put her on bottled milk almost immediately after she was born because I couldn't produce enough breast milk to satisfy her. I prayed often and hard that God would give me the strength to survive another day as her mother.

Over the years I've heard many mothers complain about having to put their children in childcare. I was not one of them. I couldn't wait for maternity leave to end so I could return to work and leave Emily in the care of professionals. My main complaint was that daycare centers only operated during the daylight hours. In order to take advantage of childcare, I needed to return to working the day shift where the pay wasn't nearly as good. There was no other option.

I was truly scared the first time we were unable to pay the electricity bill. Without sufficient funds in the bank, I had to juggle our payments—water one month, electricity the next. Or I would pay just part of a bill in the hopes of catching up the next month. Sometimes our checks bounced. It was always a crapshoot depending on how many extra shifts I was able to pick up.

No matter how bad things got, I always paid the mortgage. Until the month I couldn't. I was forced to call the bank and ask for an extension, which they graciously granted. Having no one else to turn to, I begged Earl to call his parents and ask for a loan. Reluctantly, he made the call. Earl's father consented to giving us the money we needed to stay afloat; however, he insisted on talking with me to close the deal.

"Minh, I have agreed to send you the money to cover your bills this month, but I will not do this again." I thanked him and explained that as soon as Earl finished his degree and started working again, we would be fine.

"This is not about Earl," he said. "You need to learn how to save."

I felt sucker-punched. Betrayed. I wondered what Earl had told him. No one was better at saving than me; I was an expert on how to stretch a dollar. Hurt and struggling to maintain my composure, I said, "I never spend money on myself. Believe me, if I made enough money to care for four people, we would not need your help."

The money, which was wired overnight, bought us some time. I started moonlighting with an independent health agency, picking up nursing positions on weekends and during the week where possible. Before Emily turned one, Earl completed his degree and found a job with a plant nursery working outdoors. I thought his income would allow me to cut back on work hours; it did not. Earl's workload fluctuated with the seasons and the weather, so he could never count on a steady paycheck.

The inconsistency in our work schedules and financial situation sent my stress level soaring. I preferred being at work where things were predictable than at home where things were chaotic. Toys and clothes and dirty dishes were strewn everywhere. Earl was content to sit in the muck, but I was not. Despite my exhaustion, I would turn into a whirling dervish, cleaning like a madwoman and yelling out orders. It was impossible for me to rest in the disorder.

To make matters worse, Emily would often start screaming or crying when I walked through the door. I was never sure if she was unhappy to have me home or merely imitating me. Either way, it made me feel unwelcomed.

Earl thought things would get better if I would just start attending church again. I didn't agree. Church was not going to fix our financial situation. Church was not going to pay our bills. Church was not going to clean our home or cook the meals or wash the laundry. I was drowning, and church was not throwing me a life vest. No—church was not the solution. I needed a miracle.

Martha was a junior nurse who reported to me in the vascular ward at Concord. One day, out of the clear blue, she asked me, "Do you believe in God?"

A loaded question, I surmised. There were so many ways to answer. *"I believe in Him, but He's abandoned me." "Why do you ask?" "Sometimes."* But what I actually said was, "Yes."

"Do you go to church?" Martha asked.

I smiled, recognizing that Martha was attempting to evangelize me. Her parents had been missionaries and her father was a retired pastor. Her faith was part of her attire. Though I respected her beliefs, I considered her a bit naïve.

"Martha," I said, "I believe in God, but I no longer attend church." I figured that would be the end of our conversation. It wasn't.

"Would you be interested in participating in a Bible study with some other women?" she asked.

That was not the response I expected from Martha. I could have easily dismissed an invitation to church, but her invitation to a Bible study intrigued me. I loved to learn, and it had been years since I had socialized with anyone other than Earl. My only concern was location; I was apprehensive about meeting in a church building. "Where does this Bible study meet?" I asked.

"At my friend's house," Martha stated. "There will be food and drinks too."

Something tugged at my heart. A desire to go someplace other than home, to meet with other women, to eat food I didn't prepare, and to engage in adult conversation. I didn't want to seem too interested, so I told Martha I would think about it.

Later that week, I left my car at the hospital and rode with Martha to her friend's house for Bible study. Several women were already there and warmly welcomed me in. I was leery of their friendliness and put my guard up. Perhaps they were desperate for members.

We ate cookies and drank tea. Then we gathered in the living room in a large circle. One of the women called us together in prayer. She prayed from the heart, and it was beautiful. I was the only newcomer that week. When it was time for the ladies to introduce themselves, I said something like this: "My name is Minh. I am a registered nurse at Concord Hospital where I work with Martha. I have a husband and two children, ages four and two."

I'm sure my description conjured up a picture of the perfect family, minus a dog. There was no indication that anyone would think anything else because they all smiled when I spoke and thanked me for joining them. Little did they know that my life was in turmoil—financially, emotionally, mentally, and spiritually.

I don't remember who taught the Bible lesson that night or what it was about; what I do remember is being enthralled with it. Whenever the leader read a passage from scripture and asked for feedback, a lively discussion would ensue. Some women provided scholarly responses, some shared how the text made them feel, and others asked questions rather than offer an interpretation. There were no wrong responses, and every contribution was honored.

"Minh, what do you think of the passage?" the leader asked me directly.

Though I have no memory of what I said, I do remember my answer being positively acknowledged. I was not judged, nor was I corrected. I was heard.

This Bible study offered an authentic give-and-take among the women that was sprinkled with respect and laughter. It was unlike anything I had ever experienced at church. Several ladies said they hoped I would come back the following week. I wasn't sure if they were being honest or just polite, but I didn't care. I would be coming back. I needed these women.

Wednesday night Bible study became the highlight of my week and filled a void in my life. As I studied God's word in community, the disparate pieces of my Catholic upbringing began to fit together like a 1000-piece puzzle. I discovered that the Bible texts I had heard as a child were part of a larger story that consisted of prayers and genealogies, historical people and ancient places, prophecies and long forgotten gods.

I identified strongly with the Old Testament stories, which were full of wars, famines, and destruction. That was my story. I knew what it felt like to live under those conditions and to be punished for disobedience. Like the Israelites, I longed for redemption. Encouraged by this group of women and what I was learning, I started to pray again with increased passion. Yet every time I looked in the mirror I saw someone who was unworthy of being called a child of God. I was difficult, unyielding, mean, and downright sinful. I yearned for His forgiveness, but I was pretty sure that I was unforgivable.

Then one day I heard this from the book of James: *Therefore confess your sins to each other and pray for each other so that you may be healed. The prayer of a righteous person is powerful and effective.*[21]

Martha was righteous, and I needed prayers. There was no priest in my life to confess to, so I decided to confess to Martha. I told her that I was in a miserable marriage and that I was partially to blame. She said she already knew that. Then I told her that I had accepted my fate as God's way of punishing me for my past sins. Martha appeared shocked. Looking at me with compassion she said, "If you are hurting, God is hurting too."

That did not make sense to me. Martha was revealing a side of God I knew nothing about, and it gave me pause. I realized then that I needed to go deeper in my study of scripture to understand God's heart. My once-a-week Bible study was not enough. I asked Martha to help me purchase a Bible so I could immerse myself in the Word throughout the week.

At the local Christian bookstore, Martha steered me towards a copy of the New International Version (NIV) Bible, saying it was the easiest translation to comprehend for new students. I was surprised to learn that there were numerous versions of Bible translations. While this made perfect sense, it was something I had never considered. The Bible I purchased had a conservative, brown leather cover, and all of Jesus' words were printed in red ink.

I kept my Bible in the car and read it during breaks at work. The more I read, the more scripture came alive. It was as if God was speaking directly to me. I never took my Bible inside my home because I did not want to share this part of my life with Earl. When I didn't come home on Wednesday nights, he assumed I was working extra hours. He did not know I had joined a Bible study.

At the hospital, Martha would often check in on me to see how I was doing. She did not judge my actions or provide advice; she simply prayed *for* me and *with* me. I remember her once telling me,

"Because I am a believer, I can't tell you to leave your husband, but I will stand by you through it."

Martha taught me what it meant to be a Christian friend. She listened to me, stood by me, prayed for me, and cared for me. My life became a little easier to bear when I began sharing the details of my struggles and praying about them with her. She was a bright light in my dark world.

I now know God never meant for us to bear our burdens alone. Even Jesus surrounded himself with twelve disciples. We were designed to live in community and rely on God for strength. He hopes that we will turn to Him when the journey gets rough; when we don't, He loves us enough to send angels into our lives to show us the way.

Martha was my angel.

CHAPTER 32

For by grace you have been saved through faith,
and this is not your own doing; it is the gift of God—
not the result of works, so that no one may boast.
For we are what he has made us,
created in Christ Jesus for good works,
which God prepared beforehand to be our way of life.
Ephesians 2:8-10 (NRSV)

1994–1999

Martha not only knew that I did not attend church with my family, she recognized that I needed something more than just a Bible and a Bible study to navigate the turbulence in my life. In her unassuming way, she asked me if I would like her to find a church that would suit me. It must have been summertime because Earl had to work most weekends, and he was not happy about having to miss worship services so often. If Earl didn't go to church, the kids didn't go either.

Harsh as it may sound, I remember thinking that with Earl working on Sundays, the nurture and care of the children's spiritual growth was now in my hands. The prospect of taking Eddie and Emily to church without Earl thrilled me.

"Yes," I told Martha. "Please find a church that would welcome me *and* my children."

Martha selected Solid Rock Presbyterian Community Church—a church that met in the auditorium of the primary school that Eddie and Emily already attended. That alone provided all three of us with an immediate comfort level.

I was nervous getting ready for that first church visit that included selecting attire for the kids and me. I dressed seven-year-old Eddie in dark trousers and a short-sleeved shirt; and five-year-old Emily wore a beautiful, fruit-patterned, yellow dress. Upon arrival, I noticed that most everyone was wearing jeans. It didn't faze me. My children looked beautiful, even if they were overdressed for the occasion.

Wardrobe differences not withstanding, Solid Rock was a perfect fit for us. Most of the attendees were third generation Asians who, like me, embraced our adopted Australian culture while clinging to our Asian heritage. This made me feel at home. And what a wonderful experience we all had! The kids loved their Sunday school class, and I loved the sermon that was delivered in recognizable English by a Malaysian pastor. His name was too long to say in one breath, so everyone just called him Pastor J.C.

I came home from church that Sunday with a joy in my heart that was evidently tangible. Earl felt it and got swept up in my excitement. Without thinking, I told him all about the church, its location, the congregation, the pastor, and the kids' classes.

Earl was elated to learn that I had returned to church, and he said he looked forward to worshipping with the kids and me in future weeks. But I didn't want him to. It was *my* church. He had his own church. I tried to discourage Earl from switching to Solid Rock by saying that he wouldn't fit in because all the congregants were Asian. He wasn't deterred.

"I like Asians!" he said. "After all, I married you."

Looking back, I believe Earl viewed my enthusiasm for church as a gateway to repairing our marriage and functioning as a healthy family. I did not see it that way. His attempts to impress me were always poorly executed in my eyes. He did not love me the way I needed to be loved. I wanted only one thing from Earl, and that he could not give me: safety.

Years of stressful living had made me fearful of life itself. I desperately needed Earl to have a steady job and a steady income to show me that he could care for our family if I wasn't able to. If he could do that, I would not feel like the world rested entirely on my shoulders. But Earl did not equate safety with love. And why should he? Earl had never felt unsafe. He did not know what it was like to live in fear, nor did he understand how his impulsive decisions pushed me deeper into the abyss. That's why his next move just about pushed me over the edge: Earl resigned from his weekend job at the nursery in order to attend Solid Rock Presbyterian with the kids and me.

He made this decision without consulting me. In his view, he was supporting family unity. From my view, he was failing to protect me, condemning me to longer work hours and sentencing me to a place of perpetual darkness.

It took only a few weeks for Earl to charm his way into everyone's heart at Solid Rock Presbyterian Church. I pretended to be a happy wife by forcing myself to smile through his interactions with others. However, beneath my perfect façade, I was seething and worried. I questioned how God could be so callous as to bring me to this wonderful church where I felt welcomed only to let Earl become the center of attention. It wasn't fair. I had to find my own niche at church, a place where I felt accepted apart from Earl. It began with evangelism.

Pastor J.C. was an evangelist at heart, and he often preached on the subject. No one should go through life, he said, without experiencing the hope of Jesus Christ, and it was our responsibility to introduce Him to others. All we had to do was invite people to church, and he would do the rest.

I accepted the pastor's challenge and began promoting Solid Rock Presbyterian to anyone who crossed my path—patients, neighbors, coworkers, and even the grocery store checkout clerk. No one was exempt. One of the people who accepted my invitation was Jason, a doctor at Concord of Chinese descent. Unbeknownst to me, Jason was already a committed Christian who had not yet found a church home.

Jason liked Solid Rock so much that he started bringing his fiancée to worship. Emily was also a doctor, but of Vietnamese descent. In fact, her mother was a boatperson like me. With much in common, Emily and I soon became close friends.

Jason and Emily took a particular shine to my kids, and my kids took a particular shine to Jason and Emily. My daughter in particular was tickled to meet someone who shared her name, and she nicknamed her "Big Emily." The name stuck, and all of us started calling her that.

Many times after church services ended, Jason and Big Emily would ask if they could borrow our kids. With Eddie and Emily jumping up and down with excitement, I couldn't say no even if I had wanted to. They would take the children to the park, to a movie, or out for ice cream. These were things I never did with them. Not only did such activities not enter my mind, I didn't have the time or the money for anything fun.

I was grateful on so many levels for Jason and Big Emily's willingness to be a part of the kids' lives. Their gift of time not only gave me a much-needed break, it demonstrated for Eddie and Emily what a healthy, loving relationship looked like—something Earl and I could not provide.

In addition to evangelizing, I also went overboard with both service and growth opportunities at the church by signing up for every committee that would take me. I volunteered to cook breakfasts, joined the choir, and even organized an annual church-wide retreat one year. I also signed up for an evening Bible study led by one of the church elders. Elder Ryan took us on a journey through Old Testament readings that revealed a God who judged and punished. I knew this God well. My whole life had been a series of punishing events that I assumed I deserved.

While I knew I was not a good wife or mother, I struggled to pinpoint the sins I had committed as a child that had resulted in longsuffering and torture. *Was there something I had not yet confessed? What was God still holding against me?* No matter how many times I confessed my remembered sins to God, I was unable to feel forgiven. I always felt condemned.

What I needed was the hope and salvation found in the New Testament. That was finally provided during a sermon Pastor J.C. preached on Christ's sacrificial love for the redemption of our sins. What I remember is being struck by the revelation that my sins were no worse than anyone else's, and the pastor had scripture to back that up:

> *... since all have sinned and fall short of the glory of God; they are now justified by his grace as a gift, through the redemption that is in Christ Jesus, whom God put forward as a sacrifice of atonement by his blood, effective through faith.*[22]

Pastor J.C. went on to say that there was nothing I could do to make God love me more than he already did, and there was nothing I could do to make him love me less. Once again, he presented irrefutable scripture:

> *For I am convinced that neither death, nor life, nor angels, nor rulers, nor things present, nor things to come, nor powers, nor height, nor depth, nor any-thing else in all creation, will be able to separate us from the love of God in Christ Jesus our Lord.*[23]

I wanted to believe with all my heart that God had died for my sins because he loved me beyond measure; but I couldn't under-stand how a perfect God could love an imperfect person like me. My Catholic upbringing had taught me to believe that salvation was something to be earned through repentance and good deeds. Pastor J.C.'s sermon contradicted that. I needed to know the truth, and I turned to Elder Ryan for clarification.

"Minh," he said, "we receive salvation because of what Jesus did for us on the cross. It is given freely. There is nothing we can do to earn it. It is a gift."

I remember that explanation clearly because it was the moment the scales truly fell away from my eyes. What Elder Ryan was saying was that I couldn't earn God's love through confession or acts of service because He already loved me unconditionally. I had it backwards. Confession and good works are an extension of our gratitude for what God has already done for us. This was an awesome discovery!

The apostle James summed it up perfectly when he wrote, "Show me your faith apart from your works, and I by my works will show you my faith."[24] For the first time I saw myself as God might see me: forgiven and redeemed, worthy and beloved.

While I did not cut back on my volunteer hours at the church, my attitude changed to one of gratitude. No longer was I trying to earn points toward membership in Heaven; now I was working for the sole purpose of expressing my thankfulness to God. When I reflected on my life during this time, I began to see that I *did* have much to be thankful for. I no longer lived in a communist country. I had a career that I enjoyed. I was the mother of two healthy children. I was able to provide for my family. I had friends. But try as I might, I could not feel grateful for Earl. Nor could I reconcile the feelings of anger, shame, and guilt that often wracked my mind. There was a constant rumble in my soul that would not subside and often made me feel like an egg in boiling water on the verge of cracking.

As a nurse, I knew my feelings of agitation and anxiety were not normal and that I probably needed professional help, but asking my colleagues for advice was out of the question. If I appeared unstable, I could lose my job. As the main breadwinner in the family, that was not acceptable.

I decided to take matters into my own hands. If I could self-diagnose, I thought, I might be able to treat myself without having to see a doctor. So as covertly as possible, I began to question colleagues about my symptoms by portraying them as someone else's problems. I also did extensive research in the library after hours. The information I discovered kept pointing to one thing: post-traumatic stress disorder.

I had heard of this condition, though I didn't know much about it. That was about to change. I got my hands on every medical journal available that addressed PTSD in the hopes of discovering a treatment—a simple pill perhaps. The studies were limited, and they all involved military veterans, but the message was the same: there was no cure for PTSD.

Years earlier, the members of the nursing board at Concord had denied me access to the RN program based on the fact that I experienced nightmares as a Vietnamese refugee. They had suspected something, yet there had been no follow-up to their concerns. And even though I worked in the medical field, none of my co-workers questioned my erratic and spastic behaviors, which included picking up extra shifts, refusing to take breaks, and eating as I worked. I was always on guard, skeptical of everyone else's motives, and constantly second-guessing every move I made.

My colleagues were not to blame for my problems. The notion that people could develop long-term emotional and psychological problems following exposure to extreme stress and trauma was still not widely understood, diagnosed, or accepted at this time—even in hospitals. In fact, PTSD was not documented as an official mental disorder until 1980 when the American Psychiatric Association published its third issue of the *Diagnostic and Statistical Manual*.[25] It would take some time for that report to circulate globally.

So life went on. I continued to live in a state of fear and survival while working nearly 60 hours a week, volunteering at the church, and taking classes to complete my Bachelor's Degree in Nursing. I justified my crazy schedule by blaming it on Earl who was still unemployed.

Had it not been for church and my Bible study, I don't think I could have handled the next stressful issue that presented itself. It started the day I began hearing scratching noises through the floorboards of our living room. Earl called in a specialist who gave us the bad news. Termites were eating through the supports under our house. We not only needed an exterminator, we needed to fix whatever damage the insects had already done.

Since construction was inevitable, I decided this was the best time to remodel the house. Eddie and Emily had been sharing a bedroom, and our only shower and toilet were in the shed in the backyard. It was time to build a bathroom indoors and add an extra bedroom to the back of the house. Though it was the logical thing to do, such an undertaking would be a huge financial burden under the circumstances. I went to the bank to see if I could qualify for a loan. I was approved, and construction began.

I prayed fervently that we would not default on the loan, and I prayed that no additional unforeseen disasters would unfold. I was at a breaking point and unsure whether I could handle one more thing. I was about to be tested.

One day I came home from work to learn that Earl had made an expensive business decision without consulting me first. He had seen a classified ad in the local paper for the purchase of a lawn care business, complete with tools and clients. It sounded perfect to him. There wasn't enough money in our bank account to cover the cost, so he acquired a loan from his parents to make up the difference and made the purchase.

I was beyond furious! Our arguments escalated to a whole new level. Earl's knowledge of plants and nature could not counterbalance his inability to run a company. He knew nothing about accounting, marketing, advertising, or sales, and he didn't have the business sense to know what he needed to succeed. All he saw was an opportunity to work outdoors on his own timetable. He renamed the company *E Lawn Mowing*; then he slowly proceeded to mow the business into the ground.

The descent for me was gradual. It took every bit of energy I had to maintain my composure while I continued to work and study at the hospital. When I got home, the mask came off and the witch emerged. Functioning in a perpetual state of negativity, my outbursts became more frequent and cruel. The weight of the world seemed to be entirely on my shoulders, and my family was my scapegoat. To protect them and me, I'd stay away from the house as much as possible.

Around the same time that *E Lawn Mowing* folded, I completed my BA degree. I was promoted from floor manager in the oncology unit to breast cancer specialist. This was both a blessing and a curse. With an increase in income came an increase in responsibilities.

My new role placed me at the center of many meetings with pharmaceutical companies whose representatives often conducted business after hours over dinner and drinks. I would attend these dinner meetings and polish off three or four glasses of wine. The alcohol felt good going down and helped me forget about the real issues in my life that I was not able to control. Once I was good and drunk, I would drag myself home and promptly get sick. With my head over the toilet bowl, Earl would say to the kids, "Here your mom goes again!"

I can only imagine how those memories affected my children, but I know how they affected me. The look of sadness and fear on Eddie's face is forever embedded in my brain—a picture I cannot shake. After a particularly bad night, I would look in the mirror and order myself never to drink again. Sadly, without professional help it was an order I was not able to follow.

My destructive lifestyle not only pulled me away from my children, it pulled me away from the church. There was only so much time in one day, and I was way too busy surviving to notice that I was caught in a deadly downward spiral. The lower I went the faster I slid, and the harder it became to apply the brakes.

One day when Earl wasn't home, an elder from the church and his wife came to visit me. I let them into the living room where they proceeded to counsel me on the proper role of a woman according to scripture. They told me that it was important that I allow Earl to be the man of the house, that it wasn't biblical for the wife to have the dominant role.

I listened as politely as possible while fuming on the inside. It was clear to me that Earl had hoodwinked them.

"Listen," I said. "I would prefer NOT to be in charge, but Earl is not capable. If I didn't work like I did, we would lose this house."

It was as if they didn't hear me. They just kept telling me that it was my duty to be a wife who supported her husband.

"I am a support!" I blurted out. "In fact, I do *all* the support around here! If you want to help our marriage—help Earl find a job!"

The elder appeased me by promising that he would indeed help with this. But the next thing I knew, Earl had gone solo again. This time he enrolled himself in theology classes at a local seminary. When I questioned him about this, he told me that his deepest passion was the Bible, not horticulture. His dream was to become a chaplain, and apparently the church supported him in this endeavor. I might have supported him as well, but I was too angry over the fact that he had made another decision without consulting me first.

I felt misunderstood, used, judged, and betrayed. I was angry with Earl and resented the church as an institution. Though I had been growing in my understanding of the Bible and how I fit into God's big story, from my point of view the church had failed to demonstrate Christ's love towards me. I had expected my church to be my safety net. But apparently the net was only big enough to hold one person, and it was holding Earl.

CHAPTER 33

Start children off on the way they should go,
and even when they are old, they will not turn from it.
Proverbs 22:6 (NIV)

1999–2002

I t's been said that women marry men hoping to change them, and men marry women hoping they will stay exactly the same. Inevitably, both parties are disappointed.

That was Earl and me. We were unevenly yoked from the start, and whatever feelings I had for him at the beginning of our marriage no longer existed. I did not believe in divorce and, because of the children, suicide was out of the question—though it often crossed my mind. So Earl and I stumbled along in our marriage out of duty rather than honor.

Arguments were our predominant form of communication. While this is what we modeled for the kids, I would not tolerate any fighting between Eddie and Emily. Whenever they disobeyed I would yell at them; then I would grab the wooden spoon and spank their bottoms. Earl refused to be a party to physical punishment and would retreat behind our bedroom door so he wouldn't have to watch. Later, I would feel extremely guilty for my behavior and search for extra work shifts to keep me away from home and the kids. From an early age, I taught my children to walk on eggshells in my presence, much the same way my mother had taught me.

At one point I had sense enough to suggest to Earl that we seek marriage counseling. I did not honestly expect counseling to fix our marriage, but I hoped that it would help our communication and improve our parenting practices. Unfortunately, Earl and I disagreed on the root of our problems. He believed it was tied to intimacy, or lack thereof. I believed the problem was Earl and his financial inability to provide for our family. In my mind, I didn't need intimacy; I needed help. Besides, I did not have either the time or energy for intimacy. I also felt that intimacy needed to be earned, and Earl had not earned the right to be intimate with me.

The counselor listened to us week after week without offering any useful advice. When our sessions ended, I threw myself even deeper into the one thing I could control: work.

I began attending nursing conferences, first in Australia, then around the world—New Zealand, England, Finland, and America, to name a few. I justified my time away by telling myself that the kids were better off without me. In truth, I was more comfortable in the presence of strangers than with my own family.

While on travel, I would seek out people in hotels and airports who were willing to engage in conversation, often ending our exchange by handing out my email address and phone number in the name of networking. I made it my mission to distribute 500 of my business cards annually. This was just one of the many irrelevant goals I set for myself as a way to restrain my spiraling emotions. Unfortunately, nothing I did could shake away the guilt I felt, the nightmares that plagued me, or the shame of my inadequacies as a mother.

It was during this time that Earl started his theology classes. He also initiated a youth group Bible study for Eddie and some of his peers. One night each week, about fifteen boys would gather in our living room to read the Bible, play games, and pray.

I truly wanted to support Eddie's spiritual growth, so I made it my responsibility to provide suitable snacks for these gatherings. Anyone who has spent time in the presence of teenage boys knows that they are capable of eating you out of house and home. Most of the time I couldn't keep up. I was exhausted and thus performed my self-imposed tasks with indignation. Sometimes I would pray that no kids would show up for Bible study. My inability to connect with this group, and with Emily, threw me further into an agitated state.

Eventually one of my co-workers advised me to speak to a psychiatrist. She had either noticed my distress or had finally acquired the courage to speak up. Fearing I might lose my job or my mind, I heeded her advice and made myself an appointment. Having already diagnosed my condition, I bared all my symptoms and all my emotions to the doctor so it would be easy for him to diagnose me with post-traumatic stress disorder. After several sessions, the psychiatrist diagnosed me with severe depression and prescribed a medication.

I was both shocked and relieved by the diagnosis. Depression could be managed with pills. PTSD could not.

I purchased the antidepressants as prescribed, and then I stuck them in a drawer and ignored them. In my current mental state I feared the temptation to overdose. Now that I knew what my problem was, I was sure I could manage my own care through sheer willpower rather than drugs. I put on a happy face, kept everyone at arm's length, and pretended to be someone I was not. I worked like a rat on crack, rushing from one task to another and juggling too many balls in the air without breathing. Trying to maintain this façade would eventually prove impossible.

My shell began to crack in the days leading up to Jason and Big Emily's wedding. Years earlier, in an effort to protect my children from disaster in case anything happened to me, I had dragged Earl to a lawyer's office to write up a will that named Jason and Big Emily as their guardians. So it came as no surprise when Big Emily asked if Eddie and Emily could serve as ring bearer and flower girl in her wedding. I said yes. Then Big Emily asked me to serve as her matron of honor in the wedding. I said yes. Next she asked me to oversee the sushi order that was to be delivered to the church following the reception. Once again, I said yes. Then I started to panic.

I approached Big Emily at work with the sole intention of asking to be removed from sushi duty. I practiced beforehand what I was going to say so as not to offend her in any way. I was sure I had my emotions in check, but I didn't. I broke down like a poorly constructed levee. The tears I had been damning up for years came crashing over the wall and flooded my face.

Between sobs I told Big Emily that my marriage was a wreck, that Earl was unemployed, that I was working 60 hours a week to make ends meet, and that I thought I was losing my mind. I admitted to her that I was exhausted and mean, that I didn't like going home, and that I was finding it difficult to complete simple tasks at work. I confessed that I drank until I got drunk, that I was a terrible mother and a terrible wife. And though I wanted to participate in her wedding, I acknowledged that I didn't think I was physically or mentally able to do so.

Big Emily held my hand and listened, passing me tissues every couple of minutes. My tears were cathartic. When all was said and done, I had not only been relieved of monitoring the sushi delivery, I had a new understanding of friendship. Big Emily promised to watch over the kids and me until I could get on my feet. As a doctor, she prescribed a medication for my depression—the same one the psychiatrist had ordered a year earlier. I told Big Emily that I already had the pills at home but had been afraid to take them.

"You must take them," she said. "Without them you cannot function. Without them, you could lose your job. And Minh, your children need you."

I did as Big Emily said and began taking the meds.

As the antidepressants began to kick in, I was able to see my work and home life more clearly. Things were worse than I thought. Bogged down in my own pain and consumed with trying to mask it, I had not recognized the pain in others—my patients as well as my children. No matter how much I was suffering inside, I believe Eddie and Emily were suffering more. I worked all the time. Whenever I was home, I was a tyrant, barking out orders and demanding compliance. I could not bear idleness and required the children to study or clean in my presence. It couldn't have been easy for them, and I'm sure they secretly hoped I would leave for work soon.

Though I hate to admit it, my marriage looked very much like my parents' marriage. My mother had her social circle, and I had my work. My father had given me quality time in much the same way that Earl gave our kids his attention. Like my parents, Earl and I fought all the time and, like my mother, I initiated every fight. The antidepressants had a calming effect that helped to tone down the intensity of our fights, but they didn't stop them.

There was a negative side to the drug, too. It made me feel emotionally flat. No excitement. No joy. It was as if I was wading through life as an observer, not a participant.

Thanks to the antidepressants, everything played out perfectly at Jason and Big Emily's wedding. When I look back at pictures of myself on that day, there is something ethereally beautiful and sad about me. I was model thin and my eyes appear to be searching for a faraway world.

While the drugs certainly helped me navigate a difficult time in my life, they did not cure my condition. Treated for the wrong disorder, my symptoms were simply masked rather than addressed, like putting a Band-Aid on a hemorrhaging wound. It was only a matter of time before I would bleed out.

Shortly before Emily's 13th birthday, Earl suggested that we send her to America to live with his sister's family as an international student. I listened as he explained his reasoning. It would be a good experience for Emily. It would give her a chance to get to know her cousin. It would allow Earl to focus on his classes so he could finish his degree and get a job. And it would expose Emily to an appropriate mother-child relationship, which she was not getting from me.

My heart was pounding *NO-NO-NO-NO*. Emily was too young. The journey was too unsafe. But I couldn't argue with Earl's logic. Against the desires of my heart, we shipped Emily off to North Carolina.

The house seemed strange without Emily in it. Her bedroom, with everything in its place, was awkwardly empty. Though she and I talked on the phone weekly, her aunt became the dominant influence in Emily's life. She began to polish her nails and wear makeup. From my perspective, she was too young for such things. I cursed myself for letting Emily go. I had abandoned her, just like my mother had abandoned me.

I loved Eddie and Emily deeply. I desperately wanted to be a good mother, but I had no idea how to go about it. My interactions with the kids centered more on correcting and protecting them rather than loving and nurturing them. I failed to hug them, compliment them, and encourage them. I demonstrated my love by working hard and covering their physical needs—food, clothing, and shelter. They deserved so much better than what I was giving them.

After nine long months, Emily finally returned to Australia. She was no longer the child I remembered. Gone was the shy, cautious, and obedient daughter. Emily was now outgoing, loud, free-spirited, and a bit of a know-it-all. She wore makeup and polished her nails. My little girl had grown into a young lady, and I had missed it.

CHAPTER 34

He said, "I came naked from my mother's womb,
and I will be naked when I leave.
The Lord gave me what I had, and the Lord has taken it away.
Praise the name of the Lord!"
In all of this, Job did not sin by blaming God.
Job 1:21-22 (NLT)

2002

No one understood me like my brother, Thanh. We saw the world through the same lens. It was no wonder, considering we were cut from the same cloth and had shared the same experiences and trauma as children. Even though we lived on separate continents, we had both managed to marry spouses who were unemployed, give birth to two children, and work like our lives depended on it. Whatever stress I was currently dealing with, a conversation with Thanh brought momentary joy and peace. I hadn't talked to Thanh in months, so I was grateful to receive his phone call.

"I went to the doctor," he said near the end of our conversation. "He told me I have cancer. It's in my lungs."

The wind went out of my sails. As a nurse, I knew that lung cancer was a death sentence. When I didn't say anything, Thanh continued. "They said they could treat me. I just wanted to let you know."

Thanh had never asked me for anything, but I could read his heart. We had stared down the face of death together several times— as children when the North Vietnamese invaded our home and killed our father; as prisoners tortured by the new regime; and as teens on the open seas confronting storms, pirates, and dehydration. If Thanh had to face death again, I knew he wanted me by his side.

"I will arrange my schedule so I can come and be with you," I told him.

I felt him smile across the phone lines. "That would be good," he said.

My family was used to living without me, so I took an indefinite leave of absence from the hospital and booked myself on the next flight to France. Before I left, I read every article I could find on lung cancer and spoke to every cancer doctor who crossed my path, but the verdict was always the same: there was very little to be done for lung cancer patients. My dear friend, Big Emily, dealt the hardest blow when she confirmed my darkest fear. "Minh," she said, "your brother will be lucky to make it to the end of the year."

I packed my bags for a long stay. I made a conscious decision to leave my antidepressants behind so I could be fully present with Thanh during the remainder of his life. Instead of going cold turkey, I tapered the dosage the week before the trip in an effort to avoid any side effects. Despite my precautions, I experienced one of the worst headaches of my life, which lasted almost a month.

Thanh was waiting for me at Charles de Gaulle Airport. His face broke into a beautiful smile when he saw me. Uninhibited, I ran to him and kissed him on both cheeks. We laughed, remembering how we were first introduced to this French custom in this very airport. Back then we had been shocked by such a display of affection, but now it seemed totally appropriate. It was a gesture of love as well as an acknowledgement of how far we had come in this big world. We were no longer child refugees but citizens on a global scale.

On the ride back to Thanh's apartment I asked a number of questions about his treatment and medications. Thanh readily provided answers that read like notes in one of my medical textbooks. He stopped short of sharing how he felt physically or emotionally, and I withheld any questions that might lead him down that path.

Two days after I arrived, I accompanied Thanh and his wife, Simone, to the oncologist's office. The doctor was direct and sterile in his approach as he placed an X-ray scan into the viewer to show us the extent of Thanh's cancer. I gasped silently. The cancer had not only taken over his lungs, it was evident in his bones.

A second scan showed two cancerous spots on his brain. I can't recall a single word the doctor said because it took every bit of energy I had to maintain my composure. The scans made it clear that our time together was perilously short.

Simone was the first to speak when the doctor completed his presentation. "What can we do?" she asked.

"Make him as comfortable as you can," he replied, "and enjoy what little time you have left together."

Simone looked appalled. This was not what she expected to hear. She wanted a cure.

I did not know much about the medical system in France, but I hoped that they had good hospice care. I could not bear the thought of my brother suffering any more than he had to; but hospice was the last thing Simone wanted because she was not ready to accept Thanh's death. "We will see another doctor for a second opinion," she told me.

While Simone set up additional doctor's appointments, I called my brothers back in Australia. In no uncertain terms, I explained Thanh's condition to Duc and Giang in separate phone calls telling each of them that they needed to come to France quickly if they wanted to see their brother one last time before he died.

Over the next three weeks, Simone dragged my dying brother to two more doctors. The prognosis was the same each time. The second doctor offered to do another round of chemo, though he admitted that it would probably kill Thanh. Simone gave him permission to try anyway.

I wanted to wring her neck. Chemo is not an appropriate option for people in advanced stages of cancer. It kills off healthy cells and weakens the immune system. I was angry that Simone would choose to make my brother suffer this way, but I maintained my composure. Again I encouraged her to call in hospice care, but she brushed me off. To her, that would have admitted defeat.

Thanh's spirits were raised by Duc and Giang's arrival. We reminisced about our childhood and helped Thanh plan for the care of his wife and children once he had passed. At Thanh's request, we took him for slow walks in the park across the street from where he lived knowing that each one could be his last. Though they stayed for less than a week, I believe Duc and Giang's visit brought Thanh much comfort.

Before my brothers left, Duc pulled me aside and told me to find a Catholic priest who could visit Thanh and administer last rites. I promised him I would. Thanh and his family did not belong to a church, but I knew he would appreciate the sacraments.

Later, Thanh was administered another round of chemo. As expected, it made him sicker. He had always been thin, but over the course of the next several weeks we watched in dismay as the pounds literally slipped from his body. Thanh no longer bore any resemblance to the vibrant young man who had crossed half the world with me. He was emaciated and smelled of death. Still, when I looked deeply into his eyes, I could make out the little brother I loved so much. His body was wasting away, but his soul remained very much alive.

"Sister," he said to me one day, "in your expertise, do you see people like me get well?"

I couldn't lie. "You will not live, Thanh. You will die from this disease, but we don't know when."

Thanh contemplated my answer. "Do you think my wife and children will be OK without me?" he asked. It was as if he was asking me for permission to leave them.

Thanh's daughters were 16 and 11 years of age—well beyond the ages Thanh and I had been when we were left to fend for ourselves. "You'd be surprised." I told Thanh, "I'm sure your daughters will be alright."

Several days later, Thanh completely lost his ability to speak in French. Vietnamese was the only language he could access, and I was the only person who could understand him. I was grateful to be by his side during this time and serve as his link to the world.

We moved Thanh from the bedroom to the living room where it was easier for us to care for him. He spent most days in the hospital bed that Simone had acquired, slipping in and out of consciousness. When Thanh was awake, we would converse in our native language. When he slept, I would kneel next to his bed and pray—either for a miracle or a quick death. Anything in between would be cruel.

One day, his eldest daughter, Henrietta, asked me, "What are you doing?"

"Praying," I responded.

"What do you say?" she asked.

"I'm asking God to watch over your dad." Then I added, "You can pray too."

Henrietta thought a moment. "I have a Bible," she said. She ran to her room to get it.

The Bible she handed me was brand new. Never used. I turned to Psalm 23 and read it to Thanh in French, more for Henrietta's sake than his.

The Lord is my shepherd, I shall not want. He makes me lie down in green pastures; he leads me beside still waters; he restores my soul. He leads me in right paths for his name's sake. Even though I walk through the valley of the shadow of death, I fear no evil; for you art with me; thy rod and thy staff, they comfort me.[26]

Henrietta had received her Bible when she made her first communion, but she admitted she had never used it. *Perhaps,* I thought, *it was meant for this very moment.* After all, nothing is random with God. I used Henrietta's Bible daily to pray over Thanh. I would read scripture in French when the girls were present and translate passages into Vietnamese when they weren't. One day I asked Henrietta, "Would you like to read to your dad?"

Without hesitation, she took the Bible from me and read the passage I pointed out to her. A warm sense of God's presence invaded the living room as she read the words out loud. I remember thinking that the best gift we can give the next generation is the knowledge of Jesus Christ and the hope of the resurrection. I had tried to bestow this gift on my own children, but my attempts were not always successful. Now God was providing me with an opportunity to share this gift with Thanh's children. All I could do was plant the seed. Others would need to tend the soil and prune the branches after I left.

God also laid it on my heart to speak to Thanh about his faith. With his health rapidly failing, it was more important than ever for him to reach out to God. The next time he woke, I said to him, "Look, I know you have not been going to church, but that is not a crime. You need to accept Jesus as your savior and ask for God's forgiveness so He will take you home to Heaven."

For a moment I wasn't sure if Thanh understood me, even though I was speaking in Vietnamese. Then he slowly and deliberately asked, "Do you think God will accept me?"

"Yes!" I answered, elated that Thanh was coherent. "God wants all of us!"

In the face of death, on the border between Heaven and Earth, my faith in God intensified. Jesus seemed more real to me than He had in years. I was sure He was looking down on Thanh and had heard my prayers. Knowing that God was fully present did not alleviate my fears or relieve my brother's pain, but it helped me trust that there was a plan. Thanh and I had both worked our fingers to the bone trying to create a sense of stability and safety for our families. But this world is fickle. People will disappoint. Employers will exploit. Governments will fail. Only God is constant. Only He can be trusted.

I did not speak to Simone about God since she would not let the priest in when he came knocking, but I did ask her to reconsider contacting hospice to coordinate Thanh's care. Simone was still not yet ready to let go. Instead, she made me help her transport my brother from the hospital bed to the wheelchair to the car so she could take him to yet another doctor for yet another opinion.

Thanh was wiped out when we got to the medical office, and frankly, so was I. The doctor took one look at Thanh and gave

Simone a stupefied look. "What do you want me to do for him? He's dying," he said.

Simone lost it. She was hysterical. The doctor stood up and left the room, leaving me to calm the waters. Once again I brought up hospice. I did my best to explain to her that in light of that fact that she and I were both worn out from caring for Thanh, professional help would be best. After a lengthy conversation, she finally agreed to call in a hospice nurse under one condition: morphine was not to be administered. Simone believed morphine would speed the death process, and she did not want to be responsible for anything that might hasten Thanh's demise.

It was easy for me then to find fault in Simone's decisions. I believed she was thinking only of herself. But in retrospect I can see that she loved Thanh deeply and could not envision living without him. He was her lifeline, like he had been mine so many years before. Death was too final, and she simply could not accept it. Grasping at straws was her way of loving Thanh to the end.

The hospice nurses meant well, but without morphine they were not able to provide Thanh with the care he truly needed. Morphine was the only drug that would have eased his pain. It was also the only drug that would have helped relieve his shortness of breath. Without it, Thanh struggled to take in air.

Watching him suffer was unbearable, and it tore me apart knowing there was nothing I could do to help. I stopped praying for a miracle and simply begged God to end Thanh's life and take him home to paradise. It was my final act of love.

Thanh's heart stopped beating on a Monday morning in late October. I was praying by his side when I heard the death rattle, which was soon followed by short gasps for air. Then Thanh took one last breath and died. It was over.

Simone and I lovingly washed Thanh's body. Fond memories came to mind as I went through the motions: bathing together as children before bedtime, holding on to him as he paddled like a dog toward our escape boat, and running with him into the surf after our jailbreak. We had splashed together in joy, in fear, and in relief. As I worked, I prayed—sometimes in French, more often in English, and occasionally in Vietnamese. I thanked God for making Thanh my brother and for granting me the privilege of standing by him at the end.

Then Simone and I combed Thanh's hair and dressed him in clean pajamas. His emaciated body was clear evidence that he had lived too long. But he was in Heaven now with a new body, reunited with our father and our sister and our brother. I imagined them all around me, and I smiled. Thanh was free at last. He was home.

The Catholic Church was packed the day of Thanh's funeral. I was consoled when I saw how many friends my brother had, both Vietnamese and French. But the highlight of the mass for me was hearing Henrietta read from the Bible, from the book of John:

> *Jesus said to them, "I am the bread of life; he who comes to me shall not hunger, and he who believes in me shall never thirst."*[27]

I prayed that a deep desire to know God would take hold of Henrietta's heart and that her heavenly Father's love would help her navigate the pain of losing her earthly father. I understood her grief all too well. God, and God alone, had comforted me during the darkest times of my childhood. I prayed He would do the same for her.

> *"No one can come to me unless the Father who sent me draws him; and I will raise him up at the last day."* [28]

Henrietta also shared a few personal words about her father. How hard he worked. What a good provider he had been. That she loved him for the life he had made possible for her. What she didn't share were any touching stories of laughter or joy or playfulness or fun. As I listened, I realized that Henrietta's relationship with her father was similar to the relationship I had with my own children. Devoted, but distant.

I had been in France for almost six months, choosing to be with Thanh over my own family, over my own children. I had promised God that I would never abandon them, but I had. Again. *Would God forgive me? Would Eddie and Emily forgive me?*

CHAPTER 35

Today I have given you the choice between life and death,
between blessings and curses.
Now I call on heaven and earth to witness the choice you make.
Oh, that you would choose life,
so that you and your descendants might live!
Deuteronomy 30:19 (NLT)

November 2002–2005

My brother had always encouraged me to never give up, but in the days following his death and my return to Australia, I felt defeated. A part of me had died with Thanh, and I did not know who I was or who I was supposed to be. The face I saw in the mirror was unrecognizable. Grief consumed me. I plunged into a deep depression, yearning for something I could not define and, therefore, could not grasp.

I continued to drag myself to work, but my heart wasn't in it—I was simply going through the motions. I asked my supervisors to remove me from the travel schedule for a while so I could rest and come to grips with my brother's death. Unfortunately, spending more time at home brought no relief. I felt like a stranger there, unsure of my role.

Earl watched over the children and provided them with spiritual guidance while I hovered in the background, cleaning, cooking, sleeping, and crying. Had I reached out for medical help, I'm sure doctors would have put me back on the antidepressants. However, now that I had weaned myself off of them, I wanted to stay off. Part of me was fearful that I would overdose; another part of me was fearful of being numb. Fear steered me clear of the pills and the doctors. In my pain, I turned to alcohol.

As my drinking increased, suicidal thoughts once again began to beckon. While driving home from work late at night, I would often entertain the idea of closing my eyes and simply drifting across the centerline into oncoming traffic. A semi, I speculated, would ensure instant death, and a fatal car accident would be easier for Earl to explain to the kids than an overdose of pills.

I would always change my mind when I got home and saw my children. They were my saving grace. In spite of me, Eddie and Emily were growing into dependable, compassionate individuals. I loved them so much, even though I wasn't capable of showing it.

Death would have been easy, but I chose the harder route. I chose life.

Prayer had sustained me in France as I walked through the dark valley by Thanh's side. Now, walking through my own dark valley, I turned to prayer again. More often than not, I felt like I was praying into a void where God was not present. Still, I kept praying—prayers for deliverance from my circumstances, from my fears, and from myself.

One Sunday, I decided to accompany Earl and the kids to church in the hopes of feeling God's peace again. The place was bustling with joyful activity that was too much for my crushed spirit to handle. My attempts to blend into the crowd proved fruitless; I was too far-gone to assimilate. The experience left me desolate. I didn't go back.

At the end of my rope, I made an appointment to see a different psychiatrist. No one had suggested that I do so. Not Earl. Not Big Emily. No one in my family or any of my coworkers. The credit has to go to God. He alone knew my struggles and what I needed.

Like the psychiatrist before him, this doctor diagnosed me with clinical depression and prescribed Zoloft. This antidepressant, however, works differently. It is often used in conjunction with counseling to treat PTSD. So, even though my actual condition was not being addressed, the drug did curb the severity of my symptoms—but only for a while. Then fatigue set in, which is a common side effect of the drug. For several weeks, I was able to push through the overwhelming drowsiness. Then I hit a wall.

After a long day on my feet, I came home to a mess and three family members who had left the housework for me. Exhausted, angry, sad, and depressed, I lashed out at Earl. I called him lazy and thoughtless. I accused him of taking advantage of me for years. I ranted on about the pain I felt because of him and the hole in my heart left by Thanh's death. I complained of sleepless nights and daily panic attacks that ravaged my brain and my body, pushing me to the point where I couldn't keep details straight. I revealed my fear of feeling pursued or boxed in, depending on the situation. Alcohol, I admitted, was the only thing capable of numbing my pain.

Somewhere in my tirade, I told Earl that my psychiatrists had misdiagnosed me. I was suffering from post-traumatic stress disorder—not depression. I knew it, but no one else did. I needed help.

Earl listened. He truly listened. I don't think he was surprised by anything I said except my accusation of misdiagnosis. With compassion, he promised to find me the right doctor. And he did.

A professor at the seminary Earl attended recommended Dr. Vicky. She was a Christian psychiatrist who specialized in post-traumatic stress disorder. After just four sessions with her, I got the answer I had always known.

"Normally it takes me much longer to diagnose someone with PTSD," she said, "but you are so open about your thoughts and feelings, it's easy to identify."

Initially, I wanted to blame everything on Earl. Dr. Vicky pointed out, however, that he was just my scapegoat. My issues stemmed from childhood. Dr. Vicky's experience with African children displaced by tribal wars helped me understand that traumatic experiences affect all ages for all times. With her guidance, we addressed each layer of the trauma in my life—beginning with the abuse by the gardener, followed by the brutal murder of my father and siblings, the mental abuse I suffered at my grandfather's house, my mother's lack of protection, and the sexual abuse I endured throughout my life. Several near-death experiences and the lack of a safety net in my adult years had exacerbated my condition.

Dr. Vicky explained that my angry responses to situations that were out of my control were typical for PTSD survivors whom she said live in a constant state of fear. I could identify with this assessment. I always felt like I was standing on the edge of a precipice that could give way at any moment. As I came to understand it, I had turned on a survival switch as a child, but I had never learned how to turn it off.

"Can you cure me?" I asked.

"There is no cure for PTSD," Dr. Vicky replied, "only steps to handle the disorder. First, we have to determine what triggers you."

Earl, I thought. But I was wrong. For me, the main trigger was stress. Unfortunately, all aspects of my life were stressful.

Through cognitive therapy I discovered that my biggest stress trigger was dealing with change that I had not initiated. In these situations, I automatically reacted with a fight-or-flight response. Battle or escape. Yell or run. Scream and reprimand my children or stay away from the house. Work harder or attempt suicide. Those were my choices. I could see nothing in between. For me, there was no middle ground. No compromise. Every situation was a matter of life or death.

This insight helped explain why I was driven to extreme anger and agitation every time Earl changed jobs or made a financial decision without consulting me first. He was literally thrusting me into survival mode. He wasn't a bad man; he was just a bad man for me.

I also came to realize that while I had worked hard to move up the career ladder, the extra responsibilities associated with the climb had triggered me to abuse alcohol and consider suicide. The additional money that was supposed to bring relief had actually brought more suffering because I didn't know when enough was enough.

In many ways my survival instincts had proved advantageous in the nursing profession; but just as often they had negatively affected my personal life. On the one hand, doctors wanted me on their shifts; on the other hand, subordinates and peers found it difficult to work with me. This realization was hard to bear and downright depressing.

"Will I ever be able to live a normal life?" I asked.

"Yes," Dr. Vicky assured me, "once you learn how to prevent triggers and manage symptoms. You must learn to know yourself."

Looking inward was one of the most challenging and sobering tasks I have ever attempted. I was determined to get it right and end the pain, so I stopped the drugs and alcohol cold turkey. With Dr. Vicky's help, psychotherapy became my lifeline. I felt safe in her office and was able to face some of the most frightful experiences of my past head-on. At least six things surfaced about myself that I had not been able to see and did not like.

First, I realized that I gave death the seat of honor at my life table. I did not fear death. In fact, I prepared for it—daily. I was keenly aware that the grim reaper lurked in every corner, which forced me to remain in a state of high alert. PTSD sufferers frequently talk about death because we expect it at any moment.

Second, I had projected my fears onto my children. I recall Emily once telling me, "Mom, you always tell us about the bad things to come!" She was right. I wasn't wired to expect anything good. I looked for the worst and kept my guard up waiting for it. I pushed Eddie and Emily to do more, study more, work harder, and be more productive. On my watch, they were not allowed to relax or have fun. As a result, our home environment was intense and rigid.

Third, I did not give or demonstrate love to my children. It wasn't because I didn't want to; it was because PTSD survivors do not know how to love. My way of showing love to my children was to protect them from physical harm and provide money to cover their basic needs. Providing basic needs may make a child feel safe, but it does not make them feel loved. Children feel loved when you spend time with them, show an interest in them, and encourage them in their struggles. I did none of this. Through therapy, I found myself grateful that Earl was their father because he knew how to love them appropriately.

Fourth, I showed more care for strangers than my own children. My patients had problems I could handle. I would tuck them in at night and ask them how they felt. Often, I would be there in the morning when they woke up to check on them. I did not give Eddie and Emily the same attention. They took a backseat to everyone else. I chose to work on holidays, often missing their birthdays and Christmas. And my mission to hand out an entire box of business cards each year required me to respond to dozens of emails each month. This took time and energy, two commodities I should have lavished on Eddie and Emily.

Fifth, I unfairly blamed Earl for everything. PTSD, which Earl did not cause, was the real source of my problems. Earl was kind. He was lighthearted. He was handy. He was a loving father. He was always present for the children. He was faithful. He was a follower of Christ, and he made sure that Eddie and Emily had opportunities to know Christ as well.

Last, but certainly not least, I came to realize that I was to blame for many of our financial woes, not Earl. For years I had complained that we were barely able to pay our bills due to the fact that Earl could not hold down a steady job. While this was true, there was also another truth to be acknowledged: I had been fiscally irresponsible at times.

As my career took off and my income rose, my paycheck was enough to cover the bills for a family of four. However, the bills were not my priority. I gave money away freely, the way my Dad did—to the homeless, to charities, and to friends who were down on their luck. As a nurse manager, I had purchased lavish gifts for my colleagues' birthdays and willingly picked up the tab at restaurants.

At home, I insisted that the kids have the best of everything, from designer clothes to professional music lessons. And to make sure they did not fall behind in their studies like I had, I employed several tutors to help them with each subject. I tried to teach my children the value of a dollar by giving them cold, hard cash for Christmas rather than presents. As a result, there were no packages to unwrap under the tree. In fact, there was no tree. That would have been a waste of money.

I remember one year I got home from work to discover that Emily had decorated a potted plant to serve as our Christmas tree. I was very proud of her ingenuity, but I totally missed the mark. I had denied my children the opportunity to celebrate and experience the joy of giving and receiving. I was better at giving money away than keeping it, and I did so at the expense of my children. This realization hit me the hardest.

The following Bible passage from the book of Matthew took on a whole new meaning for me:

"Why do you look at the speck of sawdust in your brother's eye and pay no attention to the plank in your own eye? How can you say to your brother, 'Let me take the speck out of your eye,' when all the time there is a plank in your own eye? You hypocrite, first take the plank out of your own eye, and then you will see clearly to remove the speck from your brother's eye."[29]

I cursed myself for not getting the help I needed years earlier. Had I been properly diagnosed with PTSD when the children were still little, the damage I inflicted on their lives might not have been so severe. Dr. Vicky repeatedly informed me that true healing was possible only if I did not dwell on past mistakes and made wise decisions going forward. She gave me hope when she told me that it was not too late to change.

My first attempts to bond with the children were disastrous. Eddie and Emily were not used to me asking personal questions or showing interest in their lives. The mother they knew was harsh, demanding, controlling, and predictable. They questioned my motives and were wary to offer a response.

Their mistrust of my intentions, however, did not deter me. Dr. Vicky had warned me that the children would push back. Emily did so more than Eddie. She became sassy and antagonistic. In her, I saw myself and fought hard against the urge to strong-arm her back into a submissive position the way my mother had controlled me.

Earl watched it all with skepticism. He tried to offer words of advice, but I wouldn't listen. Though not the cause of my problems, he was the main trigger and had the ability to exacerbate my bad behaviors.

I did not love Earl or respect him, and years of therapy were not going to change that. The bottom line was this: I was never going to be the wife Earl hoped I would be, and he was never going to be the man I needed.

Late one night, after the kids had gone to bed, I told Earl we needed to talk. "It's not working," I said. "I want a divorce."

Earl looked shocked. Despite the problems in our marriage, he never considered divorce an option. "I cannot give you a divorce," he said. Then he picked up his Bible and quoted me a passage from the Book of Matthew:

> *I tell you that anyone who divorces his wife, except*
> *for sexual immortality, makes her a victim of adultery,*
> *and anyone who marries a divorced woman commits*
> *adultery.*[30]

This was one disagreement I was not about to let him win. "Then I'll make it easy on you," I replied. "I would be happy to go out and have sex with someone else."

"That's not what I want you to do!" Earl exclaimed.

My response had clearly upset him. I saw a look of fear and hurt in his eyes. He was dependent on me for his life, much like a parasitic plant that attaches itself to a host. While he was thriving, I was dying a slow death.

"You have to let me go," I said calmly.

Earl wasn't sure he could, but I insisted. I had finished paying the penalty for my mistakes a long time ago. My sentence was up. These prison walls had no right to contain me any longer.

"Let's pray," I suggested.

To this day, I still find it odd that I suggested prayer. I can only attribute this to the Holy Spirit's long-awaited presence in our sad situation. We held hands and prayed, just like a normal Christian couple might do.

I don't remember what Earl prayed for, but I prayed for forgiveness. For all the mistakes I had made. For my anger and shame and rigidity. For all the hurts I had inflicted on the kids and on Earl. For all the times I had fallen short of being a loving wife and a nurturing mother.

It was a cleansing prayer, a prayer of deliverance that opened the door to true freedom.

CHAPTER 36

I know, Lord, that our lives are not our own.
We are not able to plan our own course.
So, correct me, Lord, but please be gentle.
Do not correct me in anger, for I would die.
Jeremiah 10:23-24 (NLT)

2005–2006

E arl and I sat the kids down after dinner. As gently as possible, we told them that we had decided to divorce. Actually, I did all the talking. Earl's silence reinforced the notion that I was the "bad" parent and divorce had been entirely my decision. Though the kids were old enough to understand my reasoning (Eddie was finishing his last year of high school, and Emily was two years behind him), they didn't take the news well.

Introverted and passive Eddie quietly stated, "I knew it would eventually come to this."

Extroverted and assertive Emily blurted out, "Where are *we* going to live?"

I assured the kids that very little would change for them. They would stay in the house with their dad and continue their education at the schools in which they were already enrolled. I would continue to pay the mortgage, but the day-to-day care of the house would now fall on their father's shoulders. He would be responsible for meals, cleaning, and laundry. I would visit as often as possible but would be living with their Uncle Giang, about 20 minutes away.

I moved the very next day.

Giang and his new wife, Hong Anh, were expecting their first child, and since Giang traveled for his job, my presence in their home proved beneficial for all parties. Hong Anh got the assistance she needed, and I got a safe place to heal. Everyone pitched in with the household chores, so the atmosphere was peaceful and supportive. When I arrived at the house after a hard day's work, Hong Anh often greeted me with a soothing cup of tea. It was so unlike the welcome I was used to receiving in my own home.

The divorce was straightforward and added just a minimal amount of stress to my life, and that's just because I had to do all the legwork. Besides initiating the separation and finding an attorney, I had to meet with the lawyer to discuss the settlement, work with Earl separately to get his signature on the documents, and drive the papers back and forth between the house and the attorney's office. All this had to be handled between my regular work hours.

I was bitter toward Earl for removing himself from the divorce process, but I was also grateful that he didn't put up a fight. We were able to come to an amicable agreement and, as a result, we never had to go to court. We simply signed the papers and the attorney filed them for us.

In a nutshell, Earl and I agreed that I would continue to pay all the bills as long as the kids were living in the house. This meant free rent for Earl for at least two more years, until Emily went off to college. In return, I could visit the kids as often as I wanted, whenever I wanted.

The day I finally received notice that I was no longer legally married, I broke down and cried tears of relief and joy. It felt as if a huge millstone had been lifted off my shoulders. I was no longer a prisoner of circumstance. I had been set free and given another chance at life.

Dr. Vicky helped me transition into my new role as a single, working mother. Together we created a navigable routine to replace the chaotic lifestyle that had once consumed me. The key was a predictable schedule that curtailed my craving for alcohol and kept me off antidepressants. With her help, the darkness and fog began to lift.

My job took up the bulk of my time. However, without the pressures of home, I found myself enjoying the work. As an oncology nurse specialist, I had to commute between several hospitals. I relished my alone time in the car and no longer felt compelled to cross the line into oncoming traffic. I was physically and emotionally stronger than I had been in years. Nonetheless, Dr. Vicky warned me that as a PTSD survivor, I was only one calamity away from a breakdown. Therefore, it was important for me to maintain counseling, stay in a routine, and avoid situations that presented stress.

That's why I visited the children no more than once or twice a week. Though I yearned to see them, I hated going to the house where the tension was palpable. Eddie was always happy to see me, but Emily was standoffish because she blamed me for breaking up our family. Earl hid in the back bedroom during my visits, which was probably best. Had he been present, I'm sure I would have lit into him over the condition of the house. There were dirty dishes in the sink, grimy countertops, unmade beds, and piles of dirty laundry. The refrigerator lacked groceries, and the bathroom smelled of mildew. The mess and disorder triggered the worst in me. I would often leave angry or in tears.

If I compared my family's new lifestyle to a dance, Eddie was the one who was willing to learn new steps; Emily was still using the old steps; and Earl had turned his back on the dance floor completely. As for me, I had already found a new rhythm and was tearing up the dance floor.

"I think Dad is moving to the U.S."

When Eddie said these words to me less than six months after the divorce was final, I just about hit the roof. Earl was doing it again: making decisions he had no right to make without consulting me first. I found him tucked away in the bedroom.

"Eddie just informed me that you are thinking of going back to the U.S." He said nothing. "Is this true?" I asked.

"Yes," he replied.

"Did you think of our children?" I chided.

"Yes," he answered. "Eddie will stay here, and Emily will come with me. We're going to live with my sister."

I felt every ounce of sanity drain from my body, and the anger boiled up in me like lava from a volcano. Earl was only thinking of himself. I could see the writing on the wall. He wanted his sister to take care of him since I was no longer willing to. I screamed profanities. I called Earl every derogatory name I could think of. I pounded the walls and would have pounded Earl into a pulp if I didn't remember Dr. Vicky telling me to turn and walk away from stressful situations.

Just when I was beginning to feel safe riding the waves of my new life, Earl pushed me from the boat, plunging me into the cold, dark sea. I sunk at such a rapid rate that I was unable to slow the descent. My brain automatically flipped into survival mode and every decision I was about to make was guided by my need to protect Emily.

I couldn't imagine anything good coming out of a move to North Carolina. Emily was angry as she struggled to deal with the divorce. The last thing she needed was to be removed from her friends and support system in her junior year of high school. She needed her mother, not her aunt. I concocted the worst-case scenarios in my head: Emily would fail in the United States; she wouldn't be able to make friends; danger lurked around every corner; she would fall behind in her studies and not be accepted into any colleges.

Earl was not capable of heading off any of these disasters. It was up to me to protect my daughter. The only logical course of action in my PTSD brain was to follow Earl and Emily to America. The idea of telling Earl to leave Emily behind in my care did not enter my mind. I had every right to forbid him from moving her out of the country, but I said nothing. I had been conditioned to respond to Earl's decisions rather than try to change them. Earl hadn't conditioned me this way—my mother had. I had been taught to obey and adapt. And so I did.

I immediately began researching jobs in North Carolina only to be reminded that my Australian nursing license would not be accepted in American hospitals or clinics. If I moved to the United States, I would have years of schooling ahead of me. Canada, on the other hand, would accept my nursing credentials.

Looking at a map, the distance between Canada and North Carolina was less than the distance between Australia and New Zealand. I decided I would have to move to Canada. I might not be able to visit Emily every weekend, but twice a month seemed possible.

When post-traumatic stress kicks into high gear, sufferers are not capable of seeing beyond the immediate situation. They just can't grasp the bigger picture. They make irrational decisions that seem logical to them and illogical to a healthy person. I was a woman in crisis, unable to see how the dominoes would fall. All I knew was that I had to go to North America to protect Emily from the dangers that awaited her, and I would move mountains to achieve that goal.

Before I knew it, Earl and Emily were gone. I immediately requested an indefinite leave of absence from the hospital in order to put all the pieces of my puzzle into place. My first objective was to sell the house. I would need the money to help pay for my move, and it was not worth keeping if both Eddie and Emily were not living there.

Ridding the house of a lifetime of memories was a monumental task. There were elementary school projects—Eddie's hand tracings with "I love you Mummy!" written beneath, and Emily's small hand pressed in clay to commemorate Mother's Day. Touching each object brought on emotions I was incapable of processing, and I cursed Earl for forcing me to decide what to keep and what to throw away. I couldn't take everything with me, yet I had nowhere to leave them. I contemplated a massive burning in the backyard, but decided against it. Finally, recognizing that I was unable to move forward on my own, I hired someone to downsize for me and make the decisions I could not make.

I also reached out to every man and woman in America and Canada with whom I had exchanged business cards. Several

311

responded with kind words of advice, yet only one offered me actual help—Paul Towner from Virginia.

I had met Paul a couple of years earlier at the Sydney airport during a particularly long flight delay. Like me, he was divorced with a young daughter. Paul responded by email immediately saying he understood my plight. He offered to put me up in a hotel in Virginia while I searched for a job. I emailed him back and told him that I needed to search for a job in Canada, not the U.S.

"Canada is more than 700 miles from North Carolina," he wrote.

"What should I do?" I asked.

Paul responded, "Move to Virginia."

I could sense that Paul was interested in getting to know me better. I chose to overlook the obvious in order to get close to Emily.

During my next session with Dr. Vicky, I informed her that I would soon be moving to Canada or the United States and would no longer be able to take advantage of her services. As I explained the situation, I felt my anger toward Earl escalating with each sentence: "It was cruel of Earl to take Emily to the U.S. Just cruel." "She won't be able to manage without me." "I am her mother. It's my job to protect her." "I will not let him poison her towards me in my absence." "I have to do whatever is necessary to prove to Emily that I love her."

As I spoke, I recognized the symptoms of PTSD, but I was not able to manage them. I was too far-gone. My survival instincts were on full speed ahead.

"I don't think it's a good idea for you to leave Australia," Dr. Vicky said calmly. "I don't think you're ready for such a big change." Though she was right, my mind was made up. Unable to alter my course, Dr. Vicky made me promise that I would find a counselor in my new country. I gave her my word that I would.

My mother and siblings were less supportive of my decision than Dr. Vicky. They told me in no uncertain terms that it was a ridiculous idea to chase Emily to America, and Eddie agreed with them. I chalked his opinion up to the fact that he was unhappy about losing his childhood home. Even Emily told me not to come, but I told myself that she was young and incapable of making sensible decisions.

It wasn't that I refused to listen to anyone; I couldn't hear them. In my mind, I was the only one capable of thinking rationally, and I had to move fast. In reality, I was in the full throes of PTSD and probably suffering a nervous breakdown as well.

I put the family home on the market and acquired a six-month tourist visa for travel in the U.S. Then I purchased a plane ticket to Virginia, packed two suitcases, withdrew enough money from the bank to cover my immediate needs, and flew halfway around the globe to try and protect my daughter who I feared was in grave danger.

PART IV
AMERICA

2006–2013

CHAPTER 37

"I have told you these things, so that in me you may have peace.
In this world, you will have trouble.
But take heart! I have overcome the world."
John 16:33 (NIV)

2006–Early 2007

W hen I arrived at Dulles International Airport in Virginia, Paul was waiting for me at the gate smiling from ear to ear. His optimism was wasted on me. I had only one thing on my mind: Emily.

It had been months since I had seen Emily's beautiful face. During our weekly phone conversations, her voice had come across as dismissive and angry. I had interpreted this as a sign of trouble, and I told Paul that I needed to see her right away. He advised me to plant roots first and find a job. I could not argue, as I was totally dependent on his good-heartedness.

Paul found me an apartment close to his house that I was able to rent on a month-to-month basis while I looked for employment. That first week I poured over job listings in the local newspapers and on several websites. When I realized I could not provide potential employers with a local phone number, Paul insisted that I use his. I was hesitant about doing this and told him I would think about it.

The following week, Paul took me to a job fair for medical professionals. Though I was not able to apply for nursing positions, I was able to apply as a private care provider for the elderly who were homebound or in nursing homes. Several companies asked me how they could reach me. I gave them Paul's number.

Following the job fair, Paul encouraged me to move into his spare bedroom. His rationale made sense: if potential employers called, I needed to be available. I cautiously packed my suitcases and moved in. Over the next few days, I did receive several calls for job interviews, which validated my decision to move into Paul's home. Paul graciously drove me to each interview, but I was not offered any of the positions.

By week three, I was feeling like a captive in Paul's house, through no fault of his. I was free to come and go as I pleased and could have rented a car, but driving in Northern Virginia frightened me. My instincts told me to drive on the left-hand side of the road, like it's done in Australia. In my state of mind, putting myself behind the wheel of a car would have been suicidal. Therefore, I was forced to rely on public transportation, which I found confusing. Oftentimes, I got lost.

I had worked myself into an extreme state of agitation, desperate to see Emily. At my wit's end, I told Paul that I couldn't wait any longer to see her, and the job hunt would have to be put on hold until I did. To me, it was a matter of life or death. This time Paul didn't argue with me. He took the next couple of days off from work so he could drive me to Emily directly.

I made arrangements with Earl over the phone to meet halfway between Northern Virginia and North Carolina at a McDonalds. It was a cold winter's day when we headed south, but the sense of relief that accompanied the trip warmed my soul.

Emily actually seemed happy to see me at first. Then she saw Paul, and that turned our visit into an awkward reunion, to say the least. I introduced him as my friend. By the sad looks on Emily and Earl's faces, I knew they suspected it was something more. I probably should have asked Paul to give me some time alone with my daughter, but after all he had done for me, I didn't feel that was appropriate.

Paul casually took a seat in the booth next to me, across from Earl. Years of conditioning had prepared my ex-husband to retreat in my presence. He stared at the table and only spoke when I asked him a direct question. I did most of the talking, which revolved around Emily's school and friends. She responded with short, curt answers that didn't contain much detail. I attributed this to the fact that she did not feel comfortable sharing in front of a stranger. Not wanting to appear as if she liked one parent more than the other, she played the neutral card and gave Earl and me equal attention.

I wanted to hug Emily when the time came for us to part, but she had already made up her mind not to. She simply said goodbye and jumped into Earl's car. My heart broke as I watched them drive off.

I had accomplished what I came to America for: to see my daughter. Unfortunately, that goal was no longer enough. I now desired to stay near her. Surely, I thought, I could find a job in North Carolina as easily as I could find one in Virginia.

The trip back to Paul's place seemed like an eternity, exacerbated by the blizzard we drove into. I felt trapped—totally reliant on Paul's driving skills, totally reliant on his goodness, totally reliant on his decisions.

I was acutely aware that my PTSD was firing on all cylinders, but I couldn't see straight on how to manage it. My mind was frenetic, jumping from one imagined disaster to another. I tried to practice the techniques Dr. Vicky had taught me by taking deep breaths and thinking of pleasanter times. Each pleasant memory, however, brought tears to my eyes and pulled me deeper into despair. If there was a clear path to follow, I could not see it.

Back in Northern Virginia, my job search was proving unsuccessful. No one wanted to hire an Australian citizen with a strong Vietnamese accent on a six-month tourist visa. It was becoming clear to me that if I wanted a job, I would have to move to America permanently.

Though my professional life was practically stalled, my relationship with Paul was developing in ways I had not anticipated. Soft-spoken and considerate, Paul gave me just what I needed—space and support. While my head was spinning out of control, he offered me encouraging words and a safe place to live. As the weeks dragged on and the job prospects diminished, I found myself depending more and more on Paul's advice. My resolve to maintain my independence was faltering.

Emily and I would talk on the phone every week. Every two or three weeks, Paul would drive me to North Carolina for a face-to-face meeting with her. None of our visits were very uplifting, but they were crucial to my mental stability. Emily's demeanor was generally angry or sad. Why I didn't scoop her up and take her back to Australia, I do not know. It just never crossed my mind.

During one of our visits, Earl pulled me aside and said, "I don't think you should visit Emily with that man unless you are married to him."

Earl knew exactly how to push my buttons. If he hadn't run off to America with our daughter, I wouldn't be visiting Emily now with "that man." It took every ounce of restraint not to scream at him. He had no idea how hard this was for me. He had no idea how hard it had been for me to be married to him. And he had no idea that his decision to move to the U.S. made everything that much harder. I didn't have a sister to run to. I didn't have a car. I didn't have a job. All I had was Paul.

As the expiration date on my tourist visa approached, I became more and more agitated. I had to make a decision: return to Australia, move to Canada and find a nursing job, or tough it out in the U.S. and find employment that had nothing to do with my skills.

"What are you going to do?" Paul asked.

Without hesitation, I replied, "I need to stay in the United States." Proximity to Emily was my priority. I was determined to protect her and show her that she mattered more to me than I had mattered to my own mother. Emily would graduate from high school in another year; then she would head to college. Our time was limited and I needed to spend it proving my love for her.

Staying in the United States was the answer Paul had been hoping for. "If you're going to stay here," he said, "let's get married."

His proposal came out of the blue. I liked Paul. I felt safe when I was with him. He was kind to me, and I had come to rely on his wisdom. But marry him? The possibility rattled me. We had a platonic relationship. Nothing more. Had I done something to inspire a proposal? The answer was yes!

I had contacted him for help. I had moved into his home when he offered me the spare room. I had relied on him to take me to visit Emily. While he worked, I took it upon myself to clean the house and cook meals for us to eat together when he got home. Without realizing it, I had been leading him on. My gratefulness had been interpreted as romantic interest. I had done it again.

I didn't respond to Paul's proposal. Instead, I said, "I need a church."

We have plenty," he said. "I'll help you find one. Does that mean you will marry me?"

Marriage to Paul was a convenient option, yet I wasn't sure it was the right thing to do. I did not love him, though I was unsure whether I was capable of loving anyone. His proposal, while not romantic, was sincere. I could say no and perhaps lose the only route I had to Emily, or I could say yes and maintain my right to refuse later. I said, "Yes."

Paul was not a church-going man. However, he eagerly took it upon himself to select churches for us to visit. He had been raised as an Episcopalian, and Paul thought that denomination would be a good fit for us because it was steeped in liturgy and mystery like Catholicism.

We attended four different Episcopalian churches four weeks in a row. Not one felt right to me. The services were too stiff, too straight-laced, or too unwelcoming. I was sure God was telling me to go home. I justified my purchase of a one-way plane ticket to Australia by telling Paul that I didn't know how long it would take for me to close out my bank account and tie up lose ends. Secretly, I wasn't sure if I would return at all.

In the weeks before my departure, I got on my knees and prayed for God to reveal His plan for me. I asked Him to either affirm my decision to marry Paul by leading us to a church that felt like home or remove my deep desire to live close to Emily. I told God, if He did not lead me to a welcoming church within the next three weeks, I would take it as a sign that I was to return to Australia permanently.

The next week Paul looked beyond the Episcopal Church. We attended a Methodist service. It felt cold. A week later, we visited a United Church of Christ. The congregation was too old. With just one Sunday left before my departure, I took it upon myself to select the last church.

Before beginning my research, I got on my knees again and prayed that God would lead me to a place where I would feel welcomed, accepted, and encouraged to grow in my faith. I honestly can't remember if I even mentioned Emily in that prayer.

I found Vienna Presbyterian Church on the Internet. It had really good reviews and was a short 15-minute drive from Paul's house. Paul had never been to a Presbyterian Church, but that was the denomination that had spoken to my heart back in Australia. Even though Solid Rock Presbyterian and I had parted ways poorly, I fondly remembered how I had been welcomed into the fold the first time I visited. My marriage to Paul depended on whether Vienna Presbyterian would be as welcoming.

It was a cool day when we pulled into the crowded church parking lot. Before I even got out of the car, I felt the spirit of God. Older couples were smiling and waving hello to each other. Younger couples were rushing to get their kids into Sunday school classrooms before the service started. Children, teens, and adults alike seemed happy to be coming to church. I got caught up in their joy and enthusiastically shook the hand of the greeter as I entered the building.

The walls on one side of the open lobby were all glass and looked directly into the sanctuary. This allowed the lobby to accommodate overflow, if necessary. I couldn't imagine the church filled to overflowing. There were enough seats to sustain a small village. With windows on every side, even behind the altar where the choir sat, the sanctuary was bathed in light. The focal point was the large wooden cross hanging over the choir loft. It was plain, simple, and empty to symbolize the risen Christ.

Paul and I found seats along the aisle. I was somewhat amazed that the laughter and fellowship continued inside the sanctuary walls. This truly was a church family, a vibrant Christian community.

I casually commented to the woman next to me that the church was beautiful and quite large. She told me that it was brand new, the result of a growing congregation. She also informed me that the balconies, which wrapped around the sides and back of the sanctuary, had just been completed. I looked up and watched as people happily found seats where no one had ever sat before.

"I have a vision," the pastor said during his sermon, "that these balconies will be filled with people who want to know the Lord."

I was drawn into his dream. I looked around and saw all white faces. Not one person looked like me, but I didn't care. The pastor said he wanted the church to be filled. He needed me. His words of hope resonated to the very core of my being. I was surviving on hope. Hope that my daughter would embrace me. Hope that I would find a job. Hope that marrying Paul was God's desire. Hope that my future would be as bright as this sanctuary.

The service ended with a rousing hymn played on a huge pipe organ. It was the music of Heaven, refreshing and invigorating. Paul and I then got caught up in the crowd as it made its way to the double doors at the back of the sanctuary. There the pastor stood shaking hands with everyone as they exited. I felt my heart leap for joy as we approached him.

Smiling from ear to ear, I shook the pastor's hand vigorously and told him how much I appreciated his message of hope. I don't think he understood what I said because I was speaking quickly in broken English with an Australian accent. Nonetheless, he looked me straight in the eye as I spoke and nodded encouragement. His polite response was the sign I had been looking for. In that moment I accepted Virginia as my new home and rested in the confidence that God was indeed watching over me.

Several days later, I flew back to Sydney on the promise that I would return as soon as possible and marry Paul.

CHAPTER 38

Consider it pure joy, my brothers and sisters,
whenever you face trials of many kinds, because you know
that the testing of your faith produces perseverance.
Let perseverance finish its work so that you may be mature and
complete, not lacking anything.
James 1:2-4 (NIV)

2007

I t was a bittersweet homecoming. My house in Australia sold quickly, which was good for me, but bad for Eddie. With his final exams approaching, he needed a stable place to live, someplace to study and call home. I used part of the proceeds from the sale of the house to pay Giang to have his basement remodeled into an apartment for him. Knowing that Eddie would be with my brother and his compassionate wife gave me incredible peace of mind.

Next I went to the hospital and formally ended my employment there. My immediate supervisor begged me to take just a year's leave of absence, to keep the door open in case I wanted to return. I couldn't envision that happening and was adamant that my future was in America. Reluctantly, she accepted my resignation and wished Earl and me success in our new life. I thanked her without taking the time to explain that Earl was no longer in the picture.

I heard the same good luck wishes as I made the rounds to say goodbye to the other doctors and nurses. Earl and I had been separated for more than a year, yet none of my coworkers seemed to know. This surprised me. The real shock came when I discovered that my closest friends — Rosie and Harry, Martha, Jason, and Big Emily — were in the same boat. Though aware that there were problems in my marriage, every one of them thought I was moving to America to be with Earl and Emily. I didn't have the heart to tell them that I was already divorced and about to marry someone else.

How had I managed to deceive so many people for so long? Why did my closest friends not know the truth about my life? Apparently, I was a master of deception. Embarrassed of the real me, I put on a mask each and every day and pretended to be someone I was not. Much like a stage actor. My deep desire to be loved and worthy of acceptance clouded my judgment and drove me to feign stability and hide my personal struggles. Keeping this charade up year after year undoubtedly contributed to my emotional and spiritual downfall.

It took me about a week to say goodbye to all my family members — Duc and Trong, Giang and Hong Anh, my Auntie Khanh and Auntie Linh, and my mother. I didn't really expect anyone to fully support my move to America, but I was taken aback when every single person asked me to reconsider. What I viewed as a selfless act of love for my daughter, they saw as a spiteful game with Earl to jockey myself into a better position with Emily. The more they tried to point out the recklessness of my decision, the more I pulled away. I was either not willing or unable to hear their rationale. I'm not sure which.

I found a cheap return ticket to the U.S. and packed everything I needed into three large suitcases. This didn't stop my friends and family from continuing their efforts to stop me. They called and they visited; they claimed my actions were rash and impulsive. They said they were trying to protect me.

My determination began to waiver. I needed to talk to someone who was unbiased, someone I could trust to give me an honest answer, someone who didn't really know my past or me. I prayed.

As I prayed, the pastor at Vienna Presbyterian Church popped into my mind. Surely he was unbiased!

I sat down at the computer and searched the Web until I found the church. Thanks to the staff directory, I was able to access email addresses and find the pastor's name. Peter. Just like the disciple on whom Jesus built his church.[31] I typed the pastor a lengthy note in broken English explaining that I was about to marry a man I did not know well in order to be near my daughter who lived in North Carolina with her father. I confessed that I was at a crossroads in my life and confused. In truth, I didn't ask the pastor for his opinion, I just asked him to pray for me.

The very next day, I found a note from the pastor in my inbox. He assured me that God would light my way as I leaned into Him for guidance. He promised to pray for me daily, and he provided me with several scripture passages for strength. An ocean and a continent apart could not diminish the compassion I felt in his words. He signed his letter simply: Pete.

Pastor Pete had given me my answer. Like the disciple for whom he was named, he was my rock. I was a lost and tired soul, and he was the kind shepherd saying, "You poor thing, come in here and find rest."

I cut all the tethers that were holding me to Australia. The ease with which everything came together was odd and seemed to confirm that I was making the right move after all. It was as if America had been beckoning me for years, and my destiny there was prearranged.

Within days of arriving back in the United States, Paul and I were at the Northern Virginia magistrate's office. We answered some questions, signed some papers, and were declared husband and wife.

I was very disappointed with the whole process. There is nothing special, and certainly nothing sacred, about being married by a government official. I found myself anxiously looking forward to Sunday when I would see Pastor Pete again and worship at Vienna Presbyterian Church. As I saw it, attending Sunday service would be the closest thing to having my marriage blessed by God.

Sunday came, and my heart filled with joyful expectation the minute Paul and I pulled into the church parking lot. We were carried along by the joyful sounds of our new surroundings—children laughing, adults greeting their friends by name, and pure notes from the pipe organ calling us inside.

The sun was bright that day, bathing the sanctuary in full light. Paul and I once again took a seat along the aisle where we had a good view of both the congregation and the choir. I tried to locate at least one other Asian in the pews, but to no avail. I alone represented the entire continent of Asia! It bothered me for only a few minutes. Once the service started, I was enveloped by the heartfelt music that filled the room, the corporate prayers, and the moving sermon delivered by Pastor Pete.

With childlike excitement I fell in line after the service with a ton of other people to shake the pastor's hand. He recognized me immediately. Vietnamese protocol not withstanding, I gave him a hug. I was giddy with joy. Pastor Pete shook Paul's hand and pointed us to the Welcome Desk where we could learn more about the church. I made a beeline for the desk, determined to find out all I could about VPC—Vienna Presbyterian Church—and the opportunities available to me.

In true Minh fashion, I wanted to sign up for every volunteer position in the church. Paul wisely advised me to wait. He thought it would be best for me to get a job first so I knew what kind of time commitment I could make. Obediently, I collected a lot of information but I didn't commit to anything.

The highs I felt at church that Sunday could not sustain me during the week. Sadness trickled in like drips from a leaky faucet, and before I knew it I was in the throes of depression. Though Paul was kind and tried to comfort me, I knew I needed something more. While searching the Help Wanted ads in the *Washington Post*, I came upon an advertisement for a clinical trial on depression. They needed subjects, and I needed help. I made the call.

After a brief phone interview, I was informed that I was a perfect candidate for the trial and was provided with details about the study. The first two phases would be conducted in a question-and-answer format. The third and last phase of the study involved an MRI. I told the interviewer that I was fine with all of this, and we set an appointment date. When I told the scheduler that I did not have transportation, she offered to pay for a taxi.

Strange as it may sound, I thoroughly enjoyed being a subject in a medical study. I felt at home in the clinical setting, and I looked forward to getting out of the house each day. To top it off, I got paid for every visit. How I wished the study would go on forever! Sadly, it came to an abrupt end the day after I had the MRI.

One of the research doctors called me at home. "Have you ever had surgery on your head?" she asked. "We found an abnormality on your MRI."

"I've never had surgery," I responded. "But I was shot in the head when I was a little girl."

There was a moment of silence before the doctor spoke again. "That makes sense. We found numerous metal fragments lodged in your skull."

"What does that mean?" I asked.

"It means that you cannot continue with the study because we cannot subject you to another MRI."

I was crushed. Without this outlet, I feared I would fall into a deeper depression. I recognized the triggers and thankfully realized that it was time for me to heed Dr. Vicky's advice and find a counselor. Dr. Adams was the answer.

Dr. Adams was familiar with, but not an expert in, PTSD. Nonetheless, he offered me wise counsel. To start, he encouraged me to stop depending on Paul for everything and to get my driver's license so I could come and go as I pleased. He also advised me to join a group where I could meet other people and make new friends. Finally, he told me to engage in some activities that would make me feel productive and useful. VPC was the answer to my doctor's orders.

I selected the church choir as my first volunteer activity. Paul drove me to rehearsal that Thursday night. The conductor was very welcoming and asked me whether I was a soprano or an alto. I had no idea, so he directed me to sit with the altos.

Sheet music was handed out, and I watched carefully to see how the other choir members organized the scores into their black, three-ring notebooks. I have to admit, I was intimidated by the sheet music. To me, it looked like a bunch of winged dots on five-tiered fence posts. I had no idea how to find pitch based on these symbols, let alone rhythm. Afraid I would hit the wrong notes, I spent the first few weeks learning the songs by mouthing the words while listening to the women around me.

After a couple weeks of rehearsal, I figured I was ready to sing on Sunday morning. The women in the choir were very kind to me and helped me find a choir robe that didn't drag on the floor. I filed into the sanctuary with the vocalists and sat in my assigned seat at the front of the church, facing the congregation. I smiled throughout the service and stood on cue when it was time to sing. Then I got cold feet. Afraid I might mess things up, I simply lip-synced my way through all the songs. Being a part of this beautiful ensemble was invigorating. I felt honored to be part of the group making holy music for God even though I wasn't actually contributing.

The following week I practiced each and every song several times at home in order to be ready to sing at the next rehearsal. Thursday night arrived; I took my assigned seat among the altos and opened my binder to the first song. The choir director cued the pianist, the music started, and we all began to sing.

"STOP!" he shouted. "We are not together. From the beginning."

We started over. Again the director yelled, "STOP! Something is not right." He asked the pianist to play the part for the altos. Someone in my section was singing offbeat. Could it be me? When he asked us to sing, I lip-synced.

"Good!" he said. "That was right! Now let's all do it together."

It *was* me! I had learned the notes, not the rhythm. There was obviously a mathematical explanation for each of the various symbols on the sheet music, but I didn't have the key to unlock their meaning. I kept up the charade for just a few more weeks. Then I forced myself to face reality. Choir was not my gift, and music was a language I did not have the energy to learn.

Several Sundays later, I waltzed into the church social hall where coffee was provided between services and asked for the person in charge. Making coffee would be easy, I suspected, since it did not require as much skill as singing. I was ushered into the kitchen to meet Gerri.

"I like to serve," I told her. "I want to learn how to make Presbyterian coffee."

Gerri laughed and showed me how it was done. I watched her closely, determined to learn it right the first time. She put me to work that very day and signed me up to make coffee for the next several weeks. I served with vigor, but I didn't enjoy the work. Making coffee, setting out the sugars and cream, cleaning up spills, and running the dishwasher reminded me of my days of waitressing in France. These were not fond memories. Once again, I was forced to face reality. Serving coffee was not my gift.

I felt terrible quitting my volunteer job knowing that people were not lined up to take my place. Gerri, with her joyful heart, took it all in stride.

"What do you think you'd like to do?" she asked.

I didn't have the faintest idea. I was a nurse, but I couldn't fathom how my nursing skills might transfer to a church setting. All I knew was that I felt alive when I was within the walls of VPC. It was a place of refuge and rejuvenation for me. What I really wanted to do was spend more time there.

"I think I'd like to work in the church part-time some day," I told her.

"Part-time work is full-time work in a church," she stated. That sounded good to me!

My next volunteer job was in the nursery. They were looking for a volunteer coordinator—someone who would willingly recruit people to care for infants and toddlers while their parents attended church services. I thought this would be a good way for me to meet others, so I applied.

I was thrilled to get the job; but Gerri was right: part-time work in a church really is full-time work. I spent a ridiculous amount of hours looking for volunteers. It was particularly hard for me to recruit people because my connections were limited. Coupled with my strange accent, people either did not know what I was saying or didn't take me seriously.

My job also required me to work in the nursery on Sunday mornings when a volunteer called in sick or didn't show up. This happened practically every week. As a result, I often had to miss my favorite church service.

Little children do not like it when their parents leave them in the care of an adult they do not know. While they would willingly go into classrooms where they recognized their teacher, they would break into tears when they saw me.

"Don't worry!" I'd tell them. "You are in America!"

The parents would laugh and the children would wail. I took this as a sign that working with children was not my gift either. After a couple of months, I resigned.

Next, I tried my hand at counting money in the Children's Ministry. Unfortunately, that didn't go well either. American coins were unfamiliar to me. At the time, I didn't even know the difference between a quarter and a dime. I simply stacked the money and let someone else calculate the total. I lasted only two short weeks in this volunteer position.

No choir. No coffee. No children. No coin counting.

Though I had yet to find a relevant place to serve, I was a permanent fixture at VPC on Sunday mornings. It was the one place where I could find rest from the demons that tormented me Monday through Saturday. (It's no wonder that the church itself is called a sanctuary.) VPC had a way of refocusing my mind on the promises of God. It fed my soul and gave me strength and hope.

My weekdays were mostly comprised of job searches and arguing with Emily over the phone. Paul took a backseat to my priorities, which did not help our new marriage. As I became more independent, I purchased a car and started visiting Emily once a month on my own. I hoped and prayed that when the school year ended, she might consider spending time with me in Virginia or enrolling in a nearby college. That did not happen.

As soon as Emily completed her final exams, she headed back to Australia. I found out about the move just a few days before she left. The news was traumatizing. I had never imagined that Emily would return to her birth country. I ignorantly assumed she would complete high school and attend college in the U.S. I had convinced myself that our relationship would blossom once she entered college and moved away from her father. Once again, I had been living in a false reality.

The loss and sadness I felt were overwhelming. I begged Emily to stay in the states. She ignored me. Like her mother, she had a mind of her own, and her mind was made up. To make matters worse, she was angry with me for selling the family house because now there was no "home" for her to go home to.

What about me? I wanted to scream. *I can be your home!* But I held my tongue knowing that I had relinquished that position to Earl a long time ago.

If there was ever a time I needed God, it was now. I didn't need a counselor or even a psychiatrist; I needed a savior. I didn't need another husband; I needed a shepherd to guide me and a flock to surround me. This was not the time to throw myself into volunteer opportunities or make any more life-changing decisions. It was time for me to relinquish control of my life to God and submit to His will. To do so, I had to slow down and listen.

For someone as high strung and as deeply wounded as me, who managed her pain by force and through sheer willpower, submission did not come easy. Mercifully, God was patient with me. Without my daughter or son nearby, without a job to report to or a mortgage to pay, without alcohol or pills, I was finally free of all the distractions that hindered me from seeking a relationship with Christ.

It was, and still is, a daily struggle for me to slow down and listen for God's voice. But when I do, I hear it.

"I can be your home! Come to me."

CHAPTER 39

...the Spirit helps us in our weakness.
We do not know what we ought to pray for,
but the Spirit himself intercedes for us through wordless groans.
And he who searches our hearts knows the mind of the Spirit,
because the Spirit intercedes for God's people
in accordance with the will of God.
And we know that in all things God works for the good of those
who love him, who have been called according to his purpose.
Romans 8:26-28 (NIV)

2007–2008

I spent the week in deep prayer. It was the only thing that brought me some relief from the overwhelming sadness in my heart and the incredible agitation in my mind. Ever thankful for Sundays, the fog finally lifted when we pulled into the VPC parking lot. Jesus's words from the Book of Matthew resonated in my head:

> *Come to me, all of you who are weary and carry*
> *heavy burdens, and I will give you rest. Take my*
> *yoke upon you. Let me teach you, because I am*
> *humble and gentle at heart, and you will find rest*
> *for your souls.*[32]

Paul and I took our usual seats on the aisle. I closed my eyes and began to pray silently. All of a sudden, the friendly noise of the sanctuary faded away, and a familiar feeling of incredible peace came upon me. I had felt this peace before and recalled each of those moments: while praying at my father's grave, while praying in my jail cell after being tortured, while praying in the middle of the South China Sea, while Neville prayed over me following my failed suicide attempt, and while praying over Thanh's body as I prepared him for burial.

Each time that I had prayed in complete brokenness, I had the pleasure of the peace that passes all understanding. Until now, the pattern had eluded me. Perhaps there had been too many distractions before for me to notice. Now there were none.

I sat in silence, bathed in the light of the sanctuary, feeling the warmth of inner peace growing inside me. I knew beyond a shadow of a doubt that the Holy Spirit was with me and in me, telling me that I was going to be OK.

This is your home. You will dwell with me now.

When church services ended, I calmly walked to the VPC Welcome Table and asked about opportunities to learn rather than serve. I was empty and needed to be filled.

The answer was a 12-week Bible study on Christian faith and doctrine. Past Bible studies had taught me that God could bring good out of bad situations. I had experienced this truth several times throughout my life, and I prayed that He would allow me to experience it again.

God did not disappoint.

With my Bible in hand, I walked into the classroom that Monday night hoping to understand why a loving God who would give so generously would take away so completely. My heart skipped a beat when I saw that the teacher was none other than Pastor Pete. I knew then that I was in the right place.

Only 19 people participated in the class—a number I considered small for such a large church. In hindsight, 19 turned out to be the perfect size; the class was intimate and safe. Pastor Pete kicked it off with a prayer and then asked everyone to briefly introduce themselves. Because the Americans had been such a prevalent presence in Vietnam, I assumed everyone would be familiar with my story. So, I casually stated what I thought was common information.

"I come from Vietnam. I left in 1975. I left by fishing boat, but I got caught and put in prison. I got out in the end. I went to Taiwan, France, and then Australia. I am here now."

Pastor Pete's expression was one of bewilderment and compassion. "Where are your parents?" he asked.

"Oh, my dad was killed," I answered.

You could have heard a pin drop. I looked at the faces around the circle. They were full of questions they dare not ask. Pastor Pete thanked me for sharing and moved on to the next person.

The very next day, Pastor Pete called me at home and asked if I would share my story with the church. VPC was in the practice of having its members share their personal testimonies of redemption on Sunday mornings. I had already heard several of these stories and was fully aware of what Pastor Pete was asking me to do. I felt honored. My English was not perfect, yet I was not uncomfortable talking in front of people. The question running through my mind was, *"Am I worthy?"*

In an instant, I remembered several people from the Bible whom God had used for His kingdom's purposes. There was a tax collector, a prostitute, a stutterer, a murderer, and several fishermen, to name a few. If God could use ordinary people to do extraordinary things, He could use me too.

I responded without hesitation. "No problem."

With the help of another church staff member, I wrote down my testimony. Its message was as pertinent for me as it was for the congregation. And so it was that I stood before the church body on a sunny Sunday morning and shared my story.

"In 1968, the Communists attacked the city where my family lived. Our house became the target in the middle of a battlefield. My dad and my younger brother—age 7, my younger sister—age 6, and I— age 11, were among the many Vietnamese people captured that day. We all lined up and waited for our turn to be interrogated."

Sharing my memories with a room filled with hundreds of strangers felt surreal. Afraid I might slip into a dark place, I glanced up from my notes to find a sea of compassionate eyes fixed on me. The body of Christ was all around me, and the Holy Spirit was alive within me. Strengthened, I continued.

> *"I remember one night, while lying on the cold cement bench in the prison cell, I asked my cell-mate if she believed in God. Her reply was NO. She explained to me that if there was a true God, He would prevent suffering and cruelty from happening to innocent people... Tears started to roll down my face as I prayed and asked God whether He really existed."*

I glanced up at the crowd. Tears were rolling down the faces of some of the women. Their compassion for me was evident.

> *"When I lost my younger brother to cancer, the brother who was imprisoned with me and who remained in France, my faith was shaken. I was again angry at God. ...How could life be so unfair?"*

People nodded to express their understanding and support. There was no condemnation here for my faith struggles.

> *"I felt God wanted me to have a relationship with Him again when my children were born. Despite having a successful professional life and a comfortable living, I was empty."*

My words surely struck a chord with at least several couples. Having worked in the VPC nursery, I had met a number of families that had returned to church following the birth of their own children. They were there for their kids' salvation, not necessarily their own.

"I suffered from depression, was diagnosed with Post Traumatic Stress Disorder—PTSD—and underwent treatment for many years. During treatment, my doctor told me that I never could be normal again..."

I shared it all. My attempts at suicide. My failed marriage. My need for counseling. My dependency on medications to get me through another day. I was an open book, but I did not feel judged.

"I now understand why my life was spared. God wants to use my experiences to bring hope to others. When I reflect back on my life, I realize how blessed I am."

And I meant it. I had lived through horrendous conditions and survived. My children and my career were a testament to the grace of God in my life. I could do nothing less than end my story with praise.

"God is indeed a loving and gracious God. He demonstrated His love to me by helping me through my ordeals. He gives me hope when I feel hopeless. He gives me strength when I feel weak. He gives me comfort when I feel hurt. He loves me uncondition-ally. His promises never fail."

The room was silent. And then the applause started. It seemed to swell to an impossible height. I felt awkward. I deserved no applause. I had not lived a righteous or holy life. The applause belonged to God and God alone. I told Him as much as I sheep-ishly returned to my seat.

I gave my testimony at all three services that Sunday morning. The reception was the same each time. I felt blessed beyond mea-sure knowing that God was telling His story through me. He was taking my garbage and turning it into something beautiful.

The old adage, *Sticks and stones may break my bones, but words will never hurt me,* is not entirely true. Proverbs 12:18 is

337

more accurate: *The words of the reckless pierce like swords, but the tongue of the wise brings healing.*

My mother's words beat me down. My father's words built me up. My grandfather's words stung like a hornet. Hubert's words wrapped me in sunlight. Angelo's words discouraged me. Matron Wheen's words strengthened me. Earl's words angered me. Paul's words protected me. And Pastor Pete's words inspired me. After I shared my testimony, I realized that I too had the power to affect people with my words.

One woman who was visiting from California asked for permission to share my story with her daughter's school. Another confessed that she had held a grudge against the Vietnamese people for the war that had taken so many American lives; she had never considered its effect on the Vietnamese children. One older gentleman offered to adopt me, to be my new father! Several Vietnam veterans approached me, many with their own stories to share. One simply stared at his hands when he thanked me for sharing mine.

"I was in your country in 1975," he said.

"Really?" I asked.

He nodded slowly. "I was a pilot on one of the last helicopters that lifted out of Saigon."

He started to tear up. In my testimony, I had not mentioned how close I had come to getting on a helicopter out of Saigon, yet God had put it on this man's heart to share his experience with me.

"There were so many people," he sobbed, "and I could not save you all."

I felt his pain. "You couldn't save us all," I consoled him. "I want to tell you, the Vietnamese people are grateful for all that you Americans did do."

He nodded his thanks, physically unable to utter another word.

"God had a plan," I assured him as he turned and walked away. I could see that now. God had a plan for each of us.

People continued to comment on my testimony for several weeks. With each encounter, I gained a clearer glimpse of God's purpose for my life. He had not led me through trials and pains to punish me, but to prepare me.

*For you, God, tested us; you refined us like silver.
You brought us into prison and laid burdens on our
backs. You let people ride over our heads; we went
through fire and water, but you brought us to a place
of abundance.*[33]

America was my place of abundance. Without family or close friends, I had to totally rely on God. I can't be sure, but I think God had been calling me to America for most of my life. I can count six times that the United States was dangled before me like fish bait. First was as a young girl when my family often spoke of marrying me off to an American soldier. Second was when my Auntie Khanh attempted to groom me in the hopes of matching me up with an American serviceman who would make me his bride after the war. Third, had I not hesitated, I might have made it onto that American helicopter in Saigon. Fourth was after my rescue at sea when I had the opportunity to become an America citizen but chose to go to France instead. Fifth was when Earl and I were starting our family and considered moving to the United States where he had a better chance of getting a job. It wasn't until my ex-husband took Emily to America that I finally took the bait. That was number six.

In light of this revelation, I stopped questioning my quick decision to marry Paul. I now believe it was God's plan all along. Accepting this as truth has allowed me to embrace my marriage. Like Jonah who was swallowed by a whale trying to escape God's call for him to go to Nineveh, there was nothing I could have done to change God's mind if He wanted me in America.[34]

So here I was in "the land of the free and the home of the brave," stripped of everything I held dear, clinging to God like a life vest. I poured over the Bible, finding comfort in the faithfulness of my savior and striving to commit certain scriptures to memory. Without the distractions of children or a job, I was able to pray daily—when I arose, throughout the day, and when I went to bed each night.

"What do you want me to do?" I would ask. *"I will go where you lead me,"* I'd promise. *"Please give me a sign,"* I begged. I fully expected God to immediately present me with some sort of quest, but He was silent, and patience was not my virtue.

Days, then weeks, then months went by. I would get angry with God, shaking my fists at Him. Then I'd fall to my knees and apologize, telling Him I was truly grateful for all He had done for me. As I vacillated between anger and thankfulness, my relationship with God blossomed. I cried out to Him, and though I did not get the answers I wanted when I wanted them, I knew God had heard me. I came to depend on Him for guidance, strength, and peace. I imagined that David, the author of most of the Psalms, might have had a similar experience. This gave me hope, for he was a man after God's own heart.

Through it all, God was refining me into the person He had created me to be from the dawn of time. The false self I had concocted was fading away, and the true child of God was being reborn. This was a crucial turning point in my faith journey because I came to understand that God's plan for my life was bigger and better than anything I could have imagined.

When the call finally came, it wasn't what I expected. Once again, God was showing me that He truly is a God of surprises!

Pastor Pete approached me after service one Sunday and asked if I would be willing to speak at a neighboring church. I joyfully accepted the invitation and shared my testimony the following week. After the service, a Vietnam veteran told me about a group that was planning a mission trip to Vietnam.

"You should go," he said. "I think it would be good for you."

"Why?" I asked. I had never given any thought to returning to Vietnam, even for a short visit. "Why would it be good for me?"

"Because someday you'll go back to Vietnam," he replied with authority, "and these connections may help."

His response triggered a strange feeling in my heart. There was nothing left in Vietnam for me to return to. My family wasn't there. The communists had stripped me of my home and my beloved father. They had tortured the people I loved and demeaned my heritage. It was a dangerous place for both Christians and former South Vietnamese citizens.

Surely God did not want me to go back there. Did He?

CHAPTER 40

Consider your own call, brothers and sisters:
not many of you were wise by human standards,
not many were powerful, not many were of noble birth.
But God chose what is foolish in the world to shame the wise;
God chose what is weak in the world to shame the strong;
God chose what is low and despised in the world,
things that are not, to reduce to nothing things that are,
so that no one might boast in the presence of God.
1 Corinthians 1:26-29 (NIV)

2009–June 2013

I was at home reading my Bible when the phone rang. On the other end of the line was a male voice inviting me to attend a meeting of like-minded Vietnamese Christians living in the Northern Virginia area. Though I wondered how this man got my name and number, I accepted his invitation without question. I took it as a sign from God since the call came while I was studying scripture.

There were twelve of us at the meeting. The biblical significance of this number did not escape me. I was the lone woman in the group. No matter how hard I tried to fade into the background, I kept getting called forward to offer my opinion. It was the female perspective they wanted to hear. Like Queen Esther[35], I wondered if I had been created for a moment such as this. I had much to say, and everything I said was accepted respectfully. When the meeting was over, I knew I had pulled my weight.

"Have you ever thought about attending seminary?" one of the men asked me.

"No!" I blurted out a little too quickly and loudly. I had been through enough schooling to last a lifetime. I was a nurse. I had already done good work for mankind and had no desire to be a pastor. Besides, I was neither fit to preach the Gospel or tell others how to live a Christian life. I knew God had a plan for me, but I didn't believe it was in ministry.

"I don't think that's for me," I added.

"Then think about it," the man said. "We need ordained people— especially women—to go back to Vietnam and tell the people there about Jesus Christ."

His words seared into my brain. *We need ordained people— especially women—to go back to Vietnam and tell the people there about Jesus Christ.* I wholeheartedly agreed, but I was absolutely the wrong person for the task. My past was riddled with mistakes, plagued with sin, and infested with anger. God would never call a person like me to such a vocation.

Yet the very next day, another man from my own church asked me, "Have you ever thought about going to seminary?"

I managed to laugh off the question, but I couldn't ignore it. The prospect had been dangled in front of me twice in one weekend. When I got home, I went to my knees and prayed for guidance. Of course, I prefaced my prayer by telling God that I was unworthy, unprepared, and not interested.

Nonetheless, I could not shake off the thought of seminary. It stuck to me like hair to Velcro. The next week I finally caught up with Pastor Pete to ask for his wise counsel. "A couple of people have asked me to think about going to seminary," I told him.

"Well, if it's God's will, you need to listen," he responded without missing a beat.

That was not the answer I was expecting. I needed the opinion of a higher authority.

Listening was not my gift. I would have to intentionally build silence into my life if I wanted to hear God's voice. Thus, I made space in each day for a long walk with God. During our time together, I would talk to Him as if He were beside me. Then I would practice listening for His response. With practice, I learned how to talk less and listen more.

One evening as I conducted online research about the current state of Vietnam, I discovered that although Christianity still existed in my homeland, it was tightly regulated and Christians were subject to persecution. My research also revealed that within the Presbyterian Church (U.S.A.), there were only two practicing female Vietnamese pastors.

I voiced my concerns to God the next day as we took our walk together. I told Him that I was disheartened by the situation in Vietnam and disappointed in the lack of female pastors of Vietnamese descent. Then I listened for his response.

The words from Isaiah 6:8 reverberated in my head.

Then I heard the voice of the Lord saying, "Whom shall I send? And who will go for us?" And I said, "Here am I. Send me!"

The message was clear. God was calling me! I did not feel worthy of such a calling, but neither had Moses or Joshua or David. Their stories reminded me that God does not send the equipped; He equips the called. If God wanted me to go into ministry, He had a lot of equipping to do!

I thoroughly expected my husband to stop me from pursuing seminary; he didn't. Though Paul was not overly enthused at the prospect of putting me through school, he did not try to talk me out of it. He did, however, play devil's advocate to help me think through the steps logically. It was a helpful exercise, but logic could not trump God's call.

With Paul's help, I submitted several applications to seminary schools across the United States. Only one of the schools called me for an interview: Pittsburgh Theological Seminary. I figured it was the only one God wanted me to attend. The school was a five-hour drive from home—close enough to occasionally visit Paul and VPC, yet far enough away to force me to rely on God alone.

The only question I remember being asked during the admission interview was whether I thought I would have a problem learning another language. I assumed they were referring to the English language since my speaking and writing skills were still rather poor. It wasn't until I was accepted into the program that I learned that they were referring to Greek and Hebrew. Oh my!

The idea of moving to a new city and having to learn ancient languages threw my PTSD into overdrive. If you can, imagine the Energizer Bunny on amphetamines. That was me. Determined to be obedient to the call, I met with my counselor back home several times to keep my emotions grounded.

To prepare myself mentally for the journey into ministry, I decided to visit Vietnam. I hadn't been there in over 35 years. If this was where God wanted me to eventually serve, I needed to experience my homeland from an adult perspective. My childhood memories had to take a backseat to what the future might hold.

On a whim, I asked Emily, who had recently graduated from high school, to join me there. She said yes.

Emily and I spent two weeks traveling between Saigon and Dalat with a humanitarian group doing construction work and caring for the children in orphanages. Emily was overwhelmed by the poverty she saw and deeply affected by the orphans who clung to her, desperate for human touch. Having lived in both locations, I caught only small glimpses of the land I once knew and loved. Desolation now dominated the landscape. Gone were the bright colors associated with growth and joy; now everything appeared dingy and sad. I took great pride in being able to point out the changes to Emily who listened with respect and compassion. Afterwards, she was able to see me through a new lens. It turned out to be a transformational trip for us both, and the beginning of a true mother-daughter relationship.

Spending time in Vietnam also inspired me to give my best to seminary school. It was as if God was telling me that He would repay me for the years the locusts had eaten.[36]

344

The apartment I moved into in Pittsburgh was small, but it was close to campus. Though I was determined to obtain a Masters Degree in Divinity, it was proving to be a stiff challenge. I struggled miserably to maintain a decent grade point average. The language barrier was wider than I had anticipated, which made the tough classes even tougher. After two terms, I was asked to take a sabbatical in order to improve my language skills. This time I assumed they meant Greek and Hebrew, but they meant English.

Paul was happy to have me back in Virginia. I did not share his feelings. I felt like a failure. My colleagues back at seminary, all of whom were decades younger than me, thought I had been treated unfairly. Though they encouraged me to continue my studies at another school, I believed God had placed me in Pittsburgh for a reason.

I took a long walk with God one afternoon and told Him in no uncertain terms that I could not continue if He did not make the path straight. Then I went to Pastor Pete and asked him to pray for me. He offered me words of encouragement that I will never forget.

"Minh," he said, "I feel God wants you to be in Pittsburgh. We Presbyterians think with our heads; you will serve as a reminder that people need to think with their hearts." If God hadn't heard my prayer, he definitely heard Pastor Pete's.

I enrolled in several English classes, and within six months I was *almost* talking like a local. At least that was how it sounded to me. I decided I would return to Pittsburgh Seminary that year rather than wait another semester. I didn't want to run the risk of forgetting what I had already learned.

Another consideration for a quick return to seminary was the financial burden of unemployment for any extended length of time. There was money in the bank that I had brought from Australia, and Paul was doing all he could to support me, but the cost of a college education was creating a strain in our new marriage. The sooner I completed my degree and found a job, the better.

Unbeknownst to me, God was working the finances out through Pastor Pete. A few weeks before I was to return to Pittsburgh, he called me into his office. The Session—the church's governing board—had met the previous evening and had approved Pastor

Pete's request to fund the rest of my education! I hadn't asked for this; I didn't know I could. I didn't even know who sat on the governing board. They were obviously not a well-informed group, I thought.

"I'm not very bright," I tried to explain. "You should use that money for something else."

Pastor Pete didn't blink an eye. "We feel convicted that God wants us to support your calling."

With the backing of my local church, I no longer felt like seminary was just a calling—it was my duty. I did not want to disappoint the Session members or Pastor Pete. Most of all, I did not want to disappoint God.

The dean at the seminary was shocked to see me back so soon. To tell the truth, I don't think he expected to see me back at all. I pleaded my case to be readmitted and proved my commitment by presenting my English certificate. The clincher was when I told the dean that my church wanted to pay for my education. They were supporting me, and I owed it to them to follow through. The dean could not turn me away.

I was a diligent student. I never missed a class, and I studied every night. Still, seminary school was difficult. Not only was it hard to learn new information at my age, I dealt with professors who believed I had no right to be a Presbyterian pastor. Apparently, I did not fit the mold. I even had one professor say to my face, "I see you study, but I don't think this is your calling." I had to tell myself over and over again to ignore such naysayers, for they did not know who had called me.

My biggest struggle in Pittsburgh was with loneliness and depression. Thankfully, God provided me with a local Christian psychiatrist who helped me battle the storms. She taught me to view PTSD as my friend who would help me stay focused on the goal that God had set before me.

God became my constant companion, and my prayer life deepened tremendously during this time. I leaned into Him for strength and comfort by praying continually throughout each day: in the mornings while I dressed, midday at meals and between classes, and each night before bed. My prayer was consistent. "All I want," I told God, "is a 3.0 average. Just enough to pass with dignity."

One warm, summer evening I took a long walk with God to enjoy the quietness of my surroundings in rural Pennsylvania. When the sun began to set, fireflies began to appear—hundreds of them. I watched in amazement as each insect's light came to life for only a few seconds before another took its place. It was like a well-synchronized dance or a well-rehearsed symphony of light—and I was the lone audience member. My heart rejoiced at the performance.

As I stood watching the fireflies appear and disappear, I was reminded of all the people I had known whose presence in my life had been short-lived. My father. My little sister and brother. Thanh. Matron Wheen. Harry. Hubert. The nuns, my teachers, and the patients I had cared for over the years. They were all flickers of bright light in my otherwise dark world. Here today and gone tomorrow, evidence of God's blessings and His enduring faithfulness.

With the help of God, my psychiatrist, and my study buddies, I became the first Asian student from Pittsburgh Theological Seminary to obtain a Masters Degree in Divinity. My fellow graduates called me a trailblazer. Though I was tickled by the title, I hoped I would simply be remembered as an obedient servant.

The highlight of my graduation was my grade point average: exactly 3.0. I had passed with dignity, thus proving that God will give you exactly what you ask for if it is in line with His will.

At the graduation ceremony I was given the award for Excellence in Pastoral Care. I accepted the honor as a sign that God was calling me to be a hospital chaplain where my skills as a nurse and my theological knowledge could intertwine. I found myself looking forward to shepherding God's people by helping them keep their eyes on Christ as they passed from this world to the next. His plan for me truly was better than anything I could have imagined.

As I look back on my life, I now see that God never stopped pursuing me over the years and across the oceans. He continually made a way for me where there was no way in order to get me back on the path He originally designed for me in my mother's womb. I have stood on the mountaintop and sunk to the depths of Sheol. I have experienced great joy and enormous sorrow. I have walked in the light and stumbled through the darkness. Through it all, one thing was constant: God's presence beside me.

As a child, I had looked to the stars for direction from my earthly father. Now as an adult, I look to my heavenly Father for guidance. Like the fireflies, He is all around me, visible yet invisible. I am still a work in progress, but I believe God and I are finally in sync.

> *If I live, I live for the Lord; and if I die, I die for the Lord. So whether I live or die, I belong to the Lord.*[37]

My journey is far from over. I am convinced that one day God will call me to be his hands and feet in mission work around the world. He will use the suffering of my past to bring hope to those who are still in bondage, for He alone is able to make beauty out of ashes. For now, I am still being refined into the person He wants me to be for His kingdom's purposes. But when He calls, I will be ready.

> *You did not choose me, but I chose you and appointed you to go and bear fruit—fruit that will last.*[38]

I am a mess; God knows this and wants me anyhow. Whatever tomorrow brings, I know that He will be right there with me. And so I am straining forward, leaving my past behind, and pressing on toward the goal to win the prize for which God has called me heavenward in Christ Jesus. He is my Savior, and He leads me on.

EPILOGUE

Now may the God of peace, who through the blood of the eternal covenant brought back from the dead our Lord Jesus, that great Shepherd of the sheep, equip you with everything good for doing his will, and may He work in us what is pleasing to him, through Jesus Christ, to whom be the glory for ever and ever. Amen.
Hebrews 13:20-21 (NIV)

After receiving her Masters of Divinity Degree from Pittsburgh Theological Seminary in 2013, Minh Phuong Towner enrolled in chaplaincy training at York Hospital in Pennsylvania and received her certificate for Clinical Pastoral Education the following year. She served as a hospice chaplain in the Lancaster area of Pennsylvania before returning to Northern Virginia where she currently serves as a hospital chaplain bringing the message of hope and peace to individuals facing the end of life.

On July 4, 2014, Minh and 101 fellow sojourners became U.S citizens on the grounds of Mt. Vernon—President George Washington's estate on the Potomac River in Virginia. A *Voice of America* reporter interviewed Minh that day and quoted her as saying, "I left Vietnam in 1975. I was one of the refugee boat people. I did not have my GPS, so I went quite a long way before I washed to America."

Minh's children, Eddie and Emily, still live in Australia and are "doing something good for mankind," as she puts it. Eddie is a senior network engineer in telecommunications, and Emily is a high school teacher in a Christian school. Earl never remarried, but Minh and Paul are approaching their 12th wedding anniversary.

From Vietnam to Taiwan to France to Australia to the United States of America—though Minh now calls Virginia home, she considers herself a citizen of God's kingdom. She is waiting for the Lord's call to carry the message of love around the world to a generation that has never been exposed to the Gospel of Jesus Christ.

Despite the progress that has been made in Vietnam over the last 40 years, religious activities are highly regulated. Groups wishing to gather for religious purposes must apply for and receive official permission from the People's Commune to operate under decree No. 92. However, because laws can vary between the national and local levels, religious controls are often inconsistent and unpredictable. The Socialist Republic of Vietnam is one of only five remaining countries in the world still ruled by a communist government.

Minh was ordained as a Presbyterian pastor in November of 2017. This made her the third Vietnamese woman to be ordained in the Presbyterian Church (USA). She has been accepted into the Doctor of Ministry program at Gordon-Conwell Theological Seminary in Massachusetts and will begin her studies in the fall of 2018.

In the meantime, Minh has found time to tackle one fun activity: she is learning how to swim. "Just in case there is swimming in Heaven," she says. "I don't want to miss anything!"

Acknowledgments

F irst and foremost, thank you to Minh, my sister in Christ, who blessed me beyond measure by granting me the privilege of writing her story. You have touched my heart, and I will never be the same.

Thank you to my precious husband, Greg, who lovingly allowed me to lock myself behind closed doors and write for hours *and years* on end. Your love and support sustained me when I was at a loss for words.

Thank you to those who read my drafts and offered wise counsel: Denise Fleissner, Robin Currie, Scott Slocum, Pete James, Loretta Frankovitch, Kate Chapman, and Greg Rahal. The credit for the clarity and focus of this book goes to each of you.

A special thanks to Jason Prater who created a captivating cover that beautifully reflects Minh's strong and determined spirit.

The names of most people and places in this book were changed, except for those who willingly gave their permission to use their identity. They alone know who they are, and to you I say, "Thank you."

A special thanks goes to Emmy and Wood Parker for providing Minh and me with a place to retreat to finalize the chapters of this book. Truly God was present in that place.

Finally, all glory and praise to the triune God for the way He weaves stories together in the fabric of life.

ENDNOTES

1   William E. Schlenger and Nida H. Corry, "Four Decades Later: Vietnam Veterans and PTSD," *The VVA Veteran*, January/February 2015, http://vvaveteran.org/35-1/35-1_long itudinalstudy.html (accessed March 3, 2018).
2   Simone Weil, *Waiting for God* (New York: Harper Collins Publishers, 1951).
3   James H. Willbanks, *The TET Offensive: A Concise History* (New York: Columbia University Press, 2007).
4   John C. McManus, "Tet Offensive: 7th Infantry Regiment in Saigon," *HistoryNet*, June 12, 2006, http://www.historynet. com/tet-offensive-7th-infantry-regiment-in-saigon.htm (accessed June 6, 2016).
5   James H. Willbanks, *Abandoning Vietnam: How America Left and South Vietnam Lost its War* (Kansas: University Press of Kansas, 2004).
6   Heather Marie Stur, *Beyond Combat: Women and Gender in the Vietnam War Era* (Cambridge University Press, 2011).
7   Matthew 18:5–6 (KJV)
8   Mark 12:41–44
9   James H. Willbanks, *Abandoning Vietnam: How America Left and South Vietnam Lost its War* (Kansas: University Press of Kansas, 2004).
10 Gregory Ball, "Operation Babylift and Frequent Wind," *Air Force Historical Support Division*, September 17, 2012, http://www.afhistory.af.mil/FAQs/Fact-Sheets/

Article/458955/1975-operation-babylift-and-frequent-wind/ (accessed July 4, 2016).

11   History.com, "Operation Frequent Wind Begins," *History. com*, April 29, 1975. https://www.history.com/this-day-in-history/operation-frequent-wind-begins (accessed July 4, 2016).

12   Luke 18:1–8

13   Jonathan Wilde, "Re-Education In Vietnam," *The Distributed Republic,* May 1, 2006. http://www. distributedrepublic.net/archives/2006/05/01/re-education-in-vietnam/ (accessed July 18, 2016).

14   Leviticus 19:8 and 9b (NLT)

15   United Nations High Commissioner for Refugees, "The State of the World's Refugees 2000: Fifty Years of Humanitarian Action," *UNHCR: The UN Refugee Agency (page 87),* January 1, 2000, http://www.unhcr. org/3ebf9bad0.html (accessed July 30, 2016).

16   Ibid 15, page 84. The exact number of boat people who died at sea following the North Vietnamese government takeover of Saigon can only be estimated. According to the United Nations High Commission for Refugees, between 200,000 and 400,000 boat people have died at sea since 1975.

17   Bill Herod, "Vietnam: Internal Commerce," *Country-data.com*, December 1987, http://www.country-data.com/ cgi-bin/query/r-14678.html (accessed August 2, 2016).

18   Felix Brender, "Like the Foam on the Stormy Sea– Vietnamese Boat People in Taiwan," *European Association of Taiwan Studies,* January 2015. (accessed August 9, 2016).

19   Migration Heritage Center, "Australia's Migration History," *Migration Heritage Center: Belongings,* http://www. migrationheritage.nsw.gov.au and Australian Government, "The Changing face of Modern Australia: 1950s to 1970s," http://www.australia.gov.au (both accessed April 24, 2016).

20   ABC.net–Australia, "Fact Check: Will Australia's Refugee Intake in 2015-16 be the Highest since WWII?" *ABC News, September 2015,* http://www.abc.net.au/

news/2015-09-29/fact-check-syria-largest-refugee-intake-julie-bishop/6786074 (accessed October 19, 2016).

21 James 5:16 (NIV)

22 Romans 3:23–25a (NRSV)

23 Romans 8:38–39 (NRSV)

24 James 2:18b (NRSV)

25 Michael R. Trimble, *Trauma and Its Wake, Volume 1: The Study and Treatment of Post-Traumatic Stress Disorder* (New York, 1985) 5–14.

26 Psalm 23:1–4 (RSVCE)

27 John 6:35 (RSVCE)

28 John 6:44 (RSVCE)

29 Matthew 7:3–5 (NIV)

30 Matthew 5:32 (NIV)

31 Matthew 16:18 (NIV)

32 Matthew 11:28–29 (NLT)

33 Psalm 66:10–12

34 In the Book of Jonah, God tells Jonah to go to Nineveh and preach against its wicked ways. Instead of complying, Jonah runs in the other direction and catches a boat bound for Tarshish. The Lord sends a violent storm, and the ship's crew cast lots to see who was responsible for it. Jonah was identified and thrown overboard where a great fish swallowed him. After three days, Jonah was spit out on the shores of Ninevah to preach repentance, just as God had planned.

35 In the Book of Esther, the title character is a beautiful Hebrew woman who becomes the queen of Persia. In a strange turn of events, she saves the Jews from annihilation when she reveals her heritage. It appears her rise in position was God's way of protecting his chosen people.

36 In the Book of Joel, the prophet laments over a great locust plague and a severe drought. This is followed by God's promise that Israel's enemies will be destroyed along with the locusts once the Jewish nation repents of its sins.

37 Romans 14:8 (NIV); the word "we" replaced with "I".

38 John 15:16

CPSIA information can be obtained
at www.ICGtesting.com
Printed in the USA
LVHW011148130519
617615LV00009B/798/P

9 781545 631638